It Only Hurts When I Sit Down

A Bicycle Adventure on Historic Route 66

Douglas L. Waterman

It Only Hurts When I Sit Down

Copyright © 2016 *It Only Hurts When I Sit Down: A Bicycle Adventure on Historic Route 66*
by Douglas L. Waterman

This book is copyrighted under the Berne Convention
All rights reserved. No reproduction without permission.

About the cover photo: The photo was taken in Oatman, Arizona. The burros are ancestors of those used by gold and silver miners. The mines were opened in the 1880s. When Franklin D. Roosevelt closed the mines in 1942, the burros were released to fend for themselves. Today the burros wander in and through the town and the tourists love it! Doug asked "a fellow tourist" to take his picture with the young burro.

ISBN: 978-0-692-76340-7
Library of Congress Control Number: 2016913206
Printed in the United States of America

Doug Waterman

For Donna

You moved our marriage to a loving high with your daily advice, emotional support and spiritual strength. Without these and your steadfast love, my adventure would not have been possible.

Table of Contents

1. In the Beginning..7
2. Goethe Inspires Me 13
3. Birth, Death and New Life 16
4. Route 66 on Index Cards....................................19
5. Setting Dates and Building Endurance 22
6. A Blessing...28
7. The Pieces are Coming Together........................30
8. To the Starting Line..34
9. Traffic, a Grump, and Family..............................38
10. The First Full Day 44
11. Strangers in the Desert..52
12. Pushed to My Limit...69
13. The Party's on in Oatman....................................79
14. Enjoying Eighty Peaceful Miles...........................89
15. Get Your Kicks on Route 66..............................100
16. Nearing Home: The Land of Enchantment 117
17. Adversity 101: The Mid-term Test....................126
18. Them Ain't Mean 133
19. Home for Mother's Day....................................138
20. Bring on the New 146
21. The Geo-Mathematical Center and Beyond 158

22.	Facing My Fear	167
23.	Music in the Old Meat Market	177
24.	Violent Weather Stalks Me…Again	183
25.	Hillbillies Only Gots White	193
26.	Life or Death – A Matter of Inches	204
27.	Kansas Route 66 – Blink and You'll Miss It	213
28.	Mizuree or Mizuruh?	217
29.	Frozen Custard Ahead	226
30.	Fear and Prejudice	236
31.	T T T	240
32.	Miss Full-of-Life	249
33.	Following Orders	255
34.	Kindness at Funks Grove	260
35.	Here and There	267
36.	A Surprise Awaits	271
37.	The End of a Wonderful Day	279
38.	Loose Ends and Celebration	283

Epilogue 293

Appendix 299

Acknowledgements 301

About the Author 303

1

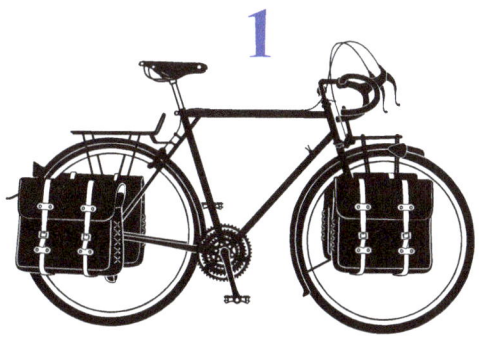

In the Beginning

The sun was edging over the crags of the distant Sierra as I kissed my wife Donna, goodbye. I cycled down our street, hollered "I love you" and waved to her one last time as I wheeled around the corner. It was already a warm day in June and I felt overdressed in shorts, a long sleeved shirt and a wind breaker. But charged by the joy and satisfaction of self-propelled speed, I ignored this minor discomfort and pedaled east-bound out of town.

The six months of preparation were finally over and I was beginning my first long distance bicycle trip. I was excited, not unlike other firsts in my life – a first kiss, driving alone for the first time, or my first pay check. I was free, eager to experience the miles ahead for which I had been planning.

But as I was soon to discover, much of what I considered preparation was naïve reasoning if not guessing. I had no idea what fourteen days on my 18-speed road bike would demand of me. I figured I'd just get on the bike and pedal 1300 miles from my hometown of Davis, California to Santa Fe, New Mexico. I would arrive there to a hero's welcome, orchestrated by my parents, sister, one brother and maybe my nephew if he could get off work. I had convinced myself that I was ready for every eventuality but tucked among all my emotions was the incessant question, "*Can I really do this*?

Fourteen hours after leaving home I arrived at Jenkinson Lake in the Sierra foothills, 3400 feet higher than when I started. I was tired but I'd achieved my rigid distance goal for the day. I washed up in the lake, laid my sleeping bag under the Ponderosa Pines and fell asleep with star light filtering through the needles above me.

The next morning, while packing the panniers in the twilight, I saw several ant battalions climbing up my tires. They had set up headquarters overnight in the two panniers that carried emergency food. After fifteen minutes of aggressive brushing, I managed to eject most of them from my café on wheels.

Finally repacked and ready to go, I resumed my uphill slog on the lightly traveled Mormon Emigrant Highway. Around noon I turned left onto Highway 88 and followed it, arriving by late afternoon at the highest all-weather crossing of the Sierra Nevada, 8573-foot Carson Pass. Exhausted, I sat on a granite boulder on the shoulder of the highway, snacked on trail mix, gulped from the only water bottle that still contained water and pondered the several less than joyful experiences I'd had during the day. Drivers had honked and some had intentionally passed close enough to force me off the road. I'd run out of water before finding a seasonal rivulet from which I half-filled one water bottle, drop by precious drop. While guzzling the refreshing liquid I tried to ignore the possibility I was imbibing giardia that could force me to seclusion in the forest, doubled up with diarrhea.

Overall I reveled in my accomplishment of reaching what would be the highest altitude from Davis to Santa Fe. My day's work was over and my next challenge would be to keep the bike from skidding out from under me as I plunged downhill at 35mph. It was the loose gravel used in keeping the roadway passable in the winter that could cause me to lose control, leaving skin and blood on the asphalt as I plowed helmet first into boulders along the highway.

In an effort to dwell on happier thoughts, I wandered to where I could look east into the distant emptiness of Nevada. A smog-free view welcomed me. The shimmering heat waves seemed to be inviting me to join them in their dance. I contemplated the states ahead: Nevada, Utah, Colorado and New Mexico, my destination 1100 desolate miles away.

While thinking of those many miles, I found it difficult to be confident. I wondered where I'd find places to eat and water to drink. I was afraid of not finding a safe place to camp every night and what I'd do if my bike broke down days from the nearest bike mechanic. The motivation, enthusiasm and anticipation that had accompanied me for these first two days were slowly being replaced by an ominous mental foreboding. Positive was changing to negative and "can-do" to "I'll never make it." It was as if I had come to an invisible line in the asphalt at that summit, the crossing of which would sever the emotional umbilical cord connecting me with the support of family and friends. Awaiting me were places I'd never been and experiences I'd never had. From here on I wouldn't be in control. Unable to trust my preparation, such as it was, I found it impossible to stop worrying.

The next morning, after fitful sleep in a grove of aspen, accompanied by droves of mosquitoes attending their regional convention in my makeshift tent, I gave up on that trip to Santa Fe. Instead, I took two days to cycle around Lake Tahoe before meeting Donna at the conference she was attending. Returning home, my tail between my legs, I wondered if I would have given up so easily if she hadn't been close enough to rescue me. Every time someone asked how my trip to Santa Fe had gone, I explained I never made it and would just have to deal with the embarrassment over my grandiose failure. But to my surprise, almost without exception friends and family encouraged me, suggesting I think of it as a practice run and that I'd make it the next time.

The following summer I headed to Santa Fe again, better prepared and with my head screwed on tighter. 1300 miles from Davis I pedaled up my parent's front driveway to a joyous family welcome which included my son, Ryan, who had arranged for enough time off to bring me back to California. It was a reunion I cherish to this day.

The months after my adventure ended were filled with memories, many of which were threatening and uncomfortable, capable of discouraging me from even thinking about riding my bike anywhere again. Packs of dogs had come out of nowhere to chase me and I was nearly hit by an unopened can of 7-Up thrown from a passing Jeep by someone with (thankfully) poor aim. I'd pushed my fully loaded bike for five miles as we both sank repeatedly into four feet of snow that hadn't yet been plowed on the Mormon Emigrant Highway. The driver of a car with dark tinted windows ran me off the road and then stopped on a city street ahead and tried to do it again. I suffered with diarrhea (not from stream water but spaghetti) and ran out of water miles from the nearest Nevada town. Heat, mountain passes, and strong headwinds led me to doubt I'd make it to the next bend. The long distance between each remote town meant few places to eat and when I reached Santa Fe fourteen days after starting, I'd lost ten pounds.

Over the weeks and months following my trip to Santa Fe, it wasn't just the frightening and difficult experiences that gave me pause. The more I thought about the struggles, the more the difficulties paled in comparison to the inspiration of having succeeded. I thought about the Baptist minister who stopped at the top of a long hill and gave me water and the excuse to stop, talk and rest. I remembered the store clerk who offered to keep an eye on my unlocked bike while I shopped and the young couple from Germany who gave me soap so I could wash my odiferous clothes in the campground laundry. When I ran out of water in Nevada, a highway department crew just happened along and one of them replenished one of my water bottles from his personal gallon jug. Crows had flown escort above me while rabbits, squirrels and kangaroo rats kept me company on the ground for short distances. One evening I bedded down under a bush in the desert and when I awoke the next morning, my sleeping bag was covered with delicate white flower petals. Before I was fully awake and heard the cattle bawling at a nearby ranch, I wondered if dying and going to heaven would be like that.

Looking back on that trip, I knew that in spite of the pain and discomfort, I'd grown emotionally. I learned that not being in control all the time freed me to enjoy the unknown. I slowly came to understand the futility of worrying my way along. In the end it was the difficult lessons and situations that taught me the most.

Seven years later, Donna and I were driving across the Mojave Desert in southern California, on our way to Santa Fe. Out of nowhere I had an idea. What would it be like to bike Route 66, 2300 miles from Santa Monica to Chicago on a highway that didn't officially exist anymore? Wanting to share my brilliant idea with Donna, I asked her, "What would you think if I took a month-long bike trip?" The miles that followed were filled with silence. I couldn't really blame her for reacting that way, knowing how she had suffered for my safety on my trip to Santa Fe. But even she knew that I was 65, recently retired, and had more time to pursue an ambitious adventure.

Several days later I was sitting with my dad in his living room in Santa Fe, my eyes wandering over his impressive collection of road maps. He and mom had traveled a lot in their lifetime but now in their old age, their deserted maps were gathering dust, fading in the morning sunlight on a bookshelf to my right. The idea crossed my mind that dad might have maps from the eight states that Route 66 had gone through. If he did, I could use them to find the old road. I leafed through every map and found four – California, Arizona, New Mexico, and Oklahoma – that were old enough to show Route 66. I felt like I'd uncovered ancient drawings, long forgotten in a museum basement drawer, each one showing the way to priceless treasure.

Dad had watched me the entire time and when I was done, I asked him, "Can I have these four?"

He nodded and asked, "Why do you want them?"

I wasn't ready to tell him what I was up to so I offhandedly said, "I'm just interested in Route 66," and figured that would be the end of that.

The next morning dad and I ate breakfast together, he a glazed-raised from Dunkin Donuts, and coffee with cream and sugar – a milkshake I called it. I had a chocolate old-fashioned, coffee black, and a bowl of granola. With a nod to mom's insistence that each day should be started with nutrition, we split a banana.

While we ate, dad mentioned he needed to run an errand downtown. I knew the incessant pain in his back made it difficult for him to get around so I considered asking him if he'd like my help. But there was something about the independence in his errand-running announcement that told me he would refuse my offer to go along. So I didn't ask.

The morning wasn't half over yet when he returned with a smile of accomplishment gracing his 93-year-old face. Using his cane to steady his gait, he walked across the living room to where I was sitting and handed me a map entitled, *Route 66 in New Mexico*. It showed all 500-plus miles of the venerable highway in New Mexico, now signed Historic Route 66. Even where it had been abandoned and I-40 or other roads had taken its place, the map showed where most of its original footprint could still be travelled. There were suggestions of historic sites to see along the way and detailed street directions through cities and towns, like Albuquerque and Gallup. Unbeknownst to dad, he had given my idea of cycling Route 66 an enormous boost.

Back home in California I pored over dad's maps. I traced the red line that represented Route 66 and imagined following it on my 18-speed road bike. What a thrill it would be to pedal from Santa Monica to Chicago, from the Pacific Ocean to the shore of Lake Michigan, my dream unfolding like the maps dad had given me.

2

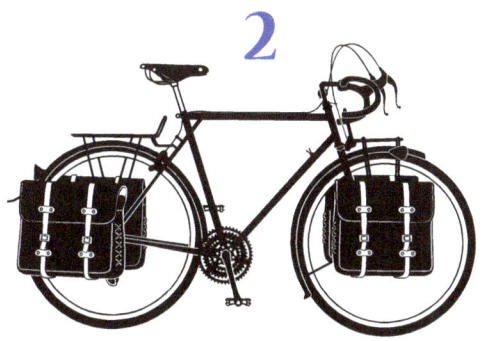

Goethe Inspires Me

My decision to cycle Route 66 resulted in a variety of unpredictable conversations. Some people had no idea where Route 66 was, a fact that surprised me. With few exceptions, those who did know would ask, "Why Route 66?" In all my answers I tried to convey the thrill awaiting me. I was anxious to experience the history of this fabled highway, to meet people who lived along what was left of it and to hear their stories.

One day it dawned on me that the following April I would turn the palindromic age of 66. Calling my ride "66 on 66" was the obvious thing to do. Several friends, with tongue in cheek, asked, "Does this mean you intend to ride the California highway numbered your age every year?" Despite my enthusiasm, I had to admit I couldn't see myself thirty-five years from then, hunched over and wobbling along in first gear, pedaling south on Highway 101 from the Oregon border to Los Angeles.

The fact that I had family living along Route 66 was another reason to cycle it. My brother Kim and his wife, Sheila, lived in Albuquerque, about one-third of the way to Chicago. My youngest brother, Chris, lived in Owasso, Oklahoma and my sister and parents were just north of Route 66 in Santa Fe. When I got to Springfield, Illinois, respite would be waiting for me at the home of my son, Ryan, and his wife, Julie. What a hoot it would be to pedal up to the front door of any of my relatives, ring the doorbell and ask if they'd like to contribute to the Chafed Fanny Foundation. At my relatives' homes I could count on hugs, a comfortable place to rest my aches and pains, home-cooked meals, a bike shop nearby if I needed one, a chance for course corrections, and a joyous sendoff.

Contemplating reasons for making this trip, I couldn't ignore the fact that it had been one year since I had retired from teaching in the Sacramento City School District. In that period of time I had struggled to accept the fact that I was now out of the loop and in the last phase of my life. For thirty-seven years, my professional life had been devoted to helping students with disabilities prepare for employment after graduation. Those years had brought immense satisfaction. At the end of every day I would drive home, confident I was making a difference – planting seeds I called it.

But when I retired, the stimulating conversations with employers, school counselors, fellow teachers, parents, and my students ended. I woke up every morning and realized that only Donna cared whether I got up or not. I had no students to place into work sites or problems to solve. I'd heard for years how men often defined their value by their work and now I understood what that meant. Without a job, my worth was dragging. But despite the emptiness, I knew I wasn't ready to be put on the shelf yet. I hungered to find new ways to be useful.

But it wasn't just the absence of a job that bothered me. Growing older brought into focus the fact that it took me longer to complete tasks. I needed glasses to see distant objects and dark glasses to protect my eyes from the UV rays that had already damaged one of them. I had orthotics in my shoes to level my posture and compensate for my life-long scoliosis. Thanks to the screeching tinnitus brought on four decades earlier while learning to fire my M1 rifle in the Army, I was nearing the time when I'd need to add hearing aids to my daily armor.

With two-thirds of my life now behind me, I wanted my trip of a lifetime to be evidence that just because I was slowing down didn't mean I was ready to be shoved off the road, literally or figuratively. I had the strong feeling that cycling to Chicago would help me find new purpose in life, starting with making it a fund-raiser for Habitat for Humanity. And since I enjoyed running competitively in 10K races, I knew I already had a head start in training for Route 66.

Despite all my reasons for wanting to take this trip, the well-meaning and the worried countered with their reasons why I shouldn't go. Some thought that turning sixty-six qualified me for increased time in a rocking chair, that I was way too old to be riding a bike. Others worried about my going alone. Some pointed out the dangers in driving a car, let alone riding a bicycle, from Santa Monica to Chicago. And others were more graphic, reminding me of what I already knew: One slight swerve by me, a passing car, or a semi, and my life would end in a congealing puddle of blood.

I knew from the start that I'd encounter danger. I'd have to ride on narrow two-lane roads and freeways where the speed limit was 75mph in some places. The broiling daylong heat, a biking challenge I'd never faced, would suck me dry as I crossed the 150 miles of the Mojave Desert in southern California. But rather than frighten me, every danger and challenge drew me in, as I visualized the thrill of achieving goal after goal. This bicycling trip of a lifetime, this dream coming true, would give me the opportunity to rebuild my self-esteem. In addition to those who encouraged me, it was the words of Goethe that inspired me:

"Whatever you think you can do or believe you can do, begin it. Action has magic, grace and power in it."

3

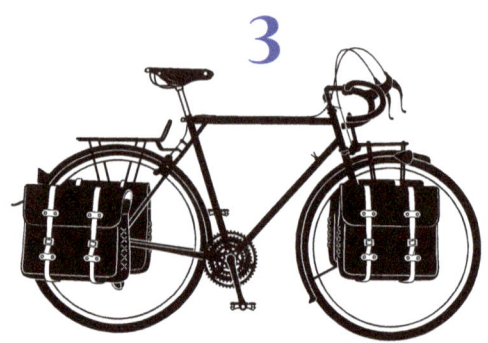

Birth, Death and New Life

The story of Route 66 began in 1921 when Congress passed the Federal Highway Act. This legislation appropriated funds to help states with their highway construction costs, but only if they designated at least seven percent of their roads as interstate highways. Within five years, our nation's first system of interstate routes had been approved and they were ready for numbering and building.

The Route from Chicago to Los Angeles was numbered 60 and then changed to 66. Route 83 would go from Canada to Mexico, Route 41 from Chicago to Florida, and Route 50 from the Atlantic to the Pacific, passing within two miles of my Davis home. Even numbered highways went east-west and odd numbered north-south, a system followed to this day in numbering United States highways. By 1937, two years before I was born, Route 66 was finished – a 2,448-mile, two-lane highway, each lane only nine feet wide.

From its beginning, Route 66 captured the imagination of America. It was given many names, including The Road of Flight, Osage Indian Trail, Mormon Trail, America's Main Street, National Old Trails, and The Grand Canyon Route. Even John Steinbeck contributed, calling it The Mother Road in his 1939 novel *The Grapes of Wrath*.

Spurred by wanderlust, tragedy, curiosity, or opportunity, people flocked to this ribbon of asphalt, concrete and brick. Travelling west to the golden state of California brought escape, a new start, and adventure. Motor courts, some built to resemble American Indian tipis, others with a garage attached to each room, and many emblazoned with neon, sprung up to accommodate the tired. Cafes and full-service filling stations were built to feed the hungry and keep their cars running. Roadside shops enticed the curious and the gullible to stop and see "a real Indian," sitting in the brutal sun, and the coyotes, scorpions, rattlesnakes, and other wild animals caged out back. To help them remember the fun they had when they got back home, tourists succumbed to buying polished rocks, arrowheads, postcards, tomahawks, ash trays, Indian blankets, petrified wood, and all manner of contrived memorabilia and novelties found along Route 66.

Thirty-five years after the birth of this classic highway, Congress passed The Interstate Highway Act of 1956. Signed by President Eisenhower, this new legislation spelled out the guidelines for a 42,500-mile interstate highway system. Drastic changes called for every interstate highway to be rebuilt. They would be wider, straighter, and have more gradual altitude gain and loss. Access would be controlled and traffic lanes going in opposite directions would be separated to prevent head-on collisions. Unfortunately, this progress in transportation would come with a high price for the people living along America's Main Street.

The old Route 66 highway alignments that couldn't be used in construction of any new interstate highway were abandoned or converted to frontage or side roads and given new alphabetical or numerical designations. Towns were bypassed by the new road, now called a freeway. If motorists wanted to leave the freeway and go into a town, their only choice was to take one of the off-ramp exits scattered farther apart than the old entrances into town had been. The day before Seligman, Arizona was bypassed in 1978, some 9,000 cars traveled through the middle of town on Route 66. The day Route 66 became Interstate 40 (I-40), not a single car took one of the two freeway exits and drove down Main Street. Over the next year, Seligman lost 70 percent of its economy. Isolated and unable to make a living, people everywhere along Route 66 abandoned their businesses and homes and became a new generation of migrants moving on.

In 1984, Williams, Arizona was the last Route 66 town bypassed. The following year, the American Association of Highway Officials met and decommissioned Route 66. It had taken nearly twelve years to build it the first time and almost thirty years the second time. Five freeways would now take its place: I-10, I-15, I-40, I-44 and I-55.

The Route 66 Associations in each of the eight states had, over the years, worked cooperatively to publicize and attract tourists to their highway. But they were powerless to alter the economic hardship and physical isolation created by the new interstate highways. In Arizona, a glimmer of hope came when the Arizona Association convinced the state legislature to install signs along the old route, attracting nostalgic tourists by naming it a Historic Route.

In 1990, Congress passed the Route 66 Study Act which created a Preservation Program to be administered by the National Park Service in Santa Fe. This program recognized Route 66 and its businesses as symbols of the American heritage of travel and therefore worthy of preservation. Business owners could apply for cost-share grants to be used toward the preservation and restoration of their historic businesses. The tide for the Mother Road was beginning to turn. Along those alignments that were still passable, the National Park Service erected brown and white signs that read, *Historic Route 66.* These signs gave visible evidence to its rebirth and helped lure tourists, soon to include me on my bike, into following it as a travel destination.

4

Route 66 on Index Cards

I wanted to make it to Chicago on Route 66 but I needed to know where the old route went. To this end, I read every Route 66 book in our city library. To fill in the many gaps, I sent away for city and state maps, magazines and other references. I knew that the success of my adventure would depend on using them all to develop a simple system of directions starting with Santa Monica and Los Angeles. Done right, this effort would reduce my chances of missing historic sights, getting lost, wandering into areas where I didn't belong, having to backtrack, or ending up on a freeway where bicyclists were forbidden.

I mulled over several ideas before deciding to type the directions I had onto 4"x6" index cards that I would clip onto a handlebar platform I hadn't yet built. This system would eliminate having to stop at intersections to pull out maps and figure out which way to go. Every time I came to a junction, all I'd have to do was glance down at the top card and follow the directions. Some friends were quick to call this system "primitive," wondering aloud why I wanted to spend so much time typing cards. But I was confident in my mile-by-mile directions, gleaned from everything I'd read. The effort in developing my cards would pay off as they kept me on Route 66 and its wandering replacements.

Several weeks later, deep into my "system," I took a break from typing my Texas cards. I rode over to Ken's Bike and Ski in Davis and asked Kurt, who knew me from previous visits, "Do you have anything I can use to keep track of my daily progress on my bike trip?"

It Only Hurts When I Sit Down

He led me down an aisle to a display case and said, "I've got just the thing." I watched as he removed a Vetta C-15 bicycle computer from its box and handed it to me. Figuring I was about to pay through the nose for an expensive, new fangled 21st century device, I asked him, "How long has this bike computer been around?"

"Oh, at least twenty years and the cost has dropped since they were first put on the market." He knew my weakness – a monetary bargain.

While I watched, with one turn of his Phillips-head screwdriver, he attached a small knob to a spoke on my front wheel. Next he secured a sensor to the front fork and aligned it with the knob. Then he wrapped the long wire from the sensor around one of the front forks, securing it with tape as he went up. At the end of the wire was an empty clip that he attached to my handlebar. In just over a minute he completed this simple assembly. He then picked up the computer, no bigger than a matchbook, and slid it into the empty clip.

Before turning me loose for a trial ride in the parking lot, he explained how the two buttons on the computer functioned. Somewhat confused, but pretending to be otherwise, I wheeled the bike outside and pushed each button as I rode around. I watched in amazement as my speed, time of day, total time of pedaling, total distance traveled, my fastest speed, and average speed all appeared on the computer screen as beckoned. With this little gizmo, I could record my numerical progress at the end of every day and then re-set it to zero, ready to gather more data the following day. Just having this new toy would bring a new sense of excitement to my adventure.

Several weeks later I completed typing forty-six index cards, (sample, Figure 1). Only two problems had cropped up. Almost without exception, everyone writing about Route 66 had done it from the perspective of driving from east to west, sometimes on one-way streets. Since I would be going the opposite direction, I had no idea which street was Route 66 eastbound.

Directions that I couldn't follow at all were those that told drivers to use urban freeways where bikes weren't allowed. Solving both of these problems would have to wait until I got to the area in question and found either Route 66 signs or residents kind enough to give me directions.

Another problem had to do with multiple alignments of Route 66. In Illinois there were three. Sometimes all three were the same road or one was longer as it meandered through rural farmland. In New Mexico, one alignment was sixty-two miles shorter and eliminated a 2,000-foot climb up La Bajada Hill between Albuquerque and Santa Fe. I solved every multiple alignment by choosing to follow the one in use in 1939, the year I was born.

As I looked at my completed stack of route cards and the maps that accompanied them, I felt like I knew the entire 2300 miles from Santa Monica to Chicago. I was excited, running at a fever pitch. The next step in getting ready was to set some tentative dates and then to get my body in condition so I could ride at least twelve hours every day. I would have to kick my discipline into high gear as I moved into this phase of my preparation.

Mi	Hwy/street/etc.	City	To See
0	Lv Tex border on I40		
22.9	I40 to Adrian exit, X to N I40 & Hwy 66 to Adrian	Adrian	HALF-WAY; Mid-pt
37.3	Hwy 66 Adrian to Vega	Vega	
63.4	Hwy 66 Vega to Cadillac Ranch, exit 62 S or I40 Enter Amar on bus loop 40,		Cadillac Ranch
	Veers N to 9th Ave, rt 9th Av becomes BshInd Av, lft	Amar	
	BshInd becomes 6th Av, rt		Gold Lght Café-40s
73.2	6th Av to Buchanan, lft		

5

Setting Dates and Building Endurance

A wet and blustery Sacramento Valley winter had slowly given way to spring. Daffodils, poppies, almond blossoms and green fields all around were collaborating to tell me the time had come to involve my bike and move my preparation outdoors. But first I wanted to huddle with my calendar and mark some dates in ink (firm) or in pencil (flexible).

The first date I penned was April 27th, the day after my 66th birthday and the day I'd leave. Next I flipped the calendar ahead to May and set aside in pencil two rest days 500 miles apart, one in Albuquerque and the other in Owasso, Oklahoma. Both were conveniently on Route 66 where my two brothers lived. In case I ran into inclement weather, mechanical problems, bodily ailments that refused to let me pedal on, or just felt inclined to take an afternoon nap under a shade tree in Missouri, I penciled in two more days to accommodate these eventualities.

From past experience, cycling an average of eighty-five miles every day was reasonable. Dividing that number into the 2300 miles to Chicago, I came up with twenty-seven days of cycling. I added the four miscellaneous off days and figured I would arrive in Chicago just in time to avoid the Memorial Day weekend surge in traffic. If I couldn't make it by then, I'd go to Plan B and enjoy the three-day holiday with my son and his wife in Springfield, Illinois before cycling the last three days from there to Chicago.

With these dates to shoot for and my anticipation growing, I moved on to the most crucial and difficult part of my preparation. It was time to start riding and take advantage of the warm spring weather and the increasing hours of daylight.

Doug Waterman

I was a recreational runner, averaging 10-15 miles every week for nearly twenty years. Occasionally I'd break up my routine and compete in 10K races. With my resting heart-beat in the high 40s and my blood pressure steady around 115/75, my doctor assured me that my cardiovascular system could meet the challenge of cycling as far as I wanted…every day. What I needed, however, was the same confidence in the rest of my body, in particular my legs. From experience I knew that my calf muscles hurt when I ran long distances and when I biked, my thigh muscles took over the complaining. So I decided to cut back on running and in its place substitute weekend training rides of increasing length starting the first Saturday in March.

I walked out the front door that morning, feeling like I was 45, not 65 and could ride forever. I slid a full water bottle into its holder, stuffed a 6-oz bag of trail mix into my handlebar bag, and pumped air into my tires until they were rock hard. I absentmindedly pressed my thumb into the seat, testing for give. I smiled at the shallow dimple my thumb made, knowing this test had never been a reliable indication of the seat's comfort. I buckled on my bike helmet, slid the computer into its clip, swung my right leg over the bike and sat down. My harmony with the seat always began comfortably, every wrinkle, bulge and protruding bone in my rear accommodated. I pushed off and wiggled my feet into their pedal toe cages. Shifting gears, my speed increased as my legs thrust effortlessly like pistons, their up-and-down movement fluid and powerful. The breeze caressed my face, while the thrill of self-powered movement, something so satisfying and simple, captivated me once again.

I followed the euphoria, the miles adding up on the computer. And then, just after my second break at twenty-five miles, the headache started in the back of my neck, followed by the hint of pain in my left thigh. Forty-three miles after starting, I wheeled back into the driveway. I dismounted and steadied myself against the bike. The sudden stiffness in my back resisted my effort to straighten up. Then came the deep pain in both thighs, a throbbing headache, and the old aching rawness in my rear end. All this pain made no sense. The roads had been flat, there was no headwind, I had no load, and I'd only been gone just under four hours. I took baby-steps into the house, flopped backward onto the bed and lay moaning while massaging my sore-to-the-touch thigh muscles for the next ten minutes. Of everything that hurt, it was my butt that worried me the least. But it hadn't always been that way.

Seven years ago on my first long distance cycling trip from Davis to Santa Fe, I'd started out completely unaware of how painful my rear would become. At the end of the second day, I made my nightly call home to Donna and told her about the pain and flaming red rash that was slowly turning my bottom into the color of a turkey vulture's head. "Try to find some *A + D Ointment* in a drug store and give it a try," she said. "We used it on the kids' diaper rash when they were babies and it should work for you." The next day I bought a tube and before I fell asleep the next two nights, I ignored any comparison between my butt and my children's and spread copious amounts on my rear. Within those two days the pain and rash were gone.

One morning several days later on that trip to Santa Fe, I parked my bicycle where I could keep an eye on it by the front door of a Farmington, New Mexico restaurant. I'd been sleeping outdoors every night, primarily because, at the end of every day there were no towns nearby. The last time I'd bathed was four days before when I washed in the boiling water flowing down a Nevada hillside from a hot spring. Not wanting to eat breakfast and offend restaurant patrons with my aroma and disheveled appearance, I had deliberately selected a table in a corner far from where others were sitting. It wasn't long, however, before a Navajo man, his hair braided in back and wearing a turquoise belt buckle and rings, walked in with a young woman. He saw the helmet and gloves on my table and deliberately headed my way. He sat down at the table next to mine, ignored my appearance and introduced himself and his daughter, Cheryl.

Following our introductory chitchat, Carlos told me, "I used to enjoy bicycling but don't much do it anymore."

"And why's that?"

"There was a problem that made the whole experience excruciating."

I'd told him that I'd ridden all the way from California so he must have decided I was some sort of an expert on anatomy and wanted to know, "How do you keep your butt from burning?"

I pondered his question, trying to decide whether to give him the honest answer or make one up on the spur of the moment. Our conversation to this point had been like that of two friends, so I decided to go with the lighthearted answer, telling him with mock seriousness, "It only hurts when I sit down."

He and Cheryl thought about that for a moment and then all three of us laughed at my non-solution to his pain problem. I went on to explain, hoping I wasn't about to embarrass his daughter, "Every night I slather *A + D Ointment* on my rear and it really works." Now lying on my bed seven years later, the ointment once again gracing my tush, the thought of that pleasant conversation many years ago came to mind and I hoped Carlos was riding again.

By the following weekend, my pains were gone. I felt strong again so I increased my mileage to fifty-seven. When I got home, I felt less sore. On the next Saturday I rode seventy-three miles with the added weight of two fully loaded rear panniers, waterproof carriers that attached to the bike with hardware specific for the front or back wheels. The following Saturday I rode eighty miles, again with two full panniers. The route I took this time had a long first gear, four-mph climb. I was tired when I got home after these last two rides but it was the kind of tired that made me feel fully alive and helped me to sleep soundly.

The following Saturday a rain storm caught me five miles from home. I hadn't packed any rain gear so I decided to wait it out on a hay bale in a farmer's barn. The intensity of the storm showed no sign of letting up after thirty minutes so I sloshed my way back home, arriving cold and drenched but thankful for the lesson on packing for inclement weather.

My ultimate training goal was to ride 100 miles in one day. Riding that distance with my bike fully loaded would give me the inner strength and endurance to go that far, even for two or three consecutive days. Folsom Lake was fifty miles away so I chose it as my turn around destination. This 100-mile round trip would stress my legs with the slight gain in elevation the first half and the resistance of a westerly headwind coming back.

I wanted the weight on this last training ride to match what it would be going to Chicago. Deciding what to take would be complicated by my age, the long distances between towns and the fact I would be alone. No one would be making motel or restaurant reservations, waiting alongside the road to rescue me with food, water, shade, or offers to carry my gear. I couldn't count on help in violent weather or with mechanical problems. I had a clear understanding of the need to pack the things I needed the most.

I started by gathering everything that would go into the four panniers. After several tries, I finally got the weight balanced. In the right front pannier I put food: two small containers of granola, a bag of trail mix, an orange, banana, whole wheat crackers, energy bars, powdered milk, plastic knife and spoon, a small plastic bowl and cup, a 6-oz jar of crunchy peanut butter and a sack lunch. In a small pouch in this pannier, I put my notebook, two road maps and the 4x6-inch route cards for Arizona and New Mexico.

The left front pannier had my SLR camera, film, first aid kit, SPF 45 sun block, zinc oxide, water purification tablets, *A + D Ointment*, snake bite kit, scissors, needle/thread, and a tube of liquid soap. Completing the load in this pannier were my toothpaste, toothbrush, ear plugs, spare tube, chain lubricant, short length of rope, a small box of tools, and my one concession to comfort, an electric razor.

The rear panniers were larger. I filled the right rear one with two long-sleeve cotton shirts, two short-sleeve t-shirts to be replaced by polyester shirts I had ordered, padded under-shorts, socks, riding shorts, one pair of jeans, a towel, dirty clothes bag, and travelers' checks. The left rear pannier contained my cold and rainy weather clothes – rain repellant jacket, pants and helmet cover, fleece shirt, gloves, sweatshirt, and windbreaker. On the back of each rear pannier I had attached a blinking red taillight.

On the rear rack I used two wide leather belts to tie down my two-person tent, sleeping bag and foam pad. I attached to the handlebar my computer, light and the wooden platform holding the 4x6-inch cards for California. In the handlebar bag I had a whistle to signal for help, a bandana, two pairs of glasses (dark and reading), Kleenex, and two readily accessible energy bars. Completing my load were three full water bottles and a rag to wipe perspiration or grease from my hands.

My packing concluded with the two deep pockets in my riding shorts. In them I had stowed away a small plastic folder that contained my driver's license, insurance card, some cash, and a laminated, two-sided card with phone numbers and addresses of family and close friends.

Before leaving on my final training ride, I was curious how much everything weighed. My gear, including water, weighed 46 pounds. My bike, with pannier racks, pump, three water bottle cages, and back rack totaled 33 pounds. Adding the 155 pounds I weighed brought the grand total to 234 pounds.

The morning of my last training ride, Davis was behind me by 6:00a.m. I followed the dedicated bike lane alongside I-80 to Sacramento. It was a pleasure not having to contend with cars. I crossed the Sacramento River, turned left and bumped my way over the cobblestones in colorful and quiet Old Sacramento. One mile later I crossed the American River, stopped in Discovery Park for a water break, and smeared sun block over the exposed skin on my face, neck, and legs.

When I started pedaling again, it was on the asphalt trail that I would follow the next forty miles to Folsom Lake. The morning was cool, there was no wind, and the songs of unseen birds serenaded me. Several wild turkeys, with nary a glance at me, ambled across the asphalt trail ahead, close enough to be run over if I hadn't braked hard. As the morning passed, I was joined by runners, walkers, and other cyclists, all of us enjoying the beauty and peacefulness of this paved trail, truly a Sacramento recreational treasure.

Several people going my direction asked, "Where ya' headed?" After I told them, "I'm training for my trip on Route 66 to Chicago," a torrent of questions always followed. I enjoyed sharing my plans, gathering advice and welcoming good wishes. Along the way I pulled up alongside a runner, slowed down, and rode with him until he completed the last mile of his half-marathon run for the morning.

I was tired and dehydrated when I got to Folsom Lake just a little after noon. I sprawled on a patch of grass, ate my peanut butter and jam sandwich, carrots, energy bar, and emptied a full water bottle. I napped for twenty minutes and then headed back home, downhill and into a light breeze. Thirteen hours after starting, with the sun now slipping behind the hills that defined the start of the Sacramento Valley west of Davis, I arrived home. I hurt but I'd achieved the boost I wanted. I had pushed my endurance to a new high and was ready to head to Chicago, capable of cycling 100 miles a day if necessary. I wanted to relax the next two weeks before leaving but I still had several problems to solve, one of which would leave me with a deep sense of gratitude.

6

A Blessing

I tore open the UPS package that arrived one afternoon after my ride to Folsom Lake. It contained two polyester cycling shirts I'd ordered from L.L. Bean. I tried them both on and immediately saw the problem with these "Made in Honduras" shirts. The sleeves hung to the tip of my fingers. I tried to picture the model for these medium-sized shirts but just couldn't imagine anyone, short of an orangutan, with arms that long.

In the past, I'd taken my clothing alteration needs to Mahin. I felt good patronizing this cheerful woman in her downtown Davis shop. I enjoyed her engaging personality and the results of her work had always met my expectations. So the next morning I gripped the handrail, climbed the twenty-eight steps to her cozy, one-room shop and asked her to perform a minor amputation on my two shirts. She directed me to her cramped changing enclosure where I put one shirt on. As she pinned the sleeves, I told her, "I'm going to wear both these shirts on my bicycle trip to Chicago." As I told her this, her smile changed to a worried frown. In an effort to reassure her, I told her about my preparations and how I was taking every precaution to be safe. Gradually she resumed her cheerful continence and promised my shirts would be ready in four days.

The morning I returned, Mahin was seated at her sewing machine, hemming a dress. She had the two windows in her shop wide open and was enjoying the cool spring morning and the varied imitations of the mocking birds singing in the tree outside. She saw me enter the open door, walked over to the clothes rack, and removed the shirts. Instead of handing them to me right away, she resumed our previous discussion about my trip. All morning I had been hurrying to finish my errands but now in Mahin's shop that urgency didn't seem so important.

"You will have a cell phone?" she both asked and instructed.

"No."

"Then how will your family know how you are?"

"I'm planning to call my wife from a pay phone or a motel phone every night."

She smiled and then told me, "I listen to mantra. I'm from India and the mantra gives me peace." She stooped over and increased the volume on the tape player that was on the floor under her sewing machine. Until then I hadn't paid any attention to the harmonious and repetitive music that was playing but now its lilt filled the room. Her features glowed and her smile widened as she told me, "The mantra means much to me and it goes into the clothes I sew. The mantra is now in your shirts, bringing you a safe trip."

With this benediction, she handed me the shirts. They had been more than altered; they had been blessed. I was overwhelmed and humbled by her concern and genuine fear for my safety.

As I pulled out my wallet to pay for the alterations, she said, "No, that's alright. This is my gift to you for your trip." I had never been a good receiver and I failed again, convincing Mahin that I needed to pay something. We settled on half the total cost. If she was disappointed in my inability to accept the generosity of her total gift, she didn't show it.

She asked me to stop in when I returned. I promised I would and as I carefully descended the steep steps, I felt an inner peace. Thanks in part to Mahin, I knew my trip would be successful.

7

The Pieces are Coming Together

When the thought of riding the length of Route 66 first played across my brain, it was accompanied by the idea of making it a charity fund raiser. If people believed in what I was doing and for whom I was doing it, their contributions would not only benefit a worthy cause but would also encourage me whenever I had those inevitable times of struggle. So with my departure nearing, I arranged to meet with Stu Bresnick, the Executive Director of Yolo County Habitat for Humanity.

Two days later I drove to meet Stu and his AmeriCorps aide, Aurora, a heightened sense of optimism riding with me. By the time we sat down, I'd convinced myself they would never think of turning down my offer. If they had any concerns about my age, relative lack of cycling experience, the danger involved on Route 66 or the fact that I would be riding by myself for 2300 miles, I figured my obvious enthusiasm would trump their reservations.

As the three of us talked, Aurora said she had travelled Route 66 and thought my idea was terrific. Stu, on the other hand, welcomed my offer but before making a final decision, he wanted to discuss it with the Habitat Board.

Leaving his office I felt like I had taken the final exam but hadn't studied hard enough to pass it. My proposal was now in the hands of "The Board" and I'd just have to be patient. Nonetheless, what was driving my disappointment was knowing I had put all my hope into this one organization and if they rejected my offer, it was too late to start the process all over again with another charity.

Two mornings later the phone rang. It was Stu. "I wanted to let you know that Habitat has agreed to back you on your trip," he said. I pantomimed a silent "Yes!" and did a little dance in the kitchen as he went on to explain, "Construction on three homes is scheduled to start in the fall so your offer is very timely. Not only will people donate but your ride will encourage volunteering in the upcoming build."

I thanked Stu for his confidence in me and when we hung up, I knew that my ride had become something special and not just a selfish jaunt across the country. The fortune in my Chinese fortune cookie from several days before said it best: *Some chance of glamour and excitement is coming to you.*

Over the next few days, Stu and Aurora created a flyer. The top portion advertised my ride and the bottom tear-off portion was for the donor to complete and mail to Habitat with their donation. He arranged for Julie Rooney, a newspaper reporter with *The Davis Enterprise*, to take my picture and write about my trip. Stu gave me a Habitat placard and I attached it to the front of my handlebar bag where it could easily be seen. On Habitat stationary, he wrote a *Letter of Introduction* for me to use if I needed help along the way. His overwhelming support inspired me, adding to my growing confidence.

During my last leisurely ride on the county roads around Davis, I could no longer ignore the binding links in my chain and the aggravating rhythmic squeak coming from the rear wheel. I was running out of time so I took the bike to Ken's bike shop and explained my litany of problems to Kurt, Ken's ace mechanic. To the things needing to be done he suggested he also adjust the brakes and give the bike an overall tune up.

Eight years earlier I'd bought this used mountain bike and ridden it problem-free to New Mexico on my first and only long-distance solo trip. Taking a nosedive off my bike at my age would likely result in broken bones so I was glad to have this sturdy bike to keep me upright even if it was several pounds heavier than the average road bike. I sacrificed speed for stability with 1.5" tires that were wide enough to keep me from falling if they slipped into parallel cracks in the road. On my training rides I'd hit potholes, jarring bumps, and railroad tracks and the bike had given me no reasons to worry.

When I picked up my bike two days later, Kurt was grinning. I'd never seen him display his feelings or speak in anything but a quiet monotone, so his visible expression of emotion caught me by surprise. "You're good to go buddy," he said. "Don't forget to mail us a postcard somewhere along your way."

My problems were now down to one. Despite my every effort, I had no idea how I'd get to the start of Route 66 in Santa Monica, 400 miles from Davis. I'd put a "ride wanted – will help with driving" ad in the newspaper and another on the ride board at the University of California – Davis. Both brought no results. I'd called five rental car agencies and they'd all told me, "Our closest Santa Monica return of a rental car is at Los Angeles International Airport (LAX)," which I knew was at least eight dangerous freeway miles from Santa Monica.

The next morning my neighbor, Jerry, and I were solving the worlds' problems in our front yards. When I told him how I was striking out on getting to Santa Monica, he volunteered, "You could always box your bike, fly it with you to LA and then take a taxi from LAX to Santa Monica." This was a possibility but I didn't want to risk my bike being damaged in transit.

Continuing his effort to be helpful he named several rental agencies and in the process mentioned one I hadn't contacted – National Car Rental. With renewed hope, I went inside, dialed National, and waited to hear their inconvenient drop-off policy. But instead, the cheerful voice on the other end explained, "You can rent a car at Sacramento International Airport and drop it off at our rental lot in Santa Monica. It's only, maybe, ten blocks from where you want to start pedaling at the ocean." Thanks to Jerry, my last problem was solved.

The day before leaving was my 66th birthday. Donna and I decided to celebrate at our favorite pasta restaurant. From the moment we sat down, we couldn't ignore the fact that, if I didn't make it back, this would be the eve of our final parting. As we talked, the mundane crowded out the meaningful. I tried to express my feelings but my words sounded empty. When we fell into silence, it was more intense than when we spoke. We had both looked forward to a long leisurely cheerful dinner but we ended up leaving sooner than we planned, our emotions still intact.

Back home, we taped to the wall a road map of Route 66. She would use it to track my progress by circling the name of the city I would call her from at the end of every day. We traced the path of Route 66, the distance daunting. Every inch of blue or red highway line on the map represented one-hundred miles on the ground, nearly a day's cycling distance.

When we finished posting the map, we sat down and reluctantly went through a folder of things she'd need to do in case I was seriously injured or killed. Discussing on my birthday the possibility of my death presented a morbid juxtaposition. But when all the family stuff was out of the way, our emotions surged to the surface. We embraced and shared how much we cared about and loved each other. And then she handed me a gift. I unwrapped it and inside was a journal. On the front page she had written:

> *Dug, my love,*
> *I will be sending you courage and strength and comfort.*
> *And most of all love. And thoughts, always positive thoughts, to smooth your way.*
>
> *I will be carrying you in my heart, and in my body, and in my very bones.*
>
> *All the time you are pedaling – like mad – on the Mother Road, may the power that created the universe, and you and me, protect and guide you, and speed you on your way.*
>
> *And may this endeavor, this challenge, be all you hope for.*
>
> *xxxooo*
> *Donna*

My tears came unbidden. I knew deep within that as my trip played itself out, her words would serve to empower and comfort me. I would be a solitary bicyclist but I would not be alone.

8

To the Starting Line

A fitful night's rest left me feeling groggy. It was still dark outside as I stood staring at my reflection in the bathroom mirror while shaving and trying to reconcile my apprehension with my excitement. As we ate breakfast, Donna commented on how confident I seemed but all I could think was, *what in heaven's name have I gotten myself into?*

Our drive to get my rental car at Sacramento International Airport took twenty minutes. Along the way I avoided talking about our nearing separation, instead reminding her to pay a bill and run an errand I'd forgotten. Goodbyes had always been difficult and this morning was no exception. At once I wanted to stay and leave, my heart and my head waging their battle.

The sun was coming up over the Sierra as we transferred my bike and gear into the trunk of the rental car. While breathing in the damp, earthy smell of spring, I used my bicycle rag to wipe the night's condensation off the windows. A passenger jet taking off interrupted the early morning quiet as we hugged. We assured one another that our upcoming time apart held the promise of new depth in our marriage. I closed my eyes and welcomed the intensity of her embrace and then her kiss. "I love you. I'll call you tonight," I said.

"I love you too. Please…be careful."

I followed her as we drove to the airport exit. She took the I-5 North on-ramp headed for work in Woodland and we waved goodbye. I wiped my tears with my shirtsleeve, merged into the traffic heading south on I-5 to Los Angeles, and accelerated to the speed limit, my mind filling with random thoughts of the adventure that had begun.

The morning hours raced toward noon and the gas gauge plunged toward empty. At the rate it was falling, I knew the full tank I'd started with was not going to be enough to get me to Santa Monica. Near the top of Tejon Pass, 325 miles from Sacramento, I decided to stop and buy a few gallons. Even with this unplanned delay, I still hoped to bike far enough inland to outrun a rainstorm forecast to move on shore overnight.

At the gas station, I became increasingly frustrated with my inability to figure out how to unlock the small door covering the gas cap. I pushed, pulled and twisted every lever, button and knob I could find inside the car, but the gas door refused to budge.

Losing patience and time, I interrupted the man pumping gas in front of me and asked him, "Could you give me a hand with my gas cap?" He shook his head, told me, "I don't have the time," and turned away.

At the other row of pumps was a tow truck driver, bending over while filling a five-gallon gas can. I approached him from behind, and from his size, I wondered what position he'd played in football. "Excuse me," I said. As he stood up and turned around I realized this was the first time I'd seen a woman tow truck operator. Thankful I hadn't betrayed my gender error out loud, I asked her, "Could you help me open the gas cap on my rental car?" If she had any pity for my incompetence, she politely hid it. "Sure, just give me a minute here."

She topped off her gas can, hefted its forty-five pounds onto the tow truck and then walked with me to my car. She opened the driver's door, bent over and flipped a lever on the floor between the door and the driver's seat. She could have found it with her eyes closed. For all I knew, since her back was turned toward me, maybe they were closed. I thanked her and with the hint of a smile, she said, "No problem."

Less than two hours later I exited the Santa Monica freeway and within ten minutes was at the National Rental lot on Broadway. The two employees, their names sewn onto their company shirt, took care of the paperwork while I unloaded the car. When they finished, it was Josh who watched me from the top of the office steps as I loaded my bike.

I attached the two small panniers to the front wheel and the two larger ones to the rear. The two belts I wrapped around the bedroll and the tent and then, with a hefty tug, cinched them tightly to the back rack. I then changed plans and tied the foam pad to the seat post, a change I would later rue. Next I clipped the first several California 4x6 inch cards onto the handlebar platform, and slid the computer, light and two full water bottles into their respective holders. I was half-way through this process when Josh straightened up, stretched and asked, "So, where ya' headed?"

I had resolved to be deliberately confident every time I was asked this question. Instead of saying, with a tinge of uncertainty, "I hope to make it to Chicago," I'd just say, "I'm goin' to Chicago." After I told Josh my destination, he resumed his silent watching. The thought crossed my mind that keeping quiet might be his way of hiding his skepticism. I put on my sun glasses to which I had mounted my side-view mirror, buckled my helmet on, and slipped on my riding gloves. During this final part of my routine, Josh's curiosity came to life again. "Where ya' from?" he asked.

"Davis. It's just west of Sacramento on the interstate to San Francisco."

"I've been to San Francisco but I don't know where Davis or Sacramento is."

I was tempted to expand my geography lesson but since I was too eager to get going, I just let the subject drop.

Route 66 once began seven blocks from the Pacific Ocean. Today it is commonly agreed that it begins where Ocean and Santa Monica Boulevards intersect at the ocean, two blocks north of the Santa Monica Pier. So I headed to the pier first, took a picture of my bike parked at the entrance, and then pushed it two blocks north to where Ocean and Santa Monica Boulevards met. As I read the 1952 plaque dedicating Route 66 as the *Will Rogers Highway*, I remembered reading that this dedication had been a promotion to publicize the movie *The Will Rogers Story* and only secondarily an effort to name the highway after Will. I looked around for a highway sign that would eliminate any doubt this was where east-bound Route 66 began but there wouldn't be one for another five years.

What I did see was a beautiful day. The sky this 27th day of April, 2005, was cloudless and the temperature in the 70s. A light westerly breeze rustled the palm fronds as people walked, jogged, and rollerbladed on the wide sidewalk separating Ocean Boulevard from the beach. I pondered joining the napping transients on the cool lush grass but when I looked at the traffic light again, it had changed. It was 3:15 p.m., and I did need to be on my way. Was I really here? I wondered. I pedaled across Ocean Boulevard and headed east on Santa Monica Boulevard. The training rides were over. This was the real thing. After a year of preparation, I was on my way to Chicago.

Starting at the Santa Monica Pier.

9

Traffic, a Grump, and Family

I'll always love you, for the rest of my life. You are my everything... Over and over I sang these words from a song made popular by Whitney Houston. It made no difference they were the only ones I could remember, the rest a guess just like the melody. Before me was a month apart from Donna and I missed her…already. With thoughts of her heavy on my mind, I joined the crush and din of delivery trucks, taxis, buses, and passenger vehicles on four-lane Santa Monica Boulevard.

Immediately I was caught up in the dangers of city cycling. Riding close to cars parked parallel, I risked being doored – slamming into a car door opening in front of me. My imagination left no doubt how that experience would wreck my bike, bringing a beautiful day and my trip to an abrupt and painful end. After the first close call, I tried to reduce, if not eliminate, this danger by looking inside every parked car to see if someone on the driver's side was preparing to get out. But the prevalence of tinted windows made it impossible to see inside most cars. So I tried keeping an open-door distance from parked cars by moving into the nearest traffic lane, exchanging the door danger to one of being sideswiped or hit from behind.

Both riding strategies were dangerous but as I rode along I found a balance. Because there was so much traffic and it was being slowed by stop lights, if I pedaled a little harder I could keep pace most of the time. When I came to unoccupied loading or no parking zones, I moved far to the right, letting vehicles pass me safely. It was these movements that I hoped would help me when I got to other heavily trafficked cities like Albuquerque, Amarillo, Oklahoma City, St. Louis and Chicago.

In Beverly Hills, Santa Monica Boulevard and I made a one block jog to the left. It was then the noise from honking cars increased. Figuring this was part of the cacophony of vehicle noise I was slowly getting used to, I just ignored it. What I couldn't ignore was the man on the sidewalk up ahead. He had been talking on his cell phone but was now flailing his arms for me to stop while also pointing behind me. I pulled up next to him, turned around, and saw cars swerving to avoid my sleeping bag pad that had come untied from the seat post and was lying in the right hand traffic lane. I leaned the bike onto the curb (it had no kick stand), thanked him, waited for a break in the traffic, and then darted into the street to retrieve the pad. While belting it securely to the back rack this time, I saw that there were no tire marks on it. This was the first of innumerable times on my trip when people looked out for me.

Sixteen miles from where Santa Monica Boulevard and I began, it ended at Sunset Boulevard in Los Angeles. With no visible evidence of having left one city and entering another, we had been together through the cities of West Los Angeles, Century City, Beverly Hills, and West Hollywood. The traffic had thinned and I was ready for my first break. I stopped at a sign directing the way to Dodger Stadium and while resting, heard someone behind me shout, "Hello." I turned around and saw a man jogging toward me. He carried a swinging briefcase and was dressed in slacks, button-down dress shirt and a tie flapping wildly over his shoulder. His next words, the same three Josh had spoken at National Car Rental, were to become the first ones spoken in nearly every conversation I'd have for the next month. "Where ya' goin?" he asked while trying to catch his breath.

"To Chicago."

"I biked to the Grand Canyon once and sprained my ankle," he said. He must have seen the perplexed look on my face but he made no effort to explain how these two events were related. "I camped there in the snow with a tent. I didn't have a sleeping bag though and froze all night. I see you've got a sleeping bag and a tent," he said.

Responding to his interest in my gear, I showed him my computer, index card directions, and the food I had packed in one front pannier. He didn't ask me about a cell phone but he did wrinkle his forehead after lifting my bike to see how heavy it was. When we parted, he wished me luck and I felt a rush of confirmation. If my interactions with people from here to Chicago were this spontaneous, funny, and unusual, I was in for a stimulating trip.

The directions I'd typed onto my 4x6-inch cards were accurate so far, confirmed from time to time by the presence of a black-and-white Historic Route 66 highway shield strapped to a light pole. I followed Sunset Boulevard to Broadway, then Figueroa Street and twenty-six miles from my start, I turned right onto Colorado Boulevard. I was

only going 15 mph but the cars on the Foothill freeway, I-210, to my left, were going even slower. I considered entering the freeway at the next on-ramp, and "speeding" past them. It was the certainty of an expensive ticket from the California Highway Patrol (CHP) and the laughter of drivers seeing that event unfold that convinced me I'd better stay off the freeway.

Nearing Glendale, Colorado Boulevard led me over the multi-arched, concrete Arroyo Seco Bridge. Built in 1913, it was at least thirteen years older than Route 66. I followed this path of the annual Rose Bowl Parade through Pasadena until in Arcadia, Route 66 became Huntington Drive. In Monrovia I passed the Aztec Hotel, built in 1926 and now on the National Register of Historic Places.

The first hours of my ride had been so much fun that I hadn't even thought about eating dinner and finding a motel for the night. A small pizza and salad at Shakeys solved the first need and a short distance later, forty miles from the Pacific, I rode up to the office of a motel named 'Motel.' It was getting dark so I decided not to take a chance on finding another motel farther on.

The office door was locked but on the wall above the door handle was a sign that read, "Push Here." The grating buzz summoned a man who emerged like an apparition out of the darkness in the back.

"Ya' want a room?" he asked in a tone that made me think he was hoping I would change my mind and move on. I shouted "Yes" into the slot in the bottom of the thick glass window that separated us, a window whose primary purpose seemed to be preventing a robbery and not to facilitate a conversation.

"It's forty dollars," a price I guessed he'd made up. Motel rates, in my experience, had never totaled to even dollars.

I briefly considered bargaining with him but decided he had already sized me up and concluded the forty dollars was what I could afford.

"I'll take it," I said.

He fumbled for a registration form and shoved it and a pen into the slot. While filling it out, I glanced up, our eyes meeting. His seemed to be sinking deeper into their sockets. He glowered at me, his glum facial expression showing no evidence of welcome. Maybe it was the bike, my gray goatee, or my helmet that reminded him of a past conflict. Or maybe he had just had a hard day and didn't want to deal with the public anymore. Whatever was going on, if I hadn't been alone, in a strange place, and hemmed in by darkness, I would have moseyed on down the road to find a more welcoming place. But under the circumstance, I wasn't going to give him any excuse to turn whatever was bothering him into my problem. I'd just be friendly and patient, leaving in my wake a smile and the impression that bicyclists are good people.

I slid the completed registration along with two twenty-dollar travelers' checks through the slot. "I need ID," he mumbled. I gave him my driver's license and waited while he compared my three fresh signatures with the used one on the driver's license. Considering the time it took him to do this, I wondered if he was scrutinizing them for evidence that I belonged in the county jail tonight, charged with trying to defraud an innkeeper.

When I'd passed his inspection, he pointed across the cracked asphalt driveway into the fading light and told me, "Your room's over there."

"What number is it?"

"Three."

"Could I have my room key?"

"Don't need one. Door's unlocked."

According to his poorly lighted motel sign, there were no in-room phones. So I explained, "I wanna lock my room when I go to make a phone call so I'll need a key to get back in."

He grumbled something unintelligible, fumbled around in a couple of drawers and reluctantly shoved the key for Room 3 into the window slot. His terse final shot was an order, "Be out by 10:00."

I smiled and said, "I will." As I headed to my room I felt his eyes following me every step of the way. I hustled my bike into the room and locked the door, feeling safe for the moment.

When I decided not to use a cell phone on my ride, Donna and I knew how important my call every evening from a pay phone or my motel room would be. It was a tangible way for us to share our daily events, solve problems, and express our love for each other. After hanging up, she would send an e-mail to our son and daughter, Ryan and Darlene, our friends, extended family and, of course, Stu Bresnick of Habitat, to give everyone an update on my progress for that day. Ryan planned to take her e-mail a step farther, adding his comments and then forwarding it to his many friends and co-workers.

When Donna and I made plans to communicate daily this way, we had no way of knowing how her e-mails would take on a life of their own, becoming a story behind the story. Responses to her e-mails were supportive, funny and loving. Daily I was reminded how important relationships were as e-mails were exchanged and my confidence grew.

I felt conspicuous and vulnerable as I left my motel room and walked down the dimly lit street to find a pay phone. As every car neared, I looked for a place to run if it stopped and someone got out to confront me. Not far from the motel I found a pay phone. It felt great to talk to Donna, her voice happy and encouraging. She gave me a brief rundown of her day and I did likewise, leaving out my evolving motel experience because I didn't want her to worry. We settled on a time for me to call tomorrow evening, said we loved each other and then goodbye. Her first e-mail this evening was short and to the point:

> *Dug finally called at 7:50. When I told him he sounded good, he said, "I feel good!" He had a nice tail-breeze for his first forty miles today. May his way be smooth and not much rain tomorrow. Blessings, Donna.*

Our conversation over, I hurried back to the motel, anticipating that every shadow held someone waiting to accost me. It took several twists on the door knob and wiggling the key in the lock before the door to my room opened. Inside I felt safe again.

Before falling asleep, I had several things I needed to do. I started with a letter from Ryan he had asked me to read at the end of this day.

> "First day of your ride! You must be excited, apprehensive, optimistic... I wish I was there to wish you well. As you start this epic journey, I hope you will grant yourself the grace to <u>enjoy</u> it. It's likely you will only do this particular trip once - <u>soak it in</u>! You are a one-of-a-kind dad...I love you and will be thinking of you often! I Wish you tough tires and a true line, with the wind always at your back!   Love, Ryan"

This was the second time today my emotions welled to tears. There would be no denying how important the encouragement of my family would be as both joy and struggle in the days ahead became pieces in the puzzle of my future.

I put Ryan's letter away, ate a PowerBar, wrote in my journal, and fell asleep. Little did I know that my night's sleep was soon to be interrupted.

10

The First Full Day

Just after midnight I was awakened by the roar of hail pounding the motel roof and slamming into the air conditioner that jutted from the window next to my bed. The Pacific storm I hoped to outrun had caught me.

It was unrealistic to think I could bicycle for one month and not run into unsafe weather. I listened to the violence raging unabated outside and knew the two days I'd set aside to wait out dangerous weather wouldn't be enough, especially if I used one of those two days this early in my trip. As I lay awake worrying, the hail gradually changed to a light rain. The song of water cascading through the downspout by the door moderated to a gentle pitter-patter that lulled me back to sleep.

Without the aid of an alarm clock, I awoke to silence at 5:45 a.m. I cracked the door and watched mist, backlit by a nearby street light, meander to the ground. The absence of wind and rain was my signal to take advantage of the improving weather. To save time, I skipped finding a café for breakfast and instead poured powdered milk and water into the bowl I carried, stirred in some granola, peeled a banana and enjoyed it with my cereal. By the time I'd finished eating, re-packed my panniers, and dropped the key into the office box it was 6:30.

The morning was invigorating, the air filled with the salty smell of the Pacific. I pedaled through shallow puddles and tiny rivulets in the street and gutter, the water leaving dark streaks on my calves. The mist soon ended but the threatening clouds still hung low, obscuring all but the base of the 10,000-foot San Gabriel Mountains to my left. About the time I thought the storm was starting to lift, the rain started. I saw an elementary school up ahead and decided to wait out the rain from under an overhang between two classrooms. This delay would give me time to look over my route cards and watch the rain as it added to the second highest yearly accumulation in history, just short of 35 inches in the Los Angeles area.

I fully expected someone on the school staff to confront me, thinking I was a transient hanging around their school. But the teachers and students all ignored me as they cheerfully hurried to their warm classrooms. The rain stopped just after the tardy bell rang and I was glad to be moving again, following Foothill Boulevard into Azusa. For the next twenty miles I rode past door-to-door businesses in Glendora, San Dimas, La Verne, Pomona, and into Claremont, all the while wondering when the congestion would end.

My 96-year-old Aunt Gertrude lived in Claremont in a retirement community for church workers. I'd been looking forward to stopping and surprising her around mid-morning. When I stepped into her room in the assisted living facility, I expected to find her reading her Bible in her favorite easy chair or even watching the stormy morning as it nourished the fragrant roses in her patio. But instead, she was asleep in bed. I said her name softly several times, gently touched her shoulder, but she didn't awaken. In the hallway I introduced myself to a nurse and asked, "Is my aunt alright?"

"She's okay," she said. "She ate her breakfast and must've gone back to sleep. Go ahead. You can wake her up." So I tried again, speaking her name louder this time. The result was the same as before. Disappointed, I asked the nurse to tell Gertrude I was sorry I'd missed her.

Several years ago Gertrude had introduced me to Virginia, a close friend who lived independently in a two-bedroom home in the same complex. Since I had the time, I decided to drop in unannounced and say "Hi." She greeted me with a hug and soon we were involved in cheerful banter over coffee accompanied by English muffins buried under thick layers of homemade strawberry jam. Our enjoyable time together passed quickly, ending with Virginia assuring me she too would tell Gertrude I had dropped by. As we walked to the door, Virginia asked, as an afterthought, "By the way, how's your bike doing?"

We hadn't talked about my bike or my trip the whole time so I decided to tell her, "I know it's foolish but I'm trying to ignore a problem with the chain. I had it worked on before I left Davis but the links have started to bind again. Are there any bicycle shops nearby?" I asked.

She didn't know of any but suggested we look through her yellow pages. She pointed out the two Competitive Edge Cyclery stores that were still ahead of me on my route through Upland and Rancho Cucamonga. Rather than taking the time to write down the phone numbers and addresses of both stores, she told me, "Just tear the page out and take it with you. I won't ever need it." So I did and was on my way again.

Wolfe's Market in Claremont was small, which partially explained why I almost missed it. I was attracted by the fact that it was still in the same location since being founded around the time Route 66 was built. Inside the market the shelves were fully stocked and the cozy aisles punctuated with friendly conversations. Only one of the three cash registers was open and two people were waiting to have their groceries rung up. To speed my single purchase, a ripe banana to eat somewhere down the road, an employee opened a register for me. Dressed casually in blue jeans and an off-yellow, three-button pullover, he rang up my total, a whopping 21 cents. As he did this, I guessed, "So this store's been here since 1932?"

With no outward sign that he was disappointed with my meager transaction or the wrong date, he said, "Actually, since 1917, nine years before Route 66." He pointed to several pictures taped to the register and said, "You can see

Wolf's Market, founded in 1917.

how the store has changed over the years." I looked at the pictures and asked, "Are you related to the owner?"

"I'm Tom Wolfe. My great-grandfather started this grocery and I'm carrying on his legacy."

I introduced myself, shook hands with Tom, and wondered silently how difficult it must be for a small independent grocery to compete with the chains. As we talked, I got a glimpse of how he did it as he greeted every customer by name, asked one how his wife was doing, and told another when he expected a special item to be in stock. As much as a grocery, Wolfe's Market was a place where friends gathered. When I asked him to sign my journal and come outside for a moment so I could take his picture, he graciously agreed to do both.

Leaving Claremont, I checked the 4x6 card that had directions for the next twenty miles. I had made a note to look for a statue, The Madonna of the Trail, in the next town of Upland. Like Wolfe's Market, I almost missed it, this time on the opposite side of Foothill Boulevard.

I crossed the wide street and circled the statue, erected here at the end of the National Old Trails Highway by the Daughters of the American Revolution. Standing on a ten-foot concrete base was the sculpture of a woman. In her left arm she cradled a baby while grasping the muzzle of a rifle with her right hand. Tugging on the hem of her dress was a young child. Imagining this woman's struggles, I wondered how I would have survived illness, child rearing, hunger and the harsh environment that so many settlers did.

Back on the bike again, I didn't see the one and one-half-inch roofing nail with a one inch square metal cap before hitting it dead-on. Firmly embedded in my front tire, it announced its presence with a repetitive click every time the tire revolved and the nail smacked the pavement. After several revolutions, the tire went flat. Now I had a second problem to add to the binding chain links. I carried a patch kit and spare inner tube to repair or replace a flat but I had no idea how to repair the chain. That problem had gotten so bad, in fact, that my foot would lurch forward several inches every time those stiff links came around and failed to engage the pedal sprocket. I figured it was only a matter of time before my foot would slip off the pedal, hit the ground and cause me to fall. It was an unreasonable expectation but I didn't want any mechanical problems on my trip. I wasn't even 24 hours into riding and I already had two, one of which had brought me to a halt. Frustration welled inside me as I wondered how I'd get both problems fixed.

Fretting over my predicament, I remembered the yellow page advertisement Virginia had insisted I tear out of her telephone directory. I pulled it out of my handlebar bag, smoothed the wrinkles, and looked at the small map that showed one of the two Cyclery stores near the intersection of Foothill and Haven streets. I looked up and saw the name of the next cross street, "Haven," suspended from the traffic light. Three blocks later, I pushed my crippled bike into the Cyclery, wondering if good fortune like this would accompany me all the way to Chicago.

Two employees were at work inside. I explained my problems and the adventure I had started yesterday. With no hesitation, Pete, with his cap on backward, set aside the repair he was working on and told me, "We'll get you back on the road in quick order."

I removed the four panniers and watched him turn the bike over and put it on a stand. For ten minutes he manipulated and lubricated the troublesome links, the movement of his hands efficient and confident. When he finished he told me, "You won't have any more trouble with your chain." I could only hope. Back in Davis, my mechanic, Kurt, had told me the same thing.

Moving on to the front tire, he threw away the inner tube, explaining, "We don't patch tubes." In its place he installed one that had slime in it, a viscous green solution that plugged small holes caused by glass and weed stickers.

Less than thirty minutes after walking into the Cyclery, my bike was ready to go. I paid the bill, thanked Pete and before leaving asked him, "If I have problems on down the road, are there any bicycle shops east of here on Route 66?"

"I don't know about San Bernardino but there's one in Victorville about fifty miles from here. From there to probably Flagstaff, about four hundred miles, you're outta luck. If I was you, if you're having problems when you get to Victorville today, I'd have them worked on before you head out into the desert."

With his advice, I was on my way again, hopeful my bicycle problems were over. And if they weren't? This experience had been a lesson in trust. If I took it to heart, there would be people helping me along, like Virginia, Pete, and the drivers yesterday who'd swerved to miss my sleeping bag pad lying in the street.

From Rancho Cucamonga, Route 66 continued straight-as-an-arrow on Foothill Boulevard through Fontana. Gradually the traffic thinned and with fewer businesses and more vacant land, I welcomed the open space. After Fontana came Rialto, home of the Wigwam Motel, built in 1949. The nineteen, 25-foot tall, conical-shaped motel rooms were once part of a seven-motel chain, the first one built in Kentucky. Helping to convey their authenticity as American Indian structures, four pine poles protruded through the top and each entryway was sculpted to give it the appearance of an open tent flap. Set a short distance apart from each other, they offered privacy not found in a typical motel where the rooms share walls. Landscaped with palm trees, grass and the statue of an American Indian outside the office, the whole atmosphere spoke "Welcome." I imagined children over the years pleading as their parents drove by, "Please, please, can we sleep in a tepee tonight?"

I continued riding east on level Foothill Boulevard until I got to San Bernardino, altitude 1,049 feet. It was early afternoon when I turned north onto the highway that paralleled I-215. Ahead of me was my first climbing challenge, the crest of 4,190-foot Cajon Pass. After ten miles of steady pedaling, I stopped for a break. Looking north I could see billowing storm clouds where I was headed. They took on the frightful form of a tsunami, its waves curling over the distant ridges. Above me towered cumulous clouds, entertaining me with the appearance of an eagle, Snoopy lying on his back, and a vanilla sundae with a whipped-cream curly-q on top.

Rehydrated and refreshed, I resumed my climb, slower now due to the increasingly steep frontage road that was now paralleling I-15 after it had merged with I-215. Eight miles later the frontage road ended. The only way to go now was up the on-ramp and onto I-15.

Freeway on-ramps in California have a sign that warns: *Pedestrians, Bicycles, Motor-driven Cycles Prohibited*. But when there is no alternate road for a bicyclist to take, the sign is modified with the word *Bicycles* blocked out. I'd worried for months over whether I'd find this modification when I got here. I walked my bike up the on-ramp and when I looked at the sign, I saw a white piece of metal covering the word *Bicycles*.

My relief was palpable as I let out a loud cheer. I sat down to rest, leaning against the sign and wondering what I would have done if I had been prohibited from riding on the freeway the final five miles to the summit. Turning around was not an option. I would have just taken my chances, hoping a CHP officer wouldn't come along and give me a citation after first asking me, "Don't you know how to read?"

Filled with renewed enthusiasm, I pedaled uphill onto the paved shoulder of the five-lane east-bound freeway. The quiet of the frontage road was now replaced by the roar of laboring engines and the noise of radial tires beating on cracked concrete. Within a mile, the feeling of fear joined that of excitement and challenge. While I had no desire to court danger, I began to understand the fascination in taking risks.

Slow, loud, lumbering eighteen wheelers kept me company in lanes four and five (numbered from left to right). I trusted each driver's ability but I still pedaled on the far right of the paved shoulder. Twice I came upon abandoned vehicles blocking the shoulder lane, stricken with mechanical problems. The only way to get around them was to pedal, at 4 mph, into lane five before the next semi came up behind me. While making this maneuver, I worried about my safety but also about making a trucker angry if he had to gear down and lose speed to avoid running over me.

I felt strong, climbing for ninety minutes to the cold, windy and intermittently overcast summit. My legs were sore but I felt a sense of accomplishment. I took a picture of the Cajon Pass sign and before I could repack my camera, the wind had dried my sweat and I was shivering. I exited the freeway at the next off-ramp and followed the frontage road for fourteen miles as it descended 1500 feet to Victorville, my destination for the night. I had traveled eighty miles today, dealt with two mechanical problems, completed my first serious climb, and gained confidence in meeting the challenges of riding on a freeway. Thankful I didn't need the bicycle repair shop I had been told was here, I looked instead for a place to eat dinner.

Long distance cycling demands the replacement of 6,000 to 7,000 calories every day. I decided to stop and capitulate to that necessity at a Mexican restaurant. I inhaled two baskets of tortilla chips with salsa, three enchiladas – asada, al pastor and pollo – rice and refried beans, two tall glasses of ice water, and, since old habits die hard, two diet cokes.

After dinner my successful search for a motel ended several blocks from the restaurant. In sharp contrast to the unwelcome I'd received last night, the manager greeted me with a welcoming smile as I walked into the office. "How ya' doin?" he asked.

"I'm fine now but it sure was cold and breezy over Cajon Pass."

"Yeah, it's a little cool for the desert this time of year. It's supposed to only get up around 72 tomorrow."

"I'll be ready for that if I can get a good night's rest. What's your rate for one person?" I asked.

"Well, let's see what we can do for you. How 'bout forty-five dollars, plus tax."

"Do you have any discounts, like AARP?"

He reached to his right and pulled his calculator over. After pushing several buttons, he told me, "With that discount it would be $42.50. Plus tax, your total will be $44.59."

"Sounds great." I filled out the registration form and decided not to pay with travelers checks this time. In my shorts pocket I had a small plastic folder where I kept my ID, insurance card, and some cash. I pulled $40 out of the folder and as I searched for a $5 bill, he said, "This is fine. Here's your key and you can put your bike in the room with you." With only a couple of exceptions, my welcoming experience in tonight's motel was to be repeated in the many nights to come.

In preparing for this adventure, I'd decided to gift myself with the comfort of a motel every night. If circumstances prevented me from doing this, I was prepared to sleep under the stars. Getting out of the weather, taking a shower, washing sweat drenched clothes, snacking, updating my journal, calling Donna, Ryan and Darlene, and getting a good night's rest would all be important in helping me make it to Chicago.

But staying in a motel didn't necessarily guarantee a night of uneventful sleep. Tonight the interruption was due to the children running in and out of the room next to mine. Their parents, with equal exuberance, were joining in the shouting. As tired as I was, blocking out the joyous commotion by putting a pillow over my head just didn't work I considered talking to the motel owner but then I remembered I'd brought my ear plugs. With them in my ears, I fell asleep, the motel as quiet as a northern California redwood forest.

11

Strangers in the Desert

Victorville was in my rearview mirror by 6:45 the next morning. Route 66 was no longer a freeway or a city street but rather a two-lane highway, the National Old Trails Highway.

Before starting my trip, I knew most of the 2300 miles to Chicago would be spent on two lane roads. What I didn't know was how dangerous these roads would be, a danger caused by speeding vehicles, narrow traffic lanes, and the consistent absence of a shoulder wide enough to accommodate me on my bicycle.

Going my direction this morning were many semis, most of them empty double hoppers hurrying to some nearby earthen pit to get their first load of the day. If there were no oncoming vehicles, each trucker would intentionally steer his rig into the opposite lane and safely barrel past me. Every time this happened, I waved my gratitude. But when faced with the situation of a vehicle coming toward us and there not being enough room for three of us abreast, some truckers wouldn't even slow down. What they did instead was blare their air-horns, sending the unmistakable message, "Get outta my way…NOW!"

When the first rolling tonnage thundered by only the length of my left arm away, I thought about the terror of being sideswiped, my body and bike ripped apart and scattered in an instant down the highway. The California Vehicle Code entitled bicycles to a narrow strip of pavement on the far right but in my present circumstance, occupying it would do me no good if it only led to my death. So from then on, when one of these belligerent bullies hurtled toward me, thinking the highway was their private racetrack, I rode off the asphalt, stopped in the detritus of the unpaved shoulder, closed my eyes, and held my breath while roadside trash and stinging grains of sand, all generated by the rush of eighteen wheels, whirled around me.

Several miles farther on, I came upon a homemade roadside memorial. Wild grass was growing among the faded plastic flowers, a cross, and a large stuffed teddy bear. The handmade sign leaning against the bear read, **Speed Kills**. I stood straddling my bike in silence while contemplating what looked like the death of a child in an auto accident. Little did I know the many times this tragic scene would be repeated between here and Chicago.

The truck traffic decreased the farther I got from Victorville. With the tension eased, my attention shifted to enjoying views of the Mojave Desert, my home ahead for the next two days. To the north the desert spread eighty miles before me, encompassing dry lake beds, the Fort Irwin National Training Center (closed to the public), the China Lake Naval Weapons Center, and hidden beyond the distant mountains, Death Valley National Park.

To the east were the Mojave National Preserve and the as yet unseen 150-mile path of Route 66 that I would follow across the Mojave Desert.

Roadside tragedy, a child's death.

The views were spectacular and I was ready for a break. I stopped on a knoll, leaned the bike against a fence post, sat down on the gravel, and sipped water. Two ravens circled overhead and a six-inch long lizard scurried to within two feet of me before stopping to see which one of us would flinch first.

As the panorama unfolded, it reminded me of the many times I'd hiked the Grand Canyon and sat on its north and south rims trying to make sense of the infinity before me. Here on the edge of the Mojave, the absolute stillness enfolded me, the quiet like an answer to a prayer for peace. With only the sound of my breathing to interrupt my reverie, I watched the azure, cloudless sky kiss the dark outlines of mountain peaks, some of which were one-hundred miles away.

The lizard and I accommodated each other, both of us remaining motionless until I got up to resume pedaling to the next town of Barstow. I was still several miles outside of town when I saw someone walking toward me. He was pushing a shopping cart, its path erratic and his efforts laborious due to the slant of the rocky shoulder. I'd read about a man named Shopping Cart Dougherty, distinctive in his turban and lush white beard. He had pushed a shopping cart containing his possessions from Chicago to Santa Monica. As I neared the man ahead, I wondered if he was Dougherty. I slowed and thought about stopping but as we passed, I settled for just saying "Hi." He never looked up or returned my greeting. As the distance between us increased, I argued back and forth with myself on whether to go back and talk with him or not. I finally decided to pass up this opportunity to enrich my morning with what I guessed could have been an interesting conversation with a stranger who had neither a turban nor a white beard.

While pedaling on, I scolded myself for not stopping. So soon I had forgotten my son Ryan's admonition of only two days before: "Grant yourself the grace to enjoy your trip, Dad. You will likely do this only once so soak it in." This was, after all, not a race to Chicago. With Ryan's words ringing in my head I resolved to take advantage of future opportunities to meet people.

The two Route 66 towns on either side of the Mojave Desert are Barstow on the west and Needles on the east. Two highways cross the Mojave and connect both towns. I would follow 150-mile Route 66, the longer and older highway. In 1973, the second highway, I-40, was

Into the Mojave Desert.

completed. Mercifully, it shortened, by thirty miles, the distance across the desert but that would do me no good since bicycles are prohibited from being on all but a few miles of the shorter I-40.

Making good time, I cycled into Barstow about mid-morning. First named Fishpond, it was later renamed Waterman's Station in honor of Robert Waterman, no known relation, the Governor of California from 1887 to 1891. In 1885 it was again renamed, this time Barstow after the President of the Southern Pacific railroad, a corporation that had a major switching yard here.

The temperature was comfortable, I guessed in the low 80s, but climbing. I found the small Route 66 museum that had been recommended in a book but it was closed. A sign indicated it was being moved to a new location. Instead I stopped at a McDonald's. I ordered a vanilla milkshake to go with the banana I'd bought yesterday at Wolfe's Market, and sat down in a booth in a railroad passenger car that had been converted into a dining room. With my plunge into the Mojave Desert just ahead, my thoughts drifted to a distant memory of another trip across the desert on Route 66. I was only eight when our family left Santa Fe at 4:00 one morning. We were headed to California for a two-week summer vacation visiting relatives. Now over fifty years later I could still hear Dad's speech the night before we left. "Hurry up and get to bed. We're leaving early tomorrow so we can get across the Mojave Desert before the temperature hits 120 degrees."

Our trip on Route 66 started comfortably enough. After the sun came up, dad read the names of states on license plates and my sister, Lynn, and I wrote them down, hoping that by the time we got to Grandma's house, our destination in Santa Monica, we would have the names of all forty-eight states. Lynn and I would also entertain ourselves by moving our fists up and down, the universal gesture that coaxed passing truckers to honk their air horns. Since the Atchison, Topeka and Santa Fe Railroad tracks often ran close to Route 66, we also made a game out of counting the cars, trying to find the longest freight.

It was when we got to Needles that things got grim. Here we confronted the oppressive heat Dad had warned us about. The cylindrical swamp cooler that hung from the front passenger window next to my mother proved to be an ineffective appliance, succeeding only in wafting warm air across her flushed face while our baby brother, Kim, wailed with discomfort in Mom's lap. Meanwhile, Lynn and I suffered in silence, trying to sleep in the back seat as we rolled through the 150-mile-long inferno toward Barstow. I felt like a chicken being roasted, little beads of sweat trickling down my forehead and chest. Even the Naugahyde seat cover made me miserable. Dressed in shorts, every time I tried to change position, the wet skin on my legs, seemingly glued to the seat, threatened to peel off.

∞

I enjoyed reminiscing my memories of Route 66 and the Mojave but I needed to get moving. I felt strong, the bike was running flawlessly and the gift of the gentle tailwind that had kept me company since Santa Monica was still clearing the way for me. My only worry was the heat that smacked me in the face as I left the air conditioned dining car.

For several miles beyond Barstow, Route 66 and I-40 were the same highway. They separated when I got to the freeway off-ramp sign that read, *Historic Route 66; Bicycles Must Exit*. From there both highways paralleled each other within a mile until the freeway crossed over Route

66 at Newberry Springs, nineteen miles from Barstow. It was noon and I'd planned to eat lunch here in the Bagdad Café where the 1988 movie of the same name had been filmed.

Within minutes, I rode past all but one of the businesses in Newberry Springs and was on my way into the desolation again. I was certain I hadn't passed the Café. But as I had already learned, it was easy to miss signs, businesses and important landmarks as I concentrated on traffic and the road hazards I was trying to avoid. The last business up ahead on my right was Deel's Heating, Air Conditioning and Plumbing. Two men and a woman were loading a pickup as I rode up and asked, "Have I passed the Bagdad Café?"

It was the tall, thin, older man who answered, "Nope. It's all by itself on the left just a couple-a miles on down Route 66 here." Before I could thank him, he continued, "If ya' don't mind my askin, what in heaven's name you doin' out here on a bicycle?"

"I'm on my way to Chicago."

"Man, I sure wouldn't cross this desert on a bicycle now or any other time to get to Chicago, or anywhere else for that matter. You ever heard of an airplane?"

We all laughed and then the younger man asked, "How old are you?"

"I just turned sixty-six. That's why I'm calling my ride, 66 on 66."

"And how old were you when you lost your sanity?"

"Musta also been when I started riding three days ago in Santa Monica."

At this point the woman saw her opening and jumped in. "I hope you have a cell phone?"

I watched her frown as I told her, "No, I sure don't."

They were sweating profusely, anxious to get out of the heat so I thanked these considerate strangers for directions to the Café and they wished me luck. As I rode on down the highway I wondered why women were usually the ones who brought up cell phones and why nobody seemed to understand that swaths of my isolated path would have no cell phone coverage, negating my need to carry one.

The fact was, up until this time in my life I had no use for a cell phone. When I'd retired from teaching two years ago in 2003, even then I had no reason to want one. Getting messages and making calls when I returned to my office at the end of every day had worked for thirty years and I saw no need to be available immediately just because others couldn't accommodate my temporarily being out of touch.

One afternoon shortly before I retired, my Instructional Assistant, Ilda, and I were on our way to check on one of our students at his work site. I mentioned off-hand that I needed to call a teacher when we got back to the office. "Why don't you just use my cell phone to call her right now?" she suggested.

She handed me her cell phone and I sat staring at it, not having the slightest idea what to do next. Out of the corner of her eye she could tell I was befuddled. So she said, "Just dial the number you want and then say, 'Send.'" So I pushed the seven number buttons and then held the phone directly in front of my mouth like it was a walkie-talkie. I paused for a second and then speaking distinctly, I said, "Send."

Ilda was a careful driver, managing not to hit any passing cars or immoveable objects alongside the street as she burst into uncontrolled laughter. Offering my pitiful defense, I told her, "Well, you told me to say send." I would just have to live with yet another story about my technological incompetence, what my wife Donna playfully called, my willful ignorance.

Cycling away from Newberry Springs, I decided the way to solve the problem of everyone being concerned about me not having a cell phone would be to pick up the next one I saw lying on the side of the road. From then on, if anyone asked if I had a cell phone, I could honestly answer "Yes," even if it wasn't working.

I'm not sure when I decided that the outside appearance of a restaurant wasn't important when choosing a place to eat. William Least Heat Moon shared his wisdom on this subject in his book, *Blue Highways*, basing his choice of restaurants on the number of calendars hanging inside. His line of reasoning is simple: The more calendars, the better the food. Of course, this procedure does entail going into the restaurant to count. Once inside, people like me find it uncomfortable to turn around and walk out, especially if it entails explaining to a restaurant employee that the reason we've decided not to eat there is because there aren't enough calendars.

My system of choosing a place to eat is less precise than Moon's. It includes asking local folks where the best Mexican-Pizza-Hamburger, etc. place is and the urgency of my hunger. Instead of the number of calendars inside, I look to see how many cars are parked outside. The words AAA Approved, Fine Dining and Inn, all intended to convey the absence of disease, are less important than seeing "Café," the four letter code word for down home cooking. I've concluded that eating establishments labeled greasy spoons are those where the inspiration for the cliché, "you can't judge a book by its cover," came from. Although unattractive, rundown and seemingly uncared for on the outside, they more often than not turn out to be comfortable places where friends meet to enjoy food that tastes good, to catch up on each other's lives, and see who can tell the most far fetched story.

I found the Bagdad Café on down the highway where I had been told it would be. Nature had paved the 150 feet between the highway and the front walk with dust and gravel. A prominent sign, visible from the highway, stood in front of the Café and on it were the words: Route 66 Roadside Attraction. To the left were the remains of the decaying motel that had been a set in the movie. From the highway the Café seemed to fit my definition of a place deserving of my business, except for the number of cars parked outside. There was only one. The Colorado license plate led me to assume that a fellow traveler was inside and, since I'd once gone to college in Colorado, we might have something in common.

I parked my bike against the front wall under the lighted Miller beer sign. The peeling dark brown paint was exposing the wall's previous color, white. Inside the Café German was being spoken by the only customers, the two women and one man traveling in the Colorado rental car.

I settled my weary self into a seat at the table nearest the door. It felt good to get off the bike and sprawl in a chair. I'd already cycled sixty miles from Victorville, and as I relaxed, I realized how much I needed this break.

The waitress, anxious for business, was prompt in arriving at my table. She'd seen me ride up and with a smile asked, "Where'd you start your trip from?"

I gave her the short answer, "Santa Monica," figuring if she didn't know where it was she would ask. Without any indication of being interested in gathering further information, she piled onto my table a thick photo album, an autograph book, and the menu.

With her load now ten pounds lighter, she asked, "What would you like to drink, honey?"

"Your tallest glass of tea filled with ice."

I wasn't in the mood to look at photographs, so while she went to pour my tea, I thumbed quickly through the album, turning three and four pages at a time. Most were of the *Bagdad Café* movie cast. I hadn't seen the movie but did recognize one of the stars, Jack Palance.

When I finished with the photo album, I looked at the walls. They were haphazardly covered with pictures, plaques, posters, cartoons and bottles. Some paid tribute to the Mother Road and others referred to the 1988 movie and the German actress, Marianne Sägebrecht, who had stared in it. I looked around for calendars but could only find two, a number that would find Least Heat Moon eating here "only if fish trophies were present," and there were none. In the midst of my wall-survey, my waitress brought my tea, complete with a thick wedge of

Bagdad Café cook.

lemon. I drowned the contents of three sugar packets in the tall glass, stirring while she took my order, a tuna fish sandwich with chips.

As she disappeared into the kitchen, I resumed looking around the room. What fascinated me most was the large map of Europe on the wall to my left by the door. The map was a mass of multicolored pins, each one stuck in the name of a European town from which a visitor to the Café had come. There was no doubt that Europeans were doing more than their share to keep this Café on Route 66 in business.

I had moved on to flipping through the pages of autograph book number six when the waitress brought my lunch and refilled my tea. While eating, I entertained myself by reading the comments in the autograph book. When I got to the last entry I added my name and a few lines about being in the desert on a bicycle, proof that I'd been here on April 29th, 2005 if anyone in my family might someday be interested.

On her next visit to my table, I gave my waitress back her library and at the same time asked her to sign my journal. She blushed and hesitated. With the roles now reversed, I guessed she wasn't used to customers, strangers at that, asking for *her* signature. Using my pen she wrote, "Best of Luck, Joanne Gonzales." Maybe it was my imagination but as she cleared all my dishes, except for the third glass of tea I was still sipping, she seemed to take on an air of newfound friendship.

As Joanne headed to the dish room, one of the three German customers turned toward me and asked, "Where you from?"

"Davis, California," I said. "It's near San Francisco."

"San Francisco. That's the last place we go, after Disneyland and Yosemite."

As our conversation warmed, he turned his back on the two women with him and faced me. From time to time he would look back at them and say something in German, but clearly his attention wasn't with them anymore. After several minutes of being ignored, the women got up, went outside, and since they didn't have the keys to the car so they could turn on the air conditioning, they wandered around the parking lot in the heat.

Meanwhile the man and I talked. His English, spoken with a heavy accent, was difficult to understand. I was impressed how much he knew about the United States, much more than I knew about Germany where

I had been stationed in the Army for twenty-six months. I suggested when they got to San Francisco that they walk out onto the Golden Gate Bridge, ride a cable car, and visit China Town. As our visit wound down, I asked him to sign my journal.

> *Hi Doug. I am pleased to hear of a cyclists tour which I can estimate having done before distances in Europe as well. In 1958, I rode from Kiel, Germany to the Brussels Worlds Fair and back via Holland. The paradise of cyclists. You'll have a wonderful trip to Chicago... Seligman a place to stay. Now Living in Hamburg as well as Nice, France. D. Rosacker*

We shook hands and after he left, Joanne kindly filled my three water bottles with ice water. Fully rested, I was ready to confront the afternoon heat of the Mojave.

Up until the Bagdad Café, Route 66 had been a lightly traveled, well maintained two-lane highway. But beyond the Café, it was a poor excuse for a road. Most of the thirty-one miles of asphalt from there to the next group of buildings in Ludlow was in complete decay. The road was a combination of wide, long, and deep cracks the size of small ditches. Where the asphalt had erupted instead of caving in, I stood on the pedals with my knees bent to cushion the shock as I hit these bumps. I was thankful for my wide tires but the ride was so jarring, much more so than on any of my training rides, that I began to wonder if the bike would shake itself apart.

I gave up riding in a straight line and zigzagged along the center stripe, the far left and right edges of the highway, the middle of the oncoming lane, and sometimes on the shoulder completely off the disintegrating asphalt. Since there were no cars, I was safe wandering all over the roadway as I searched for the path where I would be jostled the least. I passed the 20,000-year-old Pisgah Cinder Cone and shortly after 4:00 p.m., finally reached Ludlow.

Facing me from Ludlow to Needles was one-hundred miles where I was reasonably sure I would find no food or water. My last chance to fill up on both was in the Ludlow Cafe, a small building with a steeply pitched roof. It looked out of place, like it belonged at a higher altitude in a pine forest where its roof would shed tons of snow, not here where snowflakes weren't even in dreams.

I leaned my bike against the wall at the entrance. It wasn't dinnertime yet so the parking lot was empty and I was the only customer. The sign inside read, *Seat Yourself,* so I did. My hope for meeting Least Heat Moon here was dashed when I found only one calendar. The waiter eventually showed up and took my order – a hot roast beef sandwich with mashed potatoes, green beans and iced tea. Five minutes later, just as he was bringing my order, another customer came in. He sat facing the same direction I was, three booths in front of me and on the other side of the room. I heard him order coffee and a piece of pie – skip the ice cream – and then tell the waiter he was hauling a load of something – I couldn't hear what – to Maryland. His order came quickly and then the room was quiet again.

Whether motivated by discomfort with a stranger or simple boredom, the trucker decided to shed his mantle of anonymity and talk with me. He had to have noticed my bicycle near the door. It was my bike that invariably provoked curiosity and conversation as I went along. He turned sideways, raised his voice to bridge the distance between us, and asked, "So where ya' headed?"

"To Chicago."

"Well I'll be. My name's Sam; what's yours?"

"Doug."

From the comfort of my distant booth, I welcomed his friendly chatter, if for no other reason than it distracted me from my food, all of it drowning in a copious ladling of dark brown gravy into which the cook must have dumped a whole shaker of salt. The first few bites were already causing me to feel dehydrated, a condition I tried to compensate for with frequent gulps of both water and iced tea.

Every time Sam said something, he turned his body toward me just a little bit more until he was balancing his pie on his lap and his legs were no longer under the table. "Yeah," he said, I dropped a load of shoppin' carts in Oakland. Now I'm headin' to Baltimore with produce I picked up in LA. Should be there in three days, late Monday."

I pulled my pen out of my pocket and did a quick calculation on my paper napkin. Baltimore was about 2700 miles away. If he averaged 50 mph, it would take him somewhere around fifty-four hours to get there. Minus the three hours he'd lose crossing time zones, he'd have only five hours each of the next three days to sleep, eat, gas his rig and relieve his bladder.

Sam was quiet for a moment after I told him the result of my figuring. When he spoke, he said, "Stoppin' don't take much time. As I go along I just pull over on an off-ramp, truck stop, or into a vacant lot and sleep for awhile."

Sam seemed unwilling to admit or even consider that he might not make it to Baltimore in three days. But that was really his business, not mine, so I moved on to a question I'd always wanted to ask a trucker. "Don'tcha have to keep track in a log book the exact hours you drive every day?"

With my question floating in the air, he burst out laughing. "Yeah. We call them books 'funny books'. If the Highway Patrol caught me driving over the legal limit of eleven hours a day, I could get a $1,000 fine. I'm plannin' to retire when I get to 62 in a few months so it don't make no difference anyway."

And just like that, he had told me he was going to make it to Baltimore by driving nineteen hours every day, which was a total of eight hours *over* the legal daily maximum of eleven hours, a serious violation of the law.

I didn't ask and he didn't volunteer to explain how he would manipulate his "funny book" to show he was driving fewer hours than he really was. The closest he came was when he said, "Drivers being paid by the mile and those driving by themselves – both of which described Sam – are the ones most likely to fudge on their hours and miles to make them legal." As an example, he told me, "I know truckers who start driving on say a Monday but in a duplicate log book they put down they started on Tuesday."

I was enjoying talking with Sam about long-haul trucking and had one more question to ask him, this one about his engine. He explained it was built by Caterpillar and he could easily highball seventy-five mph, the speed limit for trucks in Arizona, New Mexico, and Oklahoma. Truck speed limits in other Route 66 states varied from 55 in California to 70 during the day and 65 at night in Texas. "If I need to, while pullin a full load, I can run at 85mph without havin' to keep the accelerator mashed to the floor," he said.

Sam had finished his pie and I had gagged down as much of the salty offering on my plate that I could handle. We both were ready to be on our way but before we left I walked over to his table and asked him to sign my journal.

> *Don't go fast on Bad Road's*
> *The Big Rock Lays there*
> *By Sam Peters*

Sam headed to his semi and since I was reasonably sure there were no pay phones between here and Needles, I decided to call Donna from the one just outside the restaurant entrance. As we talked about her day at work and the challenge awaiting me from here to Needles, I was startled by the blast of an air horn. I turned around and saw Sam pulling out of the parking lot. He had one thumb raised upward and was waving goodbye with his other hand.

> *Dug called about 5 p.m. from Ludlow. He's one-third of the way through the Desert. He wants our daughter Darlene and our neighbors Gail and Mark to know he has finished the last of the birthday cookies they made for him. What a treat —homemade cookies in the desert. To everyone, here is a poem he saw on a series of Burma Shave type road signs today: Better than vitamins, Better than money, A hug and a kiss, From your honey. Love to you all, Donna.*

※

When my birth family passed through Ludlow on vacation in the 1940s and 50s, Route 66 wasn't deserted like it is today. Scattered across the desert were several small towns, the most important of which were Ludlow, Amboy, Chambless and Essex. Travelers had been able to find food, water, gas, mechanical help, and in Amboy, even a motel. On one vacation in the 1940s, our 1949 Ford station wagon sprung a leak in the radiator hose. We were fortunate that less than two miles ahead was a service station that had a new hose and a mechanic to install it.

With the opening of I-40 in 1973, travelers had no reason to go thirty extra miles on two-lane Route 66 when a four-lane freeway would get them across the desert faster and safer. With the traffic siphoned off to I-40, the drawn-out closing of bypassed businesses began. Amboy was now deserted, except for the post office. (Around 2010, Roy's Motel

It Only Hurts When I Sit Down

and Restaurant in Amboy were bought and re-opened). Chambless had a few houses. I had no idea what services were in Essex, roughly thirty-seven miles from Needles, so I didn't count on any. With my three water bottles full again, I hoped they would last me the rest of today and all of tomorrow, a hope that bordered on the foolish knowing the heat I'd face.

Leaving Ludlow I settled into an easy rhythm as I watched I-40 veer off and disappear to the southeast. This time of day was a softer time to ride. The Silver Cholla (cactus), Creosote bushes, and Mesquite, with their deep water-seeking roots, broke the monotony of parched earth and rocks. I welcomed the quiet and accomplishment of the day. My enjoyment was multiplied in knowing that every cool mile I put behind me this early evening would be a scorching afternoon mile I wouldn't have to go through tomorrow, every pedal stroke putting me closer to Needles. The road surface continued to be a challenge but since the oncoming lane was in better shape, I rode there most of the

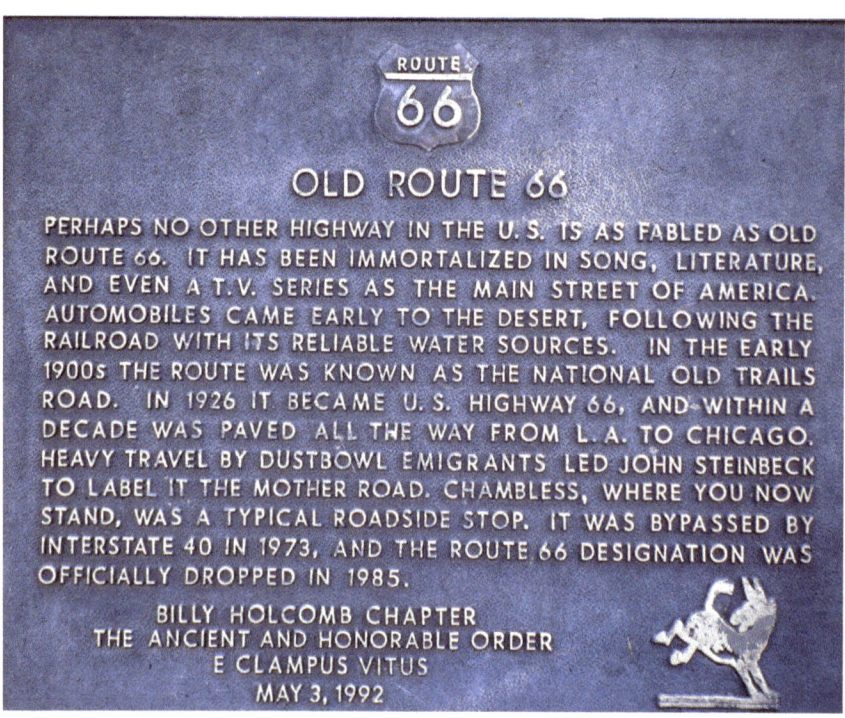

Chambless – bypassed and forgotten.

time. With an average of one car coming every half-hour from either direction, I didn't worry about traffic.

Two hours beyond Ludlow, sundown was nearing and I was having no luck in finding a secluded place to bed down. There were no dirt roads leading away from the highway to thick brush or gullies where I could hide. I was starting to feel desperate when I crossed a short bridge. Since this wasn't the rainy, flash flood time in the desert, I knew I would be both safe and comfortable sleeping under that bridge in the sand of the arroyo.

I guessed the early evening temperature to be in the high 70s, down from a high of 100-degrees. I rolled out my ground cover and bedroll. With my head just far enough out from under the bridge, when it got dark I was positioned to look up and see the stars and maybe, even a satellite. In the fading light, I snacked, wrote in my journal, and logged my progress for the day. When I shifted the functions on my computer, I saw I had pedaled 117 miles from Victorville, thanks to the absence of steep hills and the continuing presence of the gentle tailwind.

It had gotten too dark to write anymore so I repacked my journal. I was walking back to my bedroll when I heard strange noises coming from the dark under the other side of the bridge. At the same time, coming from upstream beyond the first bend in the arroyo, were sounds that sounded like someone coughing and mumbling.

Getting to where I had bedded down had entailed going down an embankment. From there I had lifted my bike over the prongs of a barbed wire fence that had been torn down. If I was about to be attacked, I knew I had no chance of getting away unless I used my flashlight to find that section of downed barbed wire before climbing the arroyo bank and pedaling away.

Summoning some sense of bravery, I decided to confront the nearest sounds, those under the bridge. I unzipped my handlebar bag, got out my bike light, and giving away my location, flashed its beam around under the bridge. The rays of the flashlight illuminated two small birds chirping while frantically flying back and forth among the bridge supports. At first I felt stupid, being fearful of two little birds. And then I felt relief, knowing when I settled down, they would too.

I doused the light, laid down on my sleeping bag again, and let my attention shift to the upstream noises. Maybe someone had gotten here before me, watched me come into the arroyo, and was now preparing to confront me. Nobody knew where I was and if I was robbed or even killed here under this bridge, I knew it would take time for my body to be found. This was the wrong time to rue not having a cell phone when I could use one.

    I decided it was too late to get dressed, gather and pack my sleeping gear, and use my bike light to find my way over the barbed wire and back to the highway. Lying quietly I could tell the upstream sounds were slowly moving away. Gradually they diminished and then ended. Maybe they too had come from birds but whatever their origin, as I fell asleep it was a relief to replace fear with watching the panoply of glorious stars as they filled the firmament above me.

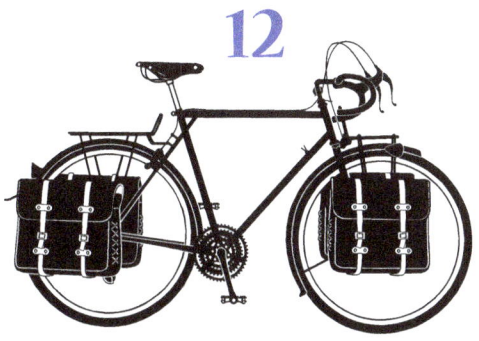

12

Pushed to My Limit

Shortly before 6:00 a.m., I awoke, sat up, looked to the east and saw a faint tinge of color in the high wispy clouds. I hurriedly slipped on my shoes, left the laces untied, and shuffled down the arroyo to a rock where I sat and watched the colorful clouds blossom and frolic, entertaining me with their graceful ebb and flow. It struck my fancy that maybe they were trying to shelter me from the heat to come. And then, as suddenly as it had begun, the Technicolor dance was over, leaving wistful strands of gray on the heavenly stage.

I ambled back to the bridge, feeling fortunate not to have spent the night in a motel room with its curtains blocking the beauty I'd just witnessed. Within thirty minutes I finished my portable breakfast, packed, and then wheeled my bike over the downed barbed wire and up the embankment. From here to Needles was sixty-five miles, a scorching distance that I felt prepared to meet head-on.

Two miles down the road I came to what was left of the town of Amboy. The motel and café were closed and fenced off. Signs warned people to **Keep Out,** but judging from the abundance of broken windows and other wanton destruction, the signs were being ignored. Several trailers and houses were abandoned and falling apart as was a small church. The living room-size building that housed the Post Office seemed to be the only legitimate reason for locals to stop. I couldn't help but wish I had been here several years ago to meet Buster Burriss while he was still alive. He had settled here in 1938 and over the years, before I-40 bypassed Amboy and Route 66, he was the heart and soul of this little oasis. The motel and café, both named Roy's after his father-in-law, had stayed open twenty-four hours a day, bustling with hungry and tired travelers.

Pedaling away from Amboy a song popped into my mind. Just like Whitney Houston's melody three days before, it was again impossible to block this mental music as it followed me around like a puppy wanting to play. This morning's tune had been made popular by the Eagles but I could remember only one line – *I want to sleep with you in the desert tonight, with a million stars all around.* As I sang this line over and over, I thought of Donna and wished she had been with me in my desert bivouac last night. The song provoked memory of the time thirty-five years ago when she and I had slept in the desert east of Fallon, Nevada. We had spread our sleeping bags out on a high-desert hillside and fallen asleep while watching a lightning storm so far away we couldn't hear the thunder. Not wanting to forget these thoughts, I stopped and in a small spiral notebook I pulled out of my handlebar bag, I wrote myself a reminder to sing these lines to Donna when I called her this evening.

Will I make it?

Eleven miles beyond Amboy I came to an unexpected house alongside the highway. Next to it were several trees, all of which had more dead branches than live. Like everything in the desert, they were trying to live with a shortage of water. Sitting on the front porch was a man tuning his guitar. I rode up to the wire gate just as another man stepped onto the porch, provoking it to creak. He sipped his steaming cup of coffee as I greeted them both and asked if they had a spigot where I could fill my water bottles. Coffee-man set his mug on the porch railing, picked up my two empty bottles and said nothing as he disappeared into the house.

Left alone with guitar-man, my attention drifted to his overall unkemptness. His face was unshaven, his pants hadn't seen soap in a long time and neither had his dirty white t-shirt with enough holes to qualify it for the rag bag. All signs indicated he knew there was no need to dress for company.

Not sure how to start our conversation, I settled on giving him a weather report. "It's warming up fast this morning," I offered.

He got up, looked at his thermometer nailed to a porch post several feet away, and said, "Yeah, it's in the 80s already. It's a little cooler in the shade of those trees behind you though."

I didn't want to disagree with him by suggesting there was no way trees with barren poles substituting for leaf clad branches could pass for shade, so I changed the subject.

"Do you see many bicyclists out here?"

He returned to his chair and pointed to a large grove of trees just up-road from their place. "In fact," he said, "two bicyclists camped out over there last night, but I think they're gone now."

Coffee-man had been gone about five minutes when he reappeared, a full bottle of water in each hand. The screen door slammed behind him as he walked over and gave both bottles filled with cold water, back to me. Little did I know how important every drop of water in those bottles would be before today would end. With coffee-man now part of the conversation, it shifted to their dream of opening a restaurant just down the road. I wondered to myself, *where in all this vacant desolation would their customers come from*? As we chatted, I had the feeling that they knew how to talk a good line but weren't quite sure how to act on it. They both had what I interpreted as a serious case of "mañana." This syndrome embodies the belief that a task, regardless of its simplicity, can always be put off to tomorrow…and tomorrow, ad infinitum.

The temperature was climbing fast and despite the temptation to sit and while the day away, capitulating to my own sense of mañana, I needed to move on. I thanked them for the conversation and for filling my water bottles. "The next time I come through here I'll repay your kindness by stopping to have a meal in your restaurant," I said.

One mile from their place I came to a plaque they had told me to look for. It gave recognition to Chambless, the town that had once been here. Several houses were all that remained, one of which was where I had stopped for water. The grocery store was boarded up, its roof peeling off with encouragement from every desert windstorm.

Prior to 1973, Route 66 had no competition as the only road across the desert. Travelers wrestling with boredom had created a clever form of entertainment that captured my attention. They had pulled off the highway and gathered rocks, coloring some with spray paint before re-positioning them on the sloped embankment. Mile-after-mile, passersby could read the word and symbol for peace, initials with the outline of a heart around them, hundreds of names and miscellaneous words.

The creativity expressed by others over the past thirty-two years was taking my mind off the heat, so I hadn't given any thought to leaving a contribution until I saw the words "Doug and Carol." Immediately I knew there was no way I could pass this by without some intentional rearrangement of the letters in Carol. After a few minutes I changed Carol to Donna. As I stood admiring my modification, it crossed my mind that if Carol came along and saw Donna's name where her name had been, she might just be a little upset. And if Doug was with her at the time, this might lead to some tension between them as he tried unsuccessfully to explain, "Honest babe, I have no idea who Donna is." I took a photograph to record my alteration in this miles-long desert signboard, and then rode away, still singing about *sleeping in the desert tonight*.

When preparing for my trip, I had anticipated the situation I was now facing. In the desert and sparsely populated areas of Arizona and New Mexico, I knew there would be long distances between grocery stores and restaurants. To deal with this eventuality, and not starve, I packed my right front pannier with food. I called it my "eat right pannier."

I rearranged the roadside rocks to spell Doug and Donna.

Noon was nearing and my stomach had been pleading for nourishment for some time. At the crest of a low hill I rode off the highway and up to the remains of a gas station. Gone were the roof, doors, windows, and gas pumps. Only walls and the concrete floor remained, providing a surface for people to stop and scrawl their graffiti, most of it with spray paint. Paper, cardboard, and broken glass were scattered everywhere. Black plastic garbage bags had been ripped open in the process of being dumped, their contents, with help from nature, strewn to distances far beyond the gas station. Some people had stopped to change their oil, draining it onto the ground where the blackened stain and acrid smell betrayed its percolating presence.

This was in no way a desirable place to eat but I welcomed the sliver of shade that covered most of my upper body while I sat on the wall in an opening where a window had been. It was that shade that made the smell and sight of the refuse tolerable. In addition to being my chair, the pumice block wall also became my table onto which I placed my lunch.

I started with my main course, using a plastic fork to spread chunky peanut butter onto multi-grain Wheat Thins. Sunflower seeds, and trail mix sufficed as my salad. For dessert I savored a Power Bar. I washed everything down with several swigs of warm water (how I longed for even one ice cube) from my last water bottle, increasing the certainty I'd run out before getting to Needles. Slowly the sun nudged the shade away from the window opening, leaving me once again bathed in direct sunlight. I wiped the perspiration from my brow and felt the sensation of sweat beads rolling through the hair on my chest. I thought about taking a short nap but with the day having gone from warm to hot, I knew if I didn't move on and find water, the meal I'd just eaten might be my last.

The next settlement, Essex, population 89, passed without excitement. The Highway Maintenance Station would have been a place to replenish my water supply but being Saturday, it was closed. The café was abandoned, the gas station deserted and the few houses seemed to be empty so I foolishly decided not to knock on doors and ask for water.

Ever so slowly Route 66 swung northward toward I-40. In the distance I could see the silver-sided semis, lined up and inching their way across the Mojave like a convoy of ants heading to their welcoming anthill. Gradually Route 66 and I-40 joined twenty-eight miles from Needles at Mountain Springs Summit. It was here, in this otherwise peaceful location, that I was about to make a serious mistake.

When planning this adventure, I'd spent the better part of a morning trying to decide which alignment of Route 66 I would take when there was more than one. I had finally decided to follow, as close as I could, the paved route in use the year I was born, 1939. But now at Mountain Springs Summit, that choice didn't seem as simple as when I'd made it sitting in the air conditioned comfort of my home.

From here to Needles there was no place to get water or food on either of the two alignments. The biggest difference between the two was that the 1939 alignment was fifteen miles longer than the 1973 I-40 alignment and those fifteen miles would add at least two hours to my struggle. If I took the longer 1939 path, I knew I wouldn't make it to Needles by dark and might not make it at all since my last water bottle was nearly empty. Ryan had suggested before I left that in addition to my three water bottles I should carry his Camel-bak, a 72-ounce reservoir of water that would double my total and ride comfortably on my back. Unfortunately, I'd made the mistake of rejecting his offer, passing it off by telling him, "My three bottles will be enough to get me across the Mojave." I had failed to accept my son's concern for his dad's safety and now I had no chance to go back and correct my rejection.

I stood on the freeway overpass watching the glut of semis pass underneath and guessed the temperature to be nearing 110. My stops had become more frequent, my breathing harder and I was sweating less. I knew from past experience that these signs and my overall fatigue were telling me to abandon my rigidity and take I-40, the shorter 1973 alignment. The decision would have been easy if I hadn't embraced the idea that going the shorter, newer way was somehow cheating. So I took one last look at the freeway underneath me and headed northeast, toward insanity on the original Route 66.

In less than 100 yards I came to a highway road sign that should have been adequate in persuading me to turn around. *Road not maintained by San Bernardino County*, it read. But I ignored it and kept going, the gradual downhill becoming steeper as I followed the increasingly fractured asphalt and pot holes, some filled with muddy water.

It was the unavoidable evidence that I was losing precious altitude, something I hated to do unless absolutely necessary, that got my attention. Not only had my path to Needles become longer but somewhere ahead, I anticipated that I would have to summon enough strength to climb another hill before getting to Needles.

I have no idea where the insistence that I stop came from but I was now standing motionless in the blazing heat, my arms braced on the handlebar, my forehead resting on the back of my hands and my eyes closed. As I pondered my situation, I finally realized that I was never going to make it to Needles, let alone Chicago, unless I started by ignoring the preposterous thought that I would be cheating if I went the shorter I-40 way.

As I turned the bike around and pushed it back uphill, I felt a tremendous sense of relief. At the I-40 on-ramp, I sipped the last of my precious water, turned left and headed east to Needles on the shorter alignment. My cousin Dick, when he later heard about my struggle at this crucial junction, breathed a sigh of relief before proclaiming, "I'm glad you weren't stuck on stupid."

It Only Hurts When I Sit Down

For every car that passed me on the freeway there was at least one semi. I welcomed their company as they pushed the air out of their way and mine, dragging me along, making it easier for me to pedal. It felt good to be back on the smooth freeway with its wide shoulder and the grooved rumble strip to my left. If a sleepy desert driver coming from behind headed off the highway toward me, his tires would emit a high-pitched whine when they hit this notched path, warning me I had a precious second or two to dive out of the way.

The final fifteen miles to Needles were mostly downhill. I was enjoying the respite from pedaling when I heard a flapping sound coming from my front tire. I stopped and saw a piece of wire sticking into it. Still attached to the wire was a small chunk of rubber that made the flapping sound when the tire revolved and smacked the road. It reminded me of the roofing nail I'd run over two days ago in Rancho Cucamonga.

I squeezed my tire to see if it would give. When it didn't I knew the tire was still fully inflated. The question now was, do I pull the wire out or leave it alone? If it had already penetrated the tube, the tire would go flat when I pulled the wire out. But if it hadn't and I continued on with the wire in the tire, it would undoubtedly work its way into the tube. I was hot, worn out, and didn't have the energy to fix a flat, even a simple one on the front tire. I finally decided to end the unknowing. I grabbed the rubber and jerked the wire out, so relieved when I didn't hear any hissing.

I pushed off, determined to be more careful as I threaded my way through the accumulation of thousands of fragments of burst steel-belted truck tires. It was impossible to see all the wires and rubber littering the shoulder and even when I did see them, I couldn't avoid hitting some of them. Over the next ten miles I stopped two more times to pull wires out of my front tire. Each time I was lucky. They too hadn't penetrated deep enough to puncture the tube. For some unknown reason, my back tire remained wire free.

Feelings of relief and accomplishment came over me as I took the first off-ramp into Needles. All three water bottles were empty, exactly how I felt. I had gained a new respect for the Mojave and I was thankful that the temperature hadn't been as hot as it could have been this time of year. While I wanted to boast that I had tamed the desert,

I knew the opposite was the truth. I'd learned an important lesson about being flexible and just how far I could push myself when under physical stress.

My experience of driving through Needles over many years had led me to wonder why anyone would want to live here. Named for the needle-like mountains to the south, I felt a more appropriate name would be *Inferno*. I remembered when, in an effort to avoid the daytime heat, our family had driven through here at night. We stopped around 1 a.m. to stretch our legs and get something to eat. I glanced at the thermometer on the restaurant wall as we went in and it read 103 degrees. I could only wonder how anyone had endured the scorching heat that day.

As I worked my way east through Needles, my intent was to find a motel. I had seen several but decided to try and find one on the east side. When I got there and hadn't found any more motels, I realized I should have stopped when I saw the first one. So I turned around and started back. I hadn't gone very far when I saw a pizza restaurant up ahead. I was fatigued physically and mentally and knew I needed to act on this opportunity to eat. My search for a motel could wait; my exhaustion couldn't.

Walking into the restaurant I ran into a blast of cold air from the air conditioning. It felt so good. I shuffled my way to a booth, slumped into it, and too tired to take off my helmet or gloves, sat with my eyes closed, my head resting on my hands. An employee interrupted my solace, first serving me a tall glass of ice water and then handing me a menu. He explained the procedure was to order at the counter. I told him I'd eventually get up and do so, but right now all I wanted was to just sit with my eyes closed in the air conditioned cool and sip ice water.

After a short while I headed to the restroom to clean up before ordering. Over and over I splashed cold water onto my face, and then leaned on the sink, letting the water run wherever it wanted. I tasted the day's accumulation of salty sweat, my tongue brushing the water dripping off my lips. I washed the grime from my hands and with it the odor from my riding gloves. Using a paper towel, I blotted my face and then looked into the mirror. Looking back at me were two hostile, red eyes, the veins of which looked like miniature meandering creeks engorged with red hot lava. I needed no further proof of how far I had pushed myself today.

An hour later nothing was left of my salad and olive/Canadian bacon, medium pizza. Their nourishment gradually altered my perspective on limits. I began to think I could still ride another two or three hours and foolishly might have if the next town had been within twenty level miles.

The restaurant employees gave me directions to several nearby motels and explained, "Most of the motels are up along the freeway, not here along the main Route 66 drag." With their directions, I left the pizza parlor and within ten minutes checked into a nearby Motel 6.

I knew I was wasting precious water but I didn't care as I stood in the shower. The thousands of drops washed away the filth, massaged my exhaustion, cooled my body temperature, and restored my sense of optimism. I wondered how, on my last bike trip, I had gone fourteen days and taken only one shower.

Feeling that I was on my way to being rational again, I called Donna using the phone in my room.

> *Dug made it through the desert to Needles. He sends these messages: Ryan, your wish for a tail wind is holding true. He asks Steve, our neighbor who has pledged $66 to Habitat for Humanity and another $66 when Dug gets to Chicago: Do I really have to get to Chicago for you to send the second amount? Bummer. Many thanks to all of you for your support. Donna.*

Before we hung up, I tried to sing the "sleeping in the desert" song to her. When I finished there was a long pause before she said, "I couldn't understand a word you said." So I resorted to speaking the lyrics, which took all the romance out of them. She knew my heart was in the right place even if I had lost my ability to simultaneously carry a tune and speak clearly.

When I flopped onto the bed, my jaw sagged, the muscles unwilling to hold my mouth closed. My extremities felt strangely detached, comfortable remaining immobile where they had landed on the mattress. What could have been a day ending with me prostrate alongside Route 66 someplace, still trying to make it to Needles, had instead ended in peace. I watched my chest rise and fall in rhythm with my breathing and in no time I was sound asleep.

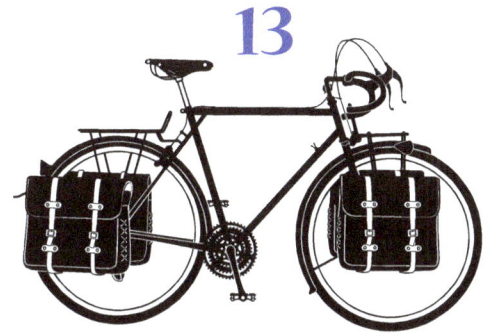

13

The Party's on in Oatman

Little things sometimes bothered me and that was how the next morning started. I had intended to write in my journal at breakfast but walking from the motel to the nearby Denny's I lost my only pen. I mentioned this to my waitress, drawing her to my "worry-abyss" when she asked, as a matter of routine, "How ya' doin?" A few minutes later she made a detour by my table, silently leaving in her wake a pen for me to keep.

Her kind gesture improved my attitude…until after breakfast. While sliding my computer into its clip on the handlebar, it slipped from my fingers, hit the asphalt hard and took several bounces. I picked it up and saw that the screen was blank. I berated myself and wondered, *now how am I going to keep track of my daily progress*? I was near to hurling the computer against a nearby concrete wall. But I knew that wouldn't bring the computer back to life, if it still had any, so I decided to try a less violent approach. As I touched the buttons with my index finger, the numbers sprang to life. There couldn't have been a happier person in Needles at that moment.

From Needles to the Colorado River, the twelve miles of freeway gradually went from level to a gentle downhill. Bicycles were forbidden on all those miles but I decided to take a chance that a Highway Patrol officer wouldn't be out this early, citations ready for distribution.

A ticketless hour later I rode to the middle of the bridge spanning the Colorado River. Semis thundered by, vibrating the bridge as they accelerated to the Arizona speed limit, 75 mph. I braced myself against the railing and took a picture of the swirling blue-green water thirty feet below. I thought of how far this life-giving current had come from the mountains of Colorado and through Utah, having coursed like me through hot and barren country to finally arrive here, the California/Arizona boundary. The cool air rose and refreshed me as I watched the eddies form and then swirl themselves apart downstream, a dance being choreographed by obstacles beneath the surface.

As I stood watching the water flow silently by, I thought about trying to find a path to the river's edge where I could dangle my feet in the water, skip flat rocks across the surface, and daydream. But there was no easy way to the river and with the heat building I knew it was time to leave California and begin the climb to the Black Mountains.

One mile beyond the Colorado River I came to a large roadside sign that eliminated any doubt that I was now in Arizona. On a blue background were the white words, "The Grand Canyon State Welcomes You." Above this greeting was an orange star with alternating yellow and red rays streaking upward, colors that would mimic those I'd see in the bluffs and canyons from here to New Mexico.

Unbridled anticipation filled me as I took the first Arizona off-ramp and headed north on the narrow two-lane road. For the next 160 miles I would be on the longest uninterrupted stretch of Route 66. My goal for noon was thirty-one miles ahead and 2,000-feet higher – the old gold mining town of Oatman.

The temperature, still under the influence of the Mojave Desert, was warming fast. As I'd done the last three days, one of my first stops was to slather sun block, SPF 45, onto the exposed areas of my face, ears, neck and legs. Because I always wore a long-sleeve shirt, I didn't worry about my arms. Last night, however, after showering I'd noticed that the ends of my fingers and a small triangular area on the back of both hands were sunburned. These spots hadn't been covered by my riding gloves so this morning I added them to my pasting routine. I laughed when I saw my face in the side-mirror, white like that of a clown until I massaged the sun block into my skin.

Continuing my uphill climb to Oatman, I recalled reading about its resident burros and how they had carried loads of gold-bearing ore, supplies and water for the miners. When their usefulness was over, many had been turned loose to fend for themselves. As a result, an estimated 1,500 burros now wandered the barren hills around Oatman. Everyday, some of them came into town to beg carrots, the recommended donkey food.

Weathered buildings, many abandoned and falling down, were the first sign that I was nearing Oatman. Conclusive evidence of my arrival came when, on the shoulder up ahead, I saw a group of people feeding two adults burros and a young one. I stopped, watched, and then asked a fellow tourist if he would take my picture with the little burro. He agreed and insisted I take one of his carrots so I could join in the feeding fun.

Beyond the family of begging burros, I ran into gridlock. Since leaving I-40, groups of classic cars and motorcycles had passed me going the opposite direction. We'd exchanged waves but I had no idea what was going on. Now in Oatman, I'd arrived at the party. Vehicles were parked on the sides of hills, in ditches, the shoulder, and even on the roadway. People were walking to and from town on the only sidewalk available – one lane of the highway. As I pedaled the steep hill into Oatman, a woman pointed at me and said, "Now I'm impressed." A short distance later another woman shouted, hopefully not referring to my smell since I was perspiring heavily, "You must be strong." I smiled and waved at everyone.

There were so many people that it was impossible to ride my bike.

I inched my way up and into the little one street town, through the wandering multitude. Many of the people were wearing the t-shirt that explained their reason for being here – *The 18th Annual, Route 66 Fun Run*. They were following the 160-mile stretch of original Route 66 just like I was, except going the opposite direction. This show on wheels had started in the town of Seligman two days before, moved on to Kingman yesterday, and now Oatman, population 200, today. I had unknowingly wandered into the last day of this annual revelry.

I was famished and the heat had again gotten the best of me. I saw two places to eat and settled on the biggest, the Oatman Hotel. Between me and the front door, the street and sidewalk were jammed with people shuffling along, intentionally going nowhere fast, parting reluctantly from time to time to let a passing car through. I too crept through the milling horde, finally reaching the hotel where I leaned my bike near the front entrance. I worried about leaving it there but I had no choice. Anyone in the meandering throng could simply unzip my panniers and take whatever they wanted. Carting off the entire eighty-pound bike with its load was also an option, locked or unlocked. I removed my camera, travelers' checks, and the two empty water bottles and walked into the hotel dining room where the joyful din intensified.

As my eyes adjusted to the darkness in the room, I saw a woman at the cash register. Assuming she was an employee, since she had on an apron, I walked up to her and speaking loud enough to be heard, asked, "I'd like to grab a bite to eat but first, do you know of a safe place where I can leave my bicycle?"

I expected her to tell me she was too busy to even give me some vague directions but instead she said, "Come with me." I followed her as she worked her way to the front door and outside into the heat and glare. She waited while I got my bike and then blazed a path for us through the mob to the entrance of the business next door, an ice cream parlor. "Wait here," is all she said before disappearing at the top of the steps. When she returned several minutes later, she explained, "The owner said it's okay to put your bike inside. At the top of the steps and to the right is a life-size carving of John Wayne sitting in a chair. Your bike should be safe behind him in the corner."

Customers leaving with their various ice cream concoctions gladly moved aside as I lifted, pushed, and dragged my unwieldy bike up the half-dozen steps into the room. With some careful jockeying, I was able to push it backward over John's outstretched legs, and lean it against the wall behind him. With my bike now in a somewhat safer location, I rejoined the woman and followed her back into the hotel dining room. Standing next to her I watched as she asked three men if I could sit at their table in the only vacant chair in the room. Their barely perceptible nods conveyed their begrudging approval.

The woman returned to her station at the cash register and I sat down. I tried to start a conversation with the three strangers but could immediately tell they were more interested in watching people – mostly scantily clad women – and drinking beer. I figured they had silently decided we had nothing in common so it wasn't worth their effort to talk with me. Looking at the people around me, I did feel a little conspicuous. I was the only one wearing baggy shorts, a bright yellow bicycling shirt, carrying a camera draped around my neck, two water bottles, and a bicycle helmet.

As I looked around the room, I saw one-dollar bills stapled to the walls, ceiling, support beams, posters, and in every nook and cranny in the room. Try as I might, I couldn't find an empty space where another dollar would fit.

A waitress eventually came to our table and took my order: the $6.95 Buffalo Burger with burro ears and a glass of iced tea. The ears were homemade potato chips, shaped like a burro's ear, and came with two dips – sour cream and salsa. Fifteen minutes later my salivating anticipation was rewarded. The food was spicy, filling and delicious. While eating, I tried once again to engage my tablemates in conversation. I succeeded in getting only grunts, single-word answers, a furtive nod or grimace. Like unprepared students in class, they would look away, hoping by so doing that I wouldn't ask them a question. So I gave up. Their unwillingness to be sociable convinced me that this was their party which they had been pressured to let me join. For whatever reasons, all they wanted was to be left alone.

The woman who had helped me with my bike was still working the cash register when I walked up to pay. "Did you enjoy your lunch?" she asked.

"It was delicious," I said. As I paid her I asked, "Would you mind filling my two water bottles?"

"Not at all." When she returned with my water bottles to her unattended cash register, I introduced myself and thanked her again for helping me find a safe place for my bike. "My name's Susie and I own this Hotel," she said. Suddenly her act of kindness earlier became more extraordinary. I asked her about the money on the walls and she told me, "There's $20,000 in one-dollar bills in this room. The hotel opened in 1924, two years before there was a Route 66 so there's been many years of dollar-bill stapling going on."

"Are the upstairs rooms in the hotel still used?"

"Just as a museum. Clark Gable and Carole Lombard spent their wedding night in room number 15 in 1939," she said.

In Clark's biography, I had read that he and Carole had no time for a honeymoon at the Oatman Hotel, or anywhere else. I decided not to mention this to Susie. Her last words to me were, "Now you come back again sometime."

Leaving the dining room, I walked under the air conditioner that was pushing cold air down and out through the wide open front door underneath it. Up until this noon, whenever I'd left my bike I always made sure I could see it from wherever I was sitting. Now headed back to my unlocked and unwatched bike, I wondered if having my bike stolen would be my third problem for the day and what I'd do if it was gone. I climbed the stairs to the ice cream parlor, turned right and saw that everything was where I'd left it. I slipped the full water bottles into their holders, gave John a pat on the shoulder, thanked him for keeping a wooden eye on my bike, and slowly wheeled it down the stairs and back into the crowd.

It was impossible to start pedaling until I got beyond the wall-to-wall pedestrian and vehicular commotion so I just pushed the bike uphill. I passed two stores whose names paid homage to the humble burros – Jackass Junction and The Classy Ass. At the entrance to another store I watched a burro come up behind a woman and nose butt her in the back, sending her stumbling through the open doorway into the store. She regained her balance and unhurt but startled, she and her friends ended up laughing. This human/burro interaction reminded me of the sign I'd seen in town that warned: **The Burros Are Wild And Can Both Bite And Kick**. However, nothing on the sign had warned about the danger of being head butted.

One-hundred yards from the Hotel the congestion eased enough so I could ride my bike again. I got on and began climbing. Two men sitting on the tailgate of a Ford Ranchero hollered, "Where ya' headn?" as I rode by. Over my shoulder I shouted, "Chicago." We continued this back-and-forth conversation, the increasing distance between us making it difficult for me to hear. I finally decided I didn't want this to be a repeat of the missed conversation with the shopping-cart-man outside Barstow. So I turned around and started coasting back to them. As I did this, they yelled, "No, no, don't come back," their directions motivated by knowing I would lose the precious altitude I'd gained and would have to do it all over again.

I've long forgotten the details of our conversation but not the fun. We laughed a lot and I was amazed at the instant affinity I had with them. Such a contrast to my sullen tablemates at lunch. After a short time, two women, their wives I assumed, returned from shopping. Everyone introduced themselves. Cindy noticed the small laminated Habitat for Humanity plaque I had affixed to the front of my handlebar bag. She asked about it and when I told her my trip was in part a fund raiser for Habitat in Yolo County California, she reached into her purse and handed me $20. I told her she didn't have to do that but she insisted. In my handlebar bag I had a small plastic baggie into which I was placing coins that I'd been finding on the pavement since Santa Monica. All the money in it would go to Habitat. She slid her donation into the baggie, I gave her a receipt, and then asked them all to sign my journal. They wrote:

> *Good Luck! – Cindy Tate*
> *Good Luck – Kees Ariens (and then his e-mail address)*
> *Ken Benton and Denise*

I thanked them for the enjoyable interlude, they wished me good luck, and I headed uphill…again.

The climb from Oatman to the top of 3556-foot Sitgreaves Pass included a two-mile, switchback-filled elevation gain of 700 feet. When the pitch got too steep, I was never too proud to get off the bike and push it, the computer registering my forward progress at 3.5 mph. When I pedaled using my lowest gear, my speed accelerated to 4 mph. I doubted a burro could pull me to the top any faster.

Nearing the summit, I came to a small puddle of water in the ditch to my right. It was being replenished by an imperceptible trickle coming from somewhere up ahead. It wasn't much farther when I saw drips seeping from the hillside shale. At the rate the drips were falling, I guessed their visible movement would be over in a day or two. I had arrived just in time to enjoy this weeping spring.

I unzipped my handlebar bag, took out the folded bandana, and walked back to the tiny pool. After dipping the cloth into the clear water, I rung it out over my head, and watched the hair on my arms stand erect as the cold water streamed down my chest and back. I repeated this several times, slowly emptying the pool. Before leaving, I draped the sopping wet bandana over my head and put my helmet on. As I resumed climbing, my forward movement created a light breeze that blew through the slots in my helmet and across the water-soaked bandana. In less than a mile, the water evaporated, taking with it how refreshed I'd felt.

As I worked my way toward the summit, I recalled reading about cars, like the Ford Model T, that had no fuel pump and had to be driven backward when climbing this pass. Other vehicles didn't have enough power in forward gears to go uphill so they too were driven backwards, reverse gear being stronger than first.

When I got to the top of Sitgreaves Pass, I leaned the bike over onto the panniers and sat down on a large rock. I gazed at the distant mountains, my destination spread out before me. I felt confident and excited. Only an accident on my part or a tragedy back home could keep me from reveling in the days that lay ahead.

The payoff for a cyclist making it to the top of any hill is the exhilarating plunge down the other side. The wind would roar as it raced through my helmet and by my ears. The only physical effort I had to make was to squeeze the brake levers hard so I didn't lose control and hurdle off the road.

Before leaving Sitgreaves summit, I gulped water and tried unsuccessfully to find a cloud or feel a breeze. I looked at the multitude of dark entrances in the hills around me, each of them marking an abandoned mine where hope and failure had played out their roles. Looking east I could see the innumerable hair pin curves in the road below and then in the far distance where the pavement straightened before its gentle uphill march to Kingman. After one last swig of water I shoved off, ready for my first Route 66 experience with speed.

To avoid the danger of running into potholes, rocks, glass and other detritus that accumulated on the right edge of the roadway, I moved into the middle of my northbound lane. Occasionally I would glance in my side-view mirror to see if a car had crept up behind me and wanted to pass. It was a thrill going thirty-four mph and I could have gone much faster if it hadn't been for the sharp curves and my fear of crashing.

It was late afternoon when I rode into Kingman and stopped at a small park. I sprawled on the grass, closed my eyes and thought back to many years ago when Donna and I had stopped here when Ryan and Darlene were young. They were glad to be out of the car, running around the park, and playing engineer while climbing on an old locomotive. I would never have believed it if someone had told me then that I'd someday be here riding my bike.

Part of the fascination in this trip was the opportunity to immerse myself in the history of Route 66. I'd prepared by reading about people, monuments, tragedies, weather, buildings, animals, and the mountains, rivers, and countryside through which I'd go. As I lay on the grass, I thought about a couple of Kingman's claims to fame. Andy Devine, the cowboy actor, grew up here. And there were Clark Gable and Carole Lombard (his third wife) who were married here on the afternoon of March 29th, 1939.

Clark had asked the MGM publicist, Otto Winkler, to *"find a remote spot where we can get married."* Otto had selected Kingman. There was a short break in the filming of Clark's movie, *Gone with the Wind*, so Otto, Clark and Carole left Los Angeles on Route 66 at 4:30 am. They took turns driving Otto's DeSoto Coupe, arriving in Kingman by mid-afternoon. The minister of the Methodist-Episcopal Church conducted the ceremony. Following the wedding, the three drove all night back to Los Angeles, arriving at 3:00 am in plenty of time for a press conference scheduled for that morning. Their honeymoon to Mexico would have to wait.

Unlike the previous evening in Needles, I knew where motels and restaurants were clustered in Kingman. Feeling rested, I headed that way and found a Chinese restaurant. Dinner was a bowl of egg flower soup and a mound of chicken fried rice. Two couples struck up a conversation with me, one of them telling me about cycling in the Netherlands. When I finished eating, my dishes were empty and in an effort to hydrate, so were my three glasses of tea.

Motel 6, a short distance down the road, was my destination after dinner. I was enjoying the last of a beautiful day, pedaling leisurely on the wide shoulder of the nearly deserted four-lane highway when a car sped past me. It was the girl in the passenger seat who leaned out her window and screamed, "Faggot!" I knew there was nothing to be gained by reacting with anger. Being on a bicycle put me in enough of a vulnerable position without making it worse. I was thankful she had split the silence with only a word and not something physically damaging. So I responded with an exuberant wave, intent on giving her and the driver the impression that I thought she was just saying, "Hello."

After my shower and before falling asleep, I used the motel phone to call Donna and then our son, Ryan. In the course of my conversation with him I mentioned feeding the baby burro in Oatman. He thought about that briefly and then told me, "The little one was a *burrito*, Dad." I laughed, wondering why I hadn't thought of that. Before hanging up, he told me that the daytime temperature forecast for tomorrow was in the 60s and 70s, and then it would drop into the 30s at night, terrific bicycling weather.

14

Enjoying Eighty Peaceful Miles

In 1978, the distance between Kingman and Seligman was shortened from eighty-four to sixty miles when I-40 bypassed Route 66. While travelers in a hurry or running out of gas welcomed the shorter interstate, the same could not be said for the people living on Route 66 in Hackberry, Valentine, Truxton, Peach Springs, and Seligman. From one day to the next, the highway that had brought them business went from busy to boring, leaving them with dwindling bank accounts. I anticipated finding the same desertion I'd seen in the similarly bypassed Mojave Desert towns of Essex, Chambless, and Amboy.

Before the sun came up in Kingman the next morning, I ate breakfast in a truck stop just across the street from the motel. Sitting in the booth ahead of me was a man spewing cigarette smoke. This was proof enough that I was out of California where smoking in a restaurant was illegal. I hurried through breakfast, trying to take my mind off the smoker by thinking about how today marked the beginning of the second phase of my trip. I was leaving the desert behind, and would, after climbing 2,000 feet, be in Seligman at 5250 feet by the end of the day. Along the way, barren earth would give way to rangeland grass that was forage for cattle, pronghorn antelope and deer. As I went higher, evergreen forests of piñon and juniper would emerge and the temperatures, as if on cue, would moderate.

Cycling northeast out of Kingman, Route 66 took me straight as an eagle's stare for twenty-three miles before gradually turning southeast. Not just a normal bend, this seven-mile arc is considered to be the longest continuous curve on any U.S. highway. It was so gradual that I had no perceptible feeling of changing direction.

Thirty-one miles from Kingman, I was ready for a break as I pedaled into what was left of Hackberry. Once a thriving silver mining town, the only remaining attraction was the old South Side Grocery, now called The Hackberry General Store. In reality, it is a curio store, catering to Route 66 tourists and selling, as the sign outside said, *"Ice, snacks, pop and souvenirs."*

The owner was deep into her routine of opening for the day. I watched as she maneuvered her red and white, classic '57 Corvette convertible onto the concrete pad outside the front door. My guess was, if all the memorabilia and signs scattered around the front and back of her business failed to coax infrequent tourists into stopping, then she knew her conspicuously parked Corvette with its "Route 66" personalized Arizona license plate, would do the trick.

I leaned my bike against the wall next to the entrance and wandered over to look at an old Mobilgas gasoline pump, its cost per leaded gallon permanently registering 15 and 9/10 cents. Six days ago when I started my trip, the cost of regular unleaded gas in Santa Monica was nudging $3.00 a gallon. To the left of the entrance was a 1929 Model A Coupe and near it were the rusting carcasses of five other old cars, long ago abandoned as reliable transportation.

The sign on the front door read: *Cowboys! Scrape shit from boots before entering.* I pushed open the screen door, letting it slam behind me. Inside, the creaking wooden floors announced my location as I wandered past an old jukebox and up and down aisles hemmed in by floor to ceiling racks jammed with jackets, sweatshirts, t-shirts and caps. Other walls and shelves were covered with cups, glasses, plaques, pictures and postcards, everything paying tribute to the attraction outside that ran east/west beyond the dirt driveway.

I considered buying a shirt but I didn't have any extra room in my panniers. What I did have room for was a Hackberry bumper decal and a sheet of Route 66 stickers, one for each of the eight states through which the old highway went. There was also an extra sticker with Route 66 on it so I affixed it to my helmet before pulling a bottle of soda out of the cooler and paying for my purchases. Buddy Holly, Nat King Cole, the Everly Brothers and Elvis sang to me from the jukebox, keeping me busy trying to remember the lyrics as I sat drinking my Coke and reading the directions on my handlebar route cards.

Meanwhile, the owner continued to bustle around, too busy to talk. I had wanted to find out from her where in this area, in the 1920s, the first pavement on Route 66 in Arizona had been put down. When I come back someday, I'll fill in this missing piece of history.

My soda finished, I went outside and into the yard behind the store. In a wooden shed was a 1919 Model T truck. It had been restored and looked ready for the road. To the left of the shed were five signs, billboards on a diet, from an old Burma Shave advertisement. This one read:

Big mistake
Many make
Rely on horn
Instead of brake
Burma Shave

The clever signs had been staked one hundred yards from each other alongside The Mother Road. I remembered seeing others in the 1940s and 50s but couldn't remember the humorous ditty that had been written on any of them.

I ambled back to my bike and took the California Route 66 sticker off the sheet. I decided that from here on, when I exited each of the remaining seven states, I would make a ritual of putting that state's sticker on my crossbar.

After Hackberry came deserted Valentine, named for a former Indian Commissioner and not the saint, and then quiet Truxton. I had no intention of stopping in either but as I passed an abandoned house in Truxton, I noticed white spray-painted words, *No Treaspassing* (sic), on the brown stucco front wall. Here was a picture that begged to be taken so I leaned my bike against the wall and in direct violation of the two words beside it, took the photograph.

As I cycled away from the house, I heard voices coming from around the corner and behind a tree. At first I thought someone was coming to chase me away but as I glanced over, I saw four men, each one sitting on a round of firewood. They were enjoying a late morning of slurred conversation while adding to the empty wine bottles scattered on the ground around them.

Just east of Truxton, a roadside sign informed me that I was entering the Hualapai (People of the Tall Pine) Indian Reservation. I passed the Music Mountain Junior/Senior High School and wondered about the origin of its unusual name. I would later learn that only sixty-seven students were enrolled in grades 7th-12th.

A short distance beyond the school was Peach Springs, population around 600. The only town on the Reservation, it now has the unenviable distinction of being the most bypassed town on Route 66. Forty-six miles west is Kingman and thirty-eight miles east is Seligman, the nearest towns in either direction. With two gas stations and only one grocery store, Peach Springs seemed to be hanging on, primarily because it was the tribal headquarters of the Hualapai Nation.

It was lunchtime and the only place I'd seen to eat was the River Runner Restaurant which adjoined the Hualapai Lodge on the east side of town. The modern buildings were highlighted by a turquoise colored roof, curved windows around the front, and stucco walls that matched the beige of the surrounding earth. I seated myself inside at an out-of-the-way corner table with a stuffed bobcat clinging to a juniper branch above me. Only two other tables in the large dining room were occupied.

Ten minutes after sitting down, no one on the wait staff had come to my table. So I got up and went to the cashier who assured me my server would be with me soon. Returning to my chair, I reminded myself that I was in the southwest now. In this land of mañana everything would happen in its good time, not forced along by the pace of an impatient and yes, hungry, bike rider from California.

Nikki's name tag eliminated the need for her to introduce herself before she took my order – vegetable soup, a tuna sandwich, a salad with blue cheese dressing, and iced tea. She seemed almost embarrassed as she spoke to me in a whisper, her soft-spokenness bordering on being shy.

While eating I wrote in my journal and looked around the room. Enlarged photographs of the Colorado River and Grand Canyon graced the walls along with another stuffed animal, a wild turkey. Scattered throughout the carpeted room were large ceramic urns, each of which contained a bush or a small tree. It was a peaceful, relaxing place, made even more so by the recording of American Indian flute music that wafted from the dining room speakers.

Nikki filled my tea glass one last time and gave me my bill. At the bottom she had written, "*Have a Beautiful Day,*" drawn a smiley face, and signed her name. As I left, the thought crossed my mind that this would be a wonderful place to bring Donna sometime.

Seven miles beyond Peach Springs, I cycled by the junction with Route 18. Unlike all the roads intersecting with Route 66 since Kingman, this one, heading north on my left, was paved. My father, and a friend, both of them spry and in their 80s, had once traveled this road, following it for sixty miles to the rim of the Grand Canyon. From there, they hiked downhill on a trail, dropping 3,000 feet in eight miles. This was the only way, other than by mule or helicopter, to get to the Havasupai Indian Reservation village of Supai, home to the most isolated Nation of American Indians in the United States.

But Supai, population 450, isn't the reason my Dad, his friend, and many others make this exhausting two-day, down and up trek. Scattered below the village, what attracts most people are five falls and the pools into which they plunge. It is the color of these pools that gives "*the people of the blue-green water,*" the Havasupai people, their name. As I passed this highway leading to the distant trailhead, I hoped to someday follow in Dad's footsteps and hike with Donna to that rugged, beautiful, and remote area.

Our family had traveled on Route 66 many times in my youth and not once had we stopped at Grand Canyon Caverns, now on my right and only seven miles past the turnoff to Supai. Maybe it was because we had been to Carlsbad Caverns National Park in New Mexico and after that awe inspiring experience, my parents had decided that every other cavern was just a hole in the ground by comparison.

The Hualapai Indians had long known of the cave's existence and had buried at least two tribal members there. Walter Peck, a woodcutter for the Atchison, Topeka and Santa Fe Railroad, rediscovered the caverns in 1927 and named them the Yampai Caverns. Subsequent owners renamed them Coconino, Dinosaur and then in 1962, Grand Canyon Caverns. I decided that linking the Caverns by name with the Grand Canyon was a deceiving marketing decision, considering that Grand Canyon National Park is eighteen miles away, as the crow flies, or thirty miles by dirt road.

The facilities at the Caverns include a motel, restaurant, and convenience market and curio store. I didn't have time to take the twenty-one story elevator ride and ¾-mile walking tour of the large underground rooms in this, the only dry limestone cave in the United States, but I did want to take a break. In the mini-mart I purchased a can of V-8 and poured it into the Styrofoam cup I'd filled with ice. I sat out front on the wooden-backed bench that faced the dirt driveway, sipped my V-8, enjoyed the view, and listened to the ravens caw to each other.

Several minutes later, my watching, listening, and sipping were interrupted by a man and two women. They were wearing badges that identified them as participants in the Yavapai College Elderhostel Program. On his badge was printed *Philip Feld, San Diego*. The squint in his eyes and the upturn to the corners of his mouth seemed engraved by years of laughter. The two women stood quietly, letting Phil take the lead in finding out what I was up to. As he and I talked, we fed off each other's desire to respond with an answer that wasn't entirely straight.

"So you started your bike ride in Davis?" he asked.

"Actually, I started in Santa Monica after I drove a rental car from Davis."

"You should have just gotten rid of the bike and kept the car."

"I thought about that but the bike wouldn't let me."

"So why are you going to Chicago on a bicycle, of all things?"

"I thought it would be fun to take a road trip and travel with the windows down all the way."

"You're a sick man, you know that?"

And so it went, laughter and smart answers back and forth until we heard a bell ring. Phil told me it was their signal to re-assemble for the next presentation in the lecture/dining room. As they left, he and his friends wished me luck.

Before leaving, I went back inside and refilled my cup with ice cubes to suck on as I went on down the road. Not long thereafter, I finally saw the elusive animal I had been looking for all day. Grazing to my right, forty feet from the highway, was a pronghorn antelope. I stopped and we stood waiting…motionless. I wanted a picture but my camera was buried in the left front pannier. In ultra-slow motion I started to reach for it and the split second I did, he took off, bounding away in silent leaps. It was as though each leg was attached to a pogo stick that thrust him forward in synchronized and rhythmic motion.

He quickly disappeared into a nearby gully, leaving me to mentally replay the sight of his entertaining gracefulness.

Since leaving Kingman this morning, I had enjoyed having the highway almost to myself. Starting tomorrow near Ash Fork and lasting until I got to Chicago, this would all change as I reentered the world of speeding freeway traffic and crowded narrow two-lane roads. While reflecting on the quiet of the past seventy miles, the silence abruptly ended. A high pitched noise, like a piece of chalk grating on a blackboard (it sounded like *chee, chee*), erupted from both sides of the road. It took a long time before I finally saw the source – prairie dogs. Blending in with the tan earth, some stood eyeing me with vigilant suspicion but most of them, in an explosion of organized panic, scurried to the nearest entrance of an underground burrow and disappeared.

I geared down, slowed to a crawl, and watched. Within seconds their curiosity got the better of most of them and they reemerged, but only far enough above ground to keep their eyes on me. I tried to imitate their high pitched cry, but soon gave up, reverting to English which at least I understood. I said hello, told them I admired their speed and how it must be fun to live in such a peaceful and beautiful place. The sound of my voice made it easier for them to keep track of me, and though it was probably my imagination, they did seem to be less frantic. In three miles, I came to the prairie dog town city limit and everything was suddenly quiet again.

In her piece entitled *Prayer Dogs,* Terry Tempest Williams wrote about the five species of prairie dogs and the fact that they are all seriously threatened with extinction. Naturalist Ernest Thompson Seaton once estimated there were five billion prairie dogs in North America in the 1900s. Today, in Colorado alone, 98% of them have been eradicated. My brief reading about these rodents had convinced me that the justification for their extermination was less indicative of their being a pest than it was about our unwillingness as humans to accommodate them as an important part of our diverse ecosystem.

It was 5:30 when, under a partly cloudy sky, I rolled into Seligman, population around 600. I could see I-40 again, less than a mile to my right. Despite its proximity to the interstate, Seligman had lost 70%

of its economy when the freeway opened. Going one mile out of their way into Seligman was just too much of an inconvenience so most travelers sped by.

I had arrived too late to stop at the only barber shop and shake the hand of semi-retired Angel Delgadillo. I felt a need to thank him for the experience I was having on Route 66. Twenty-seven years ago, from the vantage of his main street barber shop, he had watched his town shut down around him. Unwilling to give up and move on, he and his brother, Juan, and a dozen other friends met one day in the Copper Cart restaurant next door. With Angel's leadership, they decided to try and bring back The Mother Road. They founded the Historic Route 66 Association of Arizona and helped start the annual Arizona Fun Run that I'd seen in Oatman yesterday. Angel successfully lobbied the Arizona legislature to designate Route 66 as an historic highway. Following Arizona's lead, the other seven states formed their own associations which led to a national organization that put a collective voice into promoting travel on the Mother Road.

The previous two nights I'd stayed in a Motel 6, which was not my plan before starting this adventure. My intention had been to support

One year later I made a follow-up trip to meet Angel Delgadillo.

local motel owners and other out of the way businesses. Money I spent in each Route 66 town would improve in some small way a standard of living that was already on life support as evidenced by the many abandoned businesses and homes.

The sign outside the small, U-shaped, single-story motel read "Aztec." Turning into the driveway I wondered if Least Heat Moon had ever penned his criteria for picking a motel like he had done with eating establishments. Before my trip ended, if I took a shot at doing that, I would start with the tidy, clean, and freshly painted motel before me.

Inside, the office was empty. I gently thumped the desk bell twice and watched a lady walk toward me from a room in the back where a TV was broadcasting the evening news. There was something about her demeanor that conveyed the feeling that I was welcome and among friends. She wore blue jeans, and a dark grey t-shirt with four images of Minnie Mouse frolicking across the front. She wore no makeup, the lines in her face speaking of a life of hard work. When I asked, her smile and greeting were followed by, "Yes, I have a non-smoking room for you. And you get a 10% discount coupon good at the Copper Kettle restaurant just down the street."

As I filled out the registration form, she told me the story of her motel. "For many years it was closed and falling down." She paused, reached under the counter, grabbed a postcard, and as she handed it to me, she said, "I found this postcard of the original motel and used the picture on it to guide me in its restoration." She might just as well have shown me a picture of her heart, its every chamber overflowing with pride and love.

I returned the postcard, gave her my registration, paid for my room, and as she was giving me my key, she said, "There's something else I want to show you." She turned around, reached up, took a plaque off the wall and handed it to me. It was the final inspection report from the Coconino County Health Department, her legal authorization to open for business. At the bottom, the inspector had written, "This is the finest motel in Seligman."

I unlocked the door to my room and pushed my bike inside. New furniture, curtains and carpeting surrounded me. In the bathroom were a new sink and cabinets. The wallpaper around the top edge of the walls matched the rug and the bedspread. An oil painting on the wall was of an Arizona desert scene with two prairie dogs in the foreground. Everything spoke welcome, even the vase filled with plastic flowers on the nightstand. Back at the Bagdad Café, Herr Rosacker had written in my journal, "Seligman a place to stay." I wondered if this was the motel where he and his passengers had spent the night. As I looked around I thought about the financial risks and emotional worry the owner had taken on in re-opening a motel that had been abandoned.

Across the street from the Aztec is the Snow Cap drive-in restaurant, owned by Angel's younger brother, Juan. In 1953, the Delgadillo family built this restaurant out of lumber salvaged from the Santa Fe Railroad and just like Angel's barber shop, it has been a fixture on Route 66 since then. The pictures of hot dogs and ice cream cones on the outside walls, along with the words "shakes, root beer, burgers, malts, tacos," all stimulated my hunger. Also catching my eye on the front window were the words in red, "Merry Christmas" – in May. I crossed the street and saw that the Snow Cap was closed. What I didn't know was that Juan had died one year before and his drive-in was now being run by his nephew, John. Farther down the street, the Copper Kettle was also closed. I assumed there wasn't enough dinner business for either restaurant to stay open this late. I retraced the way I'd come into Seligman and found West Side Lilo's Café open. Inside, more people were smoking than not. I ordered and hurriedly finished my roast beef sandwich, mashed potatoes, salad, and wanting a change from tea, two glasses of milk. I briefly considered having a piece of homemade cherry pie but I had taken as much as I could of breathing cigarette smoke so I just paid my bill and left.

On my way back to my motel room, I saw a pay phone near the front wall of a closed gas station. I dialed and just as Donna answered, the rain started. I pulled the phone cord as far as it would stretch, trying to take advantage of the narrow overhang above me. It was futile as the wind-driven drops from a passing cloud pelted me while we talked. Always my cheerleader, when I told her about the hard climb ahead of me tomorrow from Seligman to Flagstaff, she said, "You'll make it to Flagstaff; no problem."

Back at the motel I showered, repacked my panniers, rolled the pain ointment onto my right knee, pulled back the bed covers and toppled in. I attributed my subsequent ease of falling asleep to being tired and the feeling of being at home in the welcoming and quiet motel.

> *Since Dug's 1962 Falcon hasn't been seen around town lately, there is a rumor that he has put his bike into the Falcon's trunk and is actually driving, not bicycling, Historic 66. The rumor suggests that every now and then he takes his bike out of the trunk, puts it in front of a sign, and then takes a picture. Be assured, the rumor is false.*
>
> *Dug is doing fairly well with only a minor twinge to one knee bothering him. Hopefully the pain ointment my massage therapist gave him will work.*
>
> *That's all for now, folks.*
>
> *Love, Donna*

15

Get Your Kicks on Route 66

The Copper Kettle opened at 6:00 the next morning. I walked from the motel and ordered what had become my preferred breakfast: hash browns, two eggs over hard, and two buttered slices of whole wheat toast. Feeling hungrier than usual, I added a sausage patty as a side order. I washed everything down with a large glass of orange juice and lots of water. After eating I used my ten-percent-off coupon, adding the savings to my tip. While paying, the cashier asked, "Where ya' headed?"

"Today, Flagstaff."

She rolled her brown eyes as if I was out of my mind and then informed me, "You'll have two BIG hills to climb before you get there."

It was impossible to ignore her emphasis on the word," big," as well as the seriousness in her voice when she added, "You be real careful out there on the road." It was frequent expressions of caring like hers that were deepening my connection with total strangers.

While eating breakfast I had looked over my index cards and thought I already knew about the serious climbs ahead. I'd start here in Seligman at 5250 feet, pedal to Williams at 6770 feet, and then to the top of the 7344-foot Arizona Divide. From this, the highest point on Route 66, I'd gradually descend 400 feet until, seventy-seven miles from Seligman, voilá, I'd be in Flagstaff. It seemed so easy, so matter-of-fact, and it would have been had this been my first day instead of my seventh. Because I was burning more calories than I was taking in, my energy had started to wane, and my right knee still wasn't behaving itself.

The whisper of the mile-high breeze greeted me head-on as I pedaled out of Seligman. The quiet was interrupted by an east bound freight being pulled by four engines, the first two growling as they spewed black diesel exhaust that thankfully drifted away from me. I waved at the closed window in the lead engine and the engineer honked in return. A few minutes later the engineer in a freight headed the opposite direction also exercised his air horn after I waved. For a moment we were like strangers passing on a rural dirt road, and as is the custom in such a place, the driver's wave. The action of both engineers left me feeling affirmed, our individual adventures joined.

The climb away from Seligman started gently. I eventually crested the long hill and on the other side coasted down an equally long descent that ended two hours from Seligman. The old highway looped underneath busy I-40 and as they merged, I cheered my completion of the longest and continuous 167-mile segment of Route 66. Five miles later I took the off-ramp into Ash Fork, its population, like Peach Springs and Seligman, around 600. Passing the city limit sign I saw the Ash Fork elevation listed at 5140 feet. Much to my frustration, instead of gaining elevation since leaving Seligman, I'd lost 100 feet and would have to start my climb all over again. Somehow I had read my index cards wrong at breakfast, not a good way to start my day.

Named for the three forks of Ash Creek, Ash Fork is known as The Flagstone Capital of the United States. Stacked on edge and banded onto pallets at Stoneworks, Kaibab Stone, and Dunbar Stone were thousands of square feet of yellow, red, buff and beige flagstone, all ready to be trucked away. While the town had this industry and the income it generated, it didn't seem to be enough to off-set its worn out look. Cycling the short distance through town I couldn't help but notice the many businesses and homes boarded shut and others in need of extensive repair, their lawns dead and trees dying. Unlike Seligman, access to Ash Fork from I-40 was much easier but in spite of that, there were few reasons for people to leave the freeway and wander through town as I had.

Having started today going down in altitude instead of up was really inconsequential, but it bothered me. With the primary intent of adjusting my attitude, I stopped at the Corral Market/Mustang Gas on the eastern edge of Ash Fork and bought a bottle of orange juice.

Out front the windows were being used as a bulletin board where Ash Forkians taped announcements. I drank my juice and moved from flyer to flyer, reading about lost dogs, trucks for sale, meetings at the Gospel of Faith Church, and the Aviso de la Eleccion. Other bulletins had been up so long that the morning sun had caused the ink on them to fade beyond legibility.

After catching up on Ash Fork's window pane news, I sat down to finish my juice on a bench in front of the store. Looking east I could see the start of the 1,600 foot (really) BIG climb that would take me to the next town of Williams, only twenty miles away. My frustration over losing altitude from Seligman to here had ebbed. Hydrated and relaxed, I felt ready to take on the serious grind that awaited me.

The climb to Williams began right away at the freeway on-ramp. There was no gradual increase, no opportunity to adjust. I went immediately to my lowest of eighteen gears and when not walking or stopping to snack, I pedaled steadily. Semis, geared down like I was, crept past, and occasionally a driver would honk. I would acknowledge their greeting with a wave, thankful for their blared encouragement like that of the train engineers.

In this area of northern Arizona, the evergreen forest is populated with piñons and junipers. Ahead at the higher elevation towns of Williams and Flagstaff, these trees give way to ponderosa pines and in wetter areas, aspens. As I made my way slowly uphill, it was impossible to ignore the thousands of dead piñons. Some had fallen over but the gray-black carcasses of most were still standing where they had lived their abbreviated life spans and then died. I knew this catastrophic death wasn't limited to Arizona. Aerial surveys in Colorado and New Mexico show that two million acres of piñons and 1.2 million acres of ponderosa pines are affected, including many in my parents' and sister's yards in Santa Fe. All this devastation is caused by one of six species of bark beetles.

The story of the beetles killing these trees is the story of the ebb and flow of nature. These voracious insects, each one the size of a grain of rice, are always present in the forest but it is only when the trees are stressed by drought and/or mistletoe, like they were now, that their ability to fight off the beetle's attack is compromised. When the tree has sufficient moisture, it uses its sap to push the beetle out through the hole it bored. When the tree has insufficient sap to do this, the beetles chew their way through the outer bark and feed unimpeded on the nutritious cambium, all the while emitting a chemical scent, a pheromone, which attracts other beetles to the feast. While eating and bleeding the trees to death, each generation of beetles guarantees the survival of their species by laying from one to four generations of eggs every year. A blue stem fungus the beetles carry also contributes to the death of the trees by clogging their water conducting tissues. With an assault like this it is no surprise that between two and three million piñons and ponderosa pines have been killed in Arizona alone.

Controlling the beetles by aerial spraying is ineffective because not enough spray can be delivered to the bark to kill the beetles when they attack. And once the beetles have infested a tree, there is no insecticide that is effective. The death of the trees is inevitable if they can't fight off the beetle's attack on their own.

On one of my uphill breaks, I looked around underneath several dead piñons. I was surprised to find piñon seedlings growing, already taking the place of the mother tree that had seeded them. Someday, but not likely in my lifetime, these hills will again be green, abundant with vigorous trees. It will help, of course, if precipitation returns to normal and the mistletoe dies.

Back on my bike and climbing without any lingering knee pain, I caught sight of two passenger jets streaking east above me. Streaming silently from each engine was a narrow ribbon of white fluff that invited me to gambol in it, like a child in a bouncy house. By the time each ribbon began to disintegrate and disappear, the delayed roar of the jet engines took its place above me. As I rode along, trying to watch the sky and where I was going at the same time, I tried to figure out our respective speeds.

Assuming that each jet was being assisted by the jet stream, I guessed it was flying about 550 mph. In one minute, the passengers flew nine miles, a distance it would take me one hour to pedal, if I was on level ground and not taking a nap. Looking at it another way, if I started pedaling at 6:00 a.m., took two hours of breaks, and stopped for the day at 8:00 p.m., in those fourteen hours I would cycle around 108 miles, the distance each jet would go in twelve minutes. The contrast in our respective distances and speeds surprised but didn't discourage me. I had no desire to change places with any passenger.

My climb to Williams ended at noon when I took the first I-40 exit into town. On October 13, 1984, Williams acquired the distinction of being the last city on Route 66 to be bypassed. But unlike most of the bypassed towns I'd been through, Williams was hanging on. It helped that its businesses could be seen from I-40 and off-ramp access to them was easy. Adding to the town's economic boost was the fact that Williams is only sixty-five miles from Grand Canyon National Park. This encouraged people to stop in Williams, get a motel, browse through the novelty-filled stores and purchase a memory of being on Route 66 to show their friends back home. If they had more time, travelers could enjoy the five and one-half- hour steam train ride to and from the Grand Canyon.

Except for the Buffalo Burger in Oatman, I had intentionally avoided eating fatty hamburgers and fries. But here in Williams, the convenience of enjoying a hamburger at the Dairy Queen was just too strong. I justified it as my reward for having most of the climb of the day behind me. If it had been later in the day and I wasn't sweating so much, I would have gone a little further down the main drag and eaten at Rod's Steak House, a Route 66 establishment since 1946.

In his book, *Route 66 Traveler's Guide*, Tom Snyder wrote about a section of the old highway east of Williams where travelers could ride on 1930s concrete. I wanted to do this, so after lunch I took his recommended exit from I-40 and rode along on 1990s asphalt. With no concrete in sight, I decided I must have written the directions down wrong. Resigned to my mistake, I began my search for the next freeway onramp. I cycled up a short hill and as I came over the crest, a section of white concrete several hundred yards long spread out before me. I had found Snyder's concrete.

I stopped and stood admiring the scene before me. The shoulders of both sides of the road were bordered by red volcanic cinders. Twenty-air miles directly beyond the sparkling pavement, chiseled into the deep blue as they jutted 5,000 feet above the city of Flagstaff, were Agassiz and Humphreys Peaks, the latter the highest mountain in Arizona at 12,670 feet. Now in early May, they were still covered with snow.

If ever a situation begged for rest and contemplation, this was it. So I sat down on the soft earth under a ponderosa that had so far escaped the bark beetles. A light breeze blew through its needles, creating a soft whistle as if made by an eternal presence blowing gently through opened and circled lips. I felt embraced and fully alive. Later I rode down the short hill, my tires sighing on concrete that was as smooth as a baby's cheek.

Back on the freeway, I saw flashing lights ahead. As I got closer, I could see they were coming from a Coconino County sheriff's vehicle and a City of Flagstaff police car, both moving the way I was going. In between them was a van, its three occupants shouting encouragement to three cyclists and six runners, everyone on the right shoulder of the freeway. I caught up to this official procession and as we talked they told me they were raising money for Special Olympics. It felt good to respond in kind, telling them I was riding to Chicago, raising money for Habitat.

The highway rest area in the pines several miles later gave me a chance for a needed break. I was heading back to my bike after using the restroom when a man stopped me and asked, "Where ya' goin?"

When I said, "Chicago," he jerked his head backward, opened his mouth slightly, and raised his eyebrows, miming his obvious disbelief. I went on to explain that I was following Route 66.

"And they let you go on the freeway?" he asked.

Another teachable moment had arrived. It is generally believed that the only people allowed on a freeway are those in a vehicle, but as I explained, "Bicyclists are permitted on the freeway if there is no other way for them to get from one town or frontage road to another. When you leave this rest area, look on the shoulder for the small white Arizona highway sign that has the figure of a bicycle on top. Under that you'll see the words, *use shoulder only*. This is Arizona's way of indicating it is legal for a bicycle to be on the upcoming freeway."

"I've never seen that sign but I'll look for it now."

In parting, he said, "God bless you. I'm going to say my blessings for you."

Again I was comforted by the fact that I wasn't alone. Whether I knew it or not, strangers were pulling for me, their positive thoughts helping me to feel safe.

Arizona, not to be outdone by the 7268-foot Continental Divide in New Mexico, has one of its own, the 7,344-foot Arizona Divide. I crossed this blip, the highest elevation on Route 66, and felt no altitude discomfort despite being 7300 feet higher than my hometown of Davis. More worried about the cold and rain I thought I might run into at this elevation, I'd packed some warm clothes and rain gear. But I didn't need them, at least not today. I guessed the temperature to be in the 70s, pleasant for biking.

Riding into Flagstaff, my mind was filled with memories, both happy and sad. Donna and I had gotten married in the hospital here almost thirty-eight years ago. The hospital staff had taken

Highway sign for bikes.

the furniture out of a waiting room, converting it into a simple wedding room with two large candle stands and two vases with flowers. They wheeled Donna's father in his hospital bed into the room and, with Donna's mom, her matron of honor, my parents and best man, our siblings and minister gathered around him, Donna and I said our vows and exchanged rings. Two weeks later her father lost his valiant battle with cancer at the age of forty-seven. At the cemetery in Flagstaff, we stood around him again as he was laid to rest.

I continued pedaling through Flagstaff, following Route 66 as it paralleled the railroad tracks. Seeing the traffic brought to memory the mistake I made when we were leaving town to start our honeymoon. I had accidentally turned the wrong way onto a one-way downtown street while trying to elude Donna's uncle, her brother, and several friends, all honking their horns as they followed behind us. It seems funny now but back then we were lucky not to have started our marriage riding back to the hospital in an ambulance, our car being towed to a junk yard, and every driver getting a traffic citation. Adding to the frenzy of that experience, our puppy gifted us with our first domestic chore when, unable to contain her excitement, she vomited in the car on the front floor mat.

These memories occupied me as I cycled through Flagstaff, half-heartedly looking for a motel to spend the night. I had every intention of stopping at the first motel and restaurant I came to, but like back in Needles, that plan kept changing. I kept telling myself, "I'll just go a little further." Further finally arrived when I got to the far eastern edge of town.

After dinner and before falling asleep, I used the motel room phone to make two calls, the first one to Darlene. As we talked across the miles, my confidence grew. What a privilege, I thought, to have her as my daughter. Despite her struggles with a permanent hearing loss, she had grown up to be a confident, beautiful, and loving young woman.

And then I called Donna. We talked about how fast the first week had passed and shared our memories of Flagstaff, including the winter we drove here to visit her mom. The car heater in our '62 Falcon was on the fritz so we had bundled up to try and stay warm in the bitter cold. The going was slow as we made our way, following the snow plows that left in their wake ten-foot snow banks on both sides of Route 66.

Before Donna and I hung up, she read me a column sent by Bob Cavanagh, a reporter for the *Illinois Times*. He had met Ryan one morning as they commuted to work in downtown Springfield and Ryan had told him about my upcoming Route 66 ride. Bob had called me before I left on my adventure and my answers to his questions had formed the basis of his newspaper column. While this motivated me, I was also concerned how he would explain to his readers if something went wrong and I had to abort my trip.

When I chose the motel for tonight, I failed to notice the heavily traveled street that crossed the railroad tracks directly opposite the motel. Later in the evening, the consequence of this little failure in observation woke me up. It started with the rhythmic dinging of a loud bell as the crossing arms came down and stopped cars from crossing the railroad tracks. Then the horn on the nearing train took over, the engineer blaring the standard warning of two long blasts followed by a short and then a final long. As the night played itself out, the engineer on every train had his own variation of this concert, some adding several more longs just to make sure I was awake and listening. All the noise – bells dinging, horns blaring, and the elongated roar of hundreds of railroad cars going in each direction – was so invasive that it sounded like each train was rolling through my room. This clamor continued at frequent intervals all night and by the time the sun came up, I had a new criterion to add to my list in picking a motel.

In spite of my abbreviated and erratic sleep, I was ready the next morning to begin the second week of my adventure. The air had a nip to it here at 6905 feet – I guessed it was in the low 40s – so I covered my head and ears with a thin stocking hat. The rest of my attire included riding gloves, a long sleeve cotton shirt from a Turkey Trot 10K race I'd run in Davis, a long sleeve fleece, windbreaker, and as always, shorts. I was comfortable as I left the motel, following Route 66 to the next town, Winona.

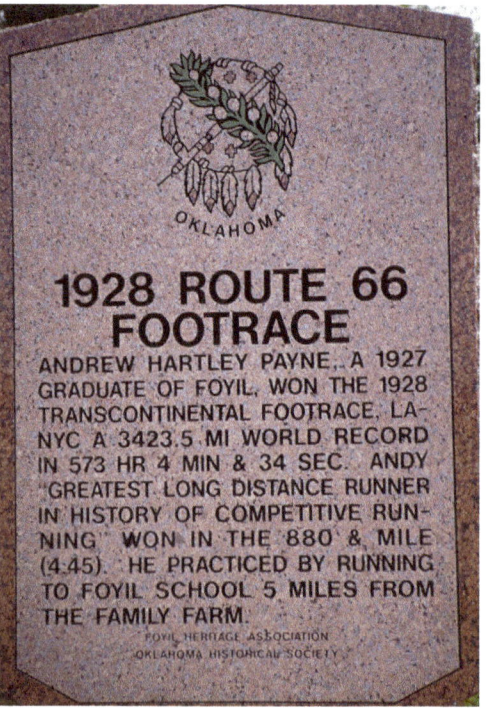

From its beginning in 1926, there was something special about Route 66. It wasn't even finished and travelers were being drawn to it. Word-of-mouth brought attention as did the *Bunion Derby*, a cross country footrace, and John Steinbeck's 1939 novel, *The Grapes of Wrath*. Adding to the romance of the road was a song, *Get Your Kicks on Route 66*, written by Bobby Troup.

After WW II, Bobby and his wife, Cynthia, left Harrisburg, Pennsylvania, headed to Los Angeles where he hoped to become a songwriter. Some years later, in his interview with Robert Townsend for the PBS video, *Great Drives, Route 66*, Bobby explained that after they'd begun their trip, Cynthia suggested he write a song about Route 40, the highway they'd started on. However, Bobby knew that after Chicago they'd be spending most of their time on Route 66 and writing about that highway seemed to be more appropriate. Sometime later when they were on Route 66, Cynthia looked at Bobby and said, "Get your kicks on Route 66." Bobby liked the line, and using it, started writing the lyrics for a song.

When they arrived in Los Angeles, his song was still unfinished. He arranged to show what he had written to Nat King Cole. Nat said he wanted to record it and urged Bobby to finish writing it. So he sat down and, with the help of road maps, completed his song using Cynthia's seven-word contribution as the refrain. Cole recorded it and it became a big hit. Since then many others have also recorded it, including Buckwheat Zydeco, The Brian Setzer Orchestra, The Rolling Stones, Charles Brown and Manhattan Transfer.

If you ever plan to motor west
Travel my way, take the highway that's the best
Get your kicks on Route Sixty-six!
It winds from Chicago to L.A.
More than two thousand miles all the way
Get your kicks on Route Sixty-six!
Now you go thru Saint Looey, Joplin, Missouri
And Oklahoma City is mighty pretty.
You'll see Amarillo, Gallup, New Mexico
Flagstaff, Arizona; don't forget Winona,
Kingman, Barstow, San Bernardino
Won't you get hip to this timely tip?
When you make that California trip.
Get your kicks on Route Sixty-six!
Get your kicks on Route Sixty-six!

Bobby didn't include any Kansas towns and overloaded it with three from Arizona. All the towns were in east-to-west order except Winona, which he placed west of Flagstaff. I decided he must have done this intentionally to solve the rhyming problem with the word Arizona.

The road to Winona passed ranchettes built among the ponderosa pines. Dogs barked and horses eyed me, circling in their paddocks as they watched me cycle by. Within half an hour of leaving Flagstaff, I knew I should have gotten to Winona by now, but there hadn't been any signs to indicate where it was. In short, I was lost. Up ahead was a country store, a perfect place to ask for directions. Inside was a lady who stood just tall enough to see over the cash register she was tending. I greeted her and asked, "Can you tell me where Winona is?"

It was obvious right away that she was unable to talk without smiling. "This whole area is Way-no-na," she explained while enunciating the town's first syllable and swinging her left arm in a wide arc at the same time.

"So I'm pronouncing it wrong when I say Wi-no-na?"

"That's okay; everyone does," she said, putting me at ease. "Way-no-na is considered by many to be the Shell Station at the freeway a couple a miles east of here. You won't miss it if you stay on this frontage road."

She wished me well and once again I was thankful for having stopped to get directions. On my way again, before reaching the gas station and freeway on-ramp 211, I came to an abandoned, steel truss bridge that crossed the creek on my left. Until the building of I-40, this now unused bridge carried Route 66 vehicles over the creek in Winona.

A gentle ripple of wind pushed me as I entered the freeway. The pain in my knee two days ago was gone now and the bike was functioning smoothly, both of us in perfect harmony. The sun, directly ahead, was high enough that drivers coming from behind could see me without being blinded. Gradually the ponderosa pines gave way to piñons, dead and alive, junipers, and then the high desert grassland of eastern Arizona. The Arizona Game and Fish Antelope Range was just ahead, giving me hope that I'd see some of these beautiful animals in the wild like I had west of Seligman.

My first cycling experience on a freeway was climbing Cajon Pass on I-15 in California. It was frightening but as I went along I gained confidence. Now, with many freeway miles behind me, riding on I-40 had become an enjoyable and even preferable route to follow. The surface was usually smoother than other roads, and I had the shoulder, which was almost as wide as a traffic lane, all to myself. Yes, the semis were loud and most were going over the 75 mph speed limit. But I welcomed the way they disrupted the air, turning the normal wind resistance into a maelstrom of wind currents that pulled me along for short distances. I also appreciated how, if each trucker saw the fast lane was open, they would move into that lane, increasing the distance between us as they passed safely. Every time that happened I would wave my appreciation and most drivers would blink their tail lights or honk in response. Friends all around.

75 mph, trucks; 10 mph, me.

I knew from past experiences driving across New Mexico and Arizona on vacation with my family, headed either to or from California, that Route 66 business owners had perfected the art of enticing gullible tourists to stop. Billboard advertising bordered on the deceptive and sometimes ridiculous. Some of it played to the ignorance of people who knew little about American Indians beyond the demeaning and sometimes fearful stereotypes acquired from watching Hollywood movies.

Up ahead was Twin Arrows, a place that fit into the creative advertising category. This compact little commercial scene was prominently marked by two, forty-foot telephone poles, painted to look like arrows and then cemented at an angle into the ground next to each other. In the movie *Forrest Gump*, these arrows can be seen in the far background when Forrest hands the yellow, mud spattered, t-shirt with the smiley-face back to its owner.

I climbed over the hip-high concrete barrier separating the abandoned buildings from the frontage road. The windows of the small diner were boarded and the red letters spelling "malts and hamburgers," were fading, flake by flake, from the wall as they were ravaged by wind, snow, rain and the searing sun. The trading post and gas station entrances were locked and blocked by tumbleweeds.

I wandered around, took several pictures and wished I'd been here before the diner had closed. In his book, *Route 66, The Mother Road*, Michael Wallis wrote that the menu had included among its delicacies, "buzzard eggs, braised rattlesnake hips, sautéed centipede legs, and lizard tongue pudding." Creative advertising indeed. And while it wouldn't become clear until later on, this diner had a historical connection with two others.

A few miles later I came to what was left of Two Guns. I pushed the bike off the freeway, leaned it against the highway fence, and got my camera. I ignored the "*No Trespassing*" signs and the padlock on the gate that blocked my entrance. Not wanting to climb over the top strands of barbed wire, ripping my clothes or skin in the process, I laid on my back and wiggled under the fence with no space to spare.

I wandered around the deserted buildings, unable to find any with roofs, windows, or doors, my hope being that I wouldn't step into a den of rattlesnakes. At the back of the property were the faded remains of the large black letters, **Mountain Lions**. The zoo here had once housed them as well as coyotes, peccaries, Gila monsters, coral snakes, cougars, bobcats and other wild animals of Arizona. I couldn't help but wonder if, as a child, I had begged my parents to stop here so I could be entertained by this exploitation before it ended sometime around 1950.

Before leaving, I parked myself on a rock that was once part of a wall. Gone were the saloons, whorehouses, dance pavilions, gambling dens and violent death. With the coming of Route 66, new businesses included a motel, restaurant, trading post/curio shop, campground, a tavern and lounge, gas station and garage. When the trading post burned down in 1934, the slow decline of Two Guns began, helped along by disagreement among the owners. Like so many other towns on Route 66, the construction of Interstate 40 fenced off access. As I sat snacking, I couldn't help wonder if some courageous soul might still come along and breathe life into the history here. Sort of like what was happening at Roy's in Ludlow, California.

Having had enough of this uncomfortable place with its history of violence and unwelcome, it was time for me to move on. I wiggled my way back under the fence and brushed the sand and weed seeds off my clothes, ready to join the traffic on the freeway.

It has been estimated that around thirty thousand years ago, a chunk of celestial flotsam composed of nickel and iron slammed into what is now northern Arizona. The resulting excavation measured nearly six hundred feet deep and three miles in circumference. I had seen Meteor Crater years before as a young boy and once with Donna and our kids. But since it is a round trip of twelve miles from Route 66, I didn't want to go out of my way to see it again. What I did want to see was the wooden fence next to the Meteor City Trading Post at the I-40 off-ramp to the Crater. The eight-foot high, 140-foot-long fence extended east from the Trading Post. Painted on it in large red letters were the words, "*World's Longest Map of U.S. Route 66.*" Below this was an undulating black line, the Mother Road from Santa Monica to Chicago. I strolled along this outdoor art gallery, looking at the representations of some of the most commonly recognized Route 66 attractions. They included the Jackrabbit Trading Post, the Red Barn, Cadillac Ranch, and the Blue Whale, all waiting for me on down the road.

Before leaving, I took a picture of the fence-map and then the Trading Post shaped like a large, white dome. The dome could have been mistaken for a flying saucer except for the fashionable yellow lightning bolt and an American Indian wearing his feather headdress, both painted on the dome and visible from the freeway.

Roughly four miles later, the freeway overpass crossed the train tracks. In the distance I saw a freight train coming so I decided to take a break and wait. The tracks curved 400 yards before the bridge overpass and as the train rounded that curve, I waved. Almost immediately the engineer blew his air horns. And as if that wasn't enough to say hello, just before he passed directly under me, he opened the window in his engine, leaned his head out, smiled and waved. He made my day.

The fifty-five miles from Flagstaff to Winslow in Navajo County had taken me just under five hours. I was whizzing along, the prevailing breeze, smooth shoulder and the gradual drop in altitude from Flagstaff, all contributing to my increased speed. My goal in Winslow was to find Standin' on the Corner Park. Its name had been taken from a line in the song, *Take it Easy*, recorded by the Eagles. Whether they intended it or not, the lyrics of their song had become another contribution, this one recent, to the romance of Route 66.

> *Well I'm a standin' on a corner in Winslow, Arizona*
> *Such a fine sight to see.*
> *It's a girl my Lord, in a flatbed Ford*
> *Slowin' down to take a look at me*
> *Come on baby, don't say maybe*
> *I've gotta' know if your sweet love*
> *Is gonna' save me.*
> *We may lose, we may win*
> *Though we will never be here again*
> *So open up I'm climbin' in*
> *So take it easy.*

America's Main Street went right by the park in the center of town. A fire on October 28, 2004 had gutted the J.C. Penney/Rasco building next to the park, leaving only its two-story walls standing. As a precaution, the little 25x60-foot park was fenced off to protect visitors from falling debris. The park featured the bronze statue of a man standing by a lamp post, his hair parted down the middle, wearing a vest, his thumbs looped into the front pockets of his jeans, and a guitar resting upright on his left boot. Behind him on the wall was a mural of a blond driving the "flatbed Ford." The real truck, a red, flatbed Ford F-500, was parked on the street behind me. As I walked along the fence and admired the truck, I hummed along with the Eagles as their music played from the curio store loudspeaker across the street.

On another corner across from the park was a drug store named Dominique's. Next to its front entrance was a second statue, this one wooden, his arms pointing straight down, palms facing his thighs. The carving included his brown boots, blue jeans with a silver belt buckle, a red shirt, yellow kerchief and a white cowboy hat. He too was "standin' on the corner," all duded up and waitin' for the girl driving the flatbed.

"Standing on the corner in Winslow, Arizona."

It was time for lunch so, several blocks past the park, I entered the Brown Mug Café and ordered a sandwich. The café was nearly empty so I had decided not to sit on a stool at the counter but instead in a four-person booth next to the front window. I had just started eating my sandwich when high school students, most of them Navajo, began arriving. Laughing and talking loudly, they headed to a large back room. When that room filled they scurried to find a place to sit in the empty booths around me. In short order, all the seats were taken. As more students arrived, they either stood waiting for an empty seat or, seeing the crowd, they left. Meanwhile, I was taking up room where four students could sit. I imagined fingers being pointed in my direction and covetous thoughts spinning behind the staring eyes.

I needed the rest but still felt selfish taking up more space than I needed. The thought of inviting some of the students to join me never crossed my mind. I took my time finishing my lunch and decided I didn't really need to look over my route cards anymore or drink a third glass of tea. So I walked to the counter and paid my bill. Like a magnet attracting iron filings, my booth was filled by six students before I reached the door. I smiled as I passed them and they returned the greeting.

A short distance beyond the café, I rode by a small diner that caught my attention. It had been painted recently, the red and white colors brilliant in the early afternoon sun. The fire hydrant on the curb in front eliminated a prime parking place, but that made no difference today since the sign in the window read *cerrado* (closed) and another sign near it read, "For Sale." I thought the diner looked vaguely familiar to the abandoned one I'd seen earlier in the day at Twin Arrows but the conclusion of this story was still to come.

The views from Route 66 were inspiring. To the far north were several buttes, like monuments, the earth around them eroded away leaving these abrupt protrusions in an otherwise flat high desert grassland. Sixty miles behind me, the majestic peaks above Flagstaff were still plainly visible. I found myself reaching out to touch them, the imaginary contact gently pricking the tips of two fingers on my right hand. I wondered what it must have been like to be a pioneer headed toward them on foot, horseback, or by wagon. They must have seemed just like they did today, so close and yet so far.

16

Nearing Home: The Land of Enchantment

The Navajo Nation Reservation encompasses a huge chunk of northeastern Arizona and smaller contiguous areas in northwestern New Mexico, and southern Utah. It sprawls across 14½-million acres, an area slightly larger than the state of West Virginia. Walking the irregular border from start to finish would be a hike of six-hundred miles. This, the largest of all reservations, is home to 300,000 Navajos who collectively call themselves Diné, the People.

When I left Twin Arrows this morning, I had no idea that the southern border of the Navajo Reservation was less than two miles away on my left. Of more concern was finding a Jackrabbit sign. The owners of the Jackrabbit Trading Post had raised advertising on Route 66 to a new standard with their iconic yellow billboards. Painted on every sign was the left profile of a sitting jackrabbit and the number of miles to the Trading Post. Up until the Highway Beautification Act of 1965, these simple signs, as prolific as rabbits themselves, could be found from one end of Route 66 to the other, building tourists' anticipation of getting to the "Jackrabbit." Perhaps this was where "Daddy, are we there yet?" got its start.

When I-40 was built, it would have been easy to cut off all access to this Trading Post and, like the retail oases at Twin Arrows and Two Guns, let it slowly crumble away. But the owner of the Jackrabbit had connections. As a result, the Trading Post survived, ending up squeezed between I-40 on the north side and Route 66 and the Santa Fe Railroad tracks on the south.

It Only Hurts When I Sit Down

I followed the off-ramp and on the shoulder south of the Trading Post, I finally saw a large yellow billboard with the familiar black jackrabbit on it. But this sign was the only one of its kind. Accompanying this rabbit were three large words, **HERE IT IS**. On the west end of the single story, pumice block trading post was a smiling ten-foot tall fiberglass jackrabbit sitting on its haunches with a red saddle blanket and brown saddle on its back. I decided not to mosey through the store but did take a picture of a family and their giggling children as they "rode" the hare.

Donna and I had driven across the Navajo Reservation many times, visiting the on-reservation trading posts at Teec Nos Pos, Two Grey Hills, Crystal, and the Hubbell Trading Post National Historic site in Ganado. We had learned about the distinctive weaving styles and dyes used by Navajo weavers (women do the weaving) in each area of the reservation, our admiration of their work leading us, over time, to purchase several rugs. We had watched the owner/trader interact with the Navajo people who came to sell their rugs and silver and turquoise jewelry. In turn, the Navajos bought food, tack, cloth, wool yarn, clothing and many other day-to-day necessities. Isolated and scattered across the Reservation, these trading posts served, within their sphere of influence, the retail needs of the Navajo people, the relationship between the trader and the Navajo being that of family.

In contrast, off-reservation Trading Posts like The Jackrabbit were more tuned in to tourists, selling them Route 66 souvenirs, petrified wood, pennants, crafts, Jackrabbit clothing, and American Indian knickknacks to take home.

A steady fifteen miles-per-hour tailwind hustled me along as I left the Jackrabbit Trading Post. Back on the freeway, I was enjoying effortless pedaling when I saw two bicyclists, the first ones on my trip. They were pushing their bikes west bound. Their loads looked heavier than mine and they had the misfortune of cycling into the wind. I waved but neither of them returned my greeting. It was apparent that the tailwind I had hoped for and gotten was bringing them struggle. I felt vaguely guilty as I pedaled along, even coasting from time to time. As I thought about my effortless pedaling, I knew that regardless of the weather conditions, some people would be thankful while others would bemoan their misfortune. Little did I know that my turn to struggle with the environment was nearing.

On the second day of my adventure, I had passed the Wigwam Motel in Rialto, California. Now just ahead in Holbrook, I was nearing its twin, The Wigwam Village. These two motels were the last in a chain of seven and the only two built on Route 66. Not well known is the fact that these motels were improperly named. A wigwam is a short hut framed by arched poles with bark and hides laid over them, a type of housing built by American Indians from the Great Lakes eastward. The tall cone-shaped structures of the Holbrook motel are similar to those constructed by Plains Indians – the Blackfeet, Arapahoe, Cheyenne, Kiowa, and Sioux – and are properly called tepees.

Tepees

Route 66 and I exited the freeway and in a matter of minutes arrived at the misnamed Wigwam Village, built in the late 1940s. The differences between the individual tepees here in Holbrook and those in Rialto were mostly color, beige in Rialto and white here, and the choice of landscaping. The emphasis in Rialto had been on palm trees and asphalt while here it was junipers and rocks. But there was another difference that caught my eye right away. Parked in front of every Holbrook tepee was a classic car. One was a 1949 two-door Ford coupe that brought back memories of the 1949 Ford four-door sedan that had transported our family when we drove by here back in the early

1950s. I wanted to stay here tonight, basking in the ambiance, but the "No Vacancy" sign was already lighted at mid-afternoon, testimony to the motel's attraction.

The next to last motel on the northeastern edge of Holbrook was the Relax Inn. Thanks to the daylong tailwind, I had ridden ninety-three miles and averaged 12.8 mph for the day. I accepted my early arrival for what it was, a chance to hand-wash my dirty clothes, dry them over the motel heater, have an unhurried dinner and then a long phone conversation with Donna before getting to bed early.

As I checked in, the desk clerk greeted my attempts at conversation with mumbling and no eye contact. Even my bicycle failed to provoke its usual stream of questions. Walking to my first floor room, I wondered how this grumpy, obviously unhappy man had been picked as the welcoming bridge between exhausted travelers and their having a good night's sleep. Thinking back, he was the second motel clerk to fail in his responsibility to be hospitable. I hoped he would be the last.

Entering the state of Arizona four days ago, I crossed an invisible line that marked the beginning of the Mountain Time Zone. I would have reset my watch forward one hour but since Arizona stays on Mountain Standard Time year-round, the time across The Grand Canyon State is the same as California when it changes to Pacific Daylight Saving Time. The most obvious result of not changing the time on my watch was that the farther east I went, both sunrise and sunset came earlier, disrupting my biorhythm.

The following morning, first light was at 5:00. Like every other morning, I had no lack of motivation when it came to getting started. The earlier I got going, the more I could lollygag along and enjoy this once in a lifetime trip.

My daily routine usually started when I parted the motel curtains and looked outside to see if the sky was overcast, clear or drippy. Some mornings I could see the wind blowing trees and bushes and if so, from what direction. This morning my meteorological assessment didn't come until I got dressed and stepped outside. Walking to a nearby restaurant for breakfast under a sky filled with wispy clouds, I felt a light breeze blowing out of the east, a head wind. Not good. But by the time I'd finished eating and started biking at 5:50, the clouds were gone and the breeze was now blowing from the southeast, pushing against me at an angle. The tail wind I'd enjoyed every day up until today had spoiled me but I wasn't about to complain, even though I knew today I had a long gradual climb of 1500 feet to my evening destination, Gallup, New Mexico.

I followed the frontage road to the freeway one mile from the motel, pedaled up the on-ramp and passed a sign that gave Route 66 yet another name: The Purple Heart Trail. A short distance down the road, unusual advertising for a nearing roadside business cropped up along the freeway fence. It took three forms: imitation Pueblo Indian kivas, petrified trees, and replicas of vicious dinosaurs. I understood the economic necessity of using these eye catching symbols to persuade travelers to exit the freeway and spend their money. What I couldn't accept was the use of ladders as one of the forms of enticement. They had been stuck into the ground with only their top several rungs visible, leaving the erroneous impression that each ladder led to an underground kiva.

Growing up in New Mexico I knew that a kiva was an underground, circular, ceremonial chamber, a sacred and ritual center for Pueblo Indians where tribal elders prayed for rain, health, crops, and good hunting. They gathered in the kiva to retell their oral history, chant, teach, and make tribal decisions. In this setting, the fake ladders didn't belong and should never have been used to advertise the entrance to a sacred structure that didn't exist.

Twenty-five miles from Holbrook, I passed the freeway exits to the Painted Desert, Petrified Forest National Park and the Painted Desert Indian Center, the latter beckoning tourists with tepees and flying flags. I rode past both off-ramps, anxious to reach my next planned stop, the historic Painted Desert Trading Post, abandoned in the 1950s.

Several miles further on, I exited I-40 at Pinta Road, crossed over the freeway, ignored the Dead End sign, and headed north, swerving to miss the potholes in the rutted dirt road. Within half-a-mile I came to a disintegrating strip of asphalt, an early alignment of Route 66. I turned left and headed west into the wind, bumping along on what was left of the narrow highway, now one car-width wide due to the encroaching vegetation. The quiet was frequently interrupted by flocks of mourning doves that erupted from the grass, chamisa and rabbit brush alongside the road. As they flew away, they made a squeaking

Decaying Painted Desert Trading Post.

sound, a sure sign, I decided, that their wing hinges needed a squirt of WD-40. Following the single lane, I relished the peace of the high desert and the cumulous clouds that were trying, unsuccessfully so far, to gather and deliver precious rain.

The single story Trading Post stood alone, deteriorating like so many rural buildings I'd seen along Route 66. Unlike the Jackrabbit Trading Post, no influential politician had come to lobby on its behalf. Its east side was cracked and sagging. The windows and doors were gone but it still had a roof. Its name on the front no longer included the words "Painted" or "Post." The "ng" in the word Trading was also missing, having fallen off with the white painted plaster that had once held it aloft. Still adorning the exterior were the red words, "cold drinks, rugs, curios, and jewelry." Two Route 66 black and white highway shields had been painted on either side of the front doorway. I was surprised to see no graffiti. When preparing for my trip, one source estimated that no more than one hundred people leave the freeway every year to visit this Trading Post, falling down and all but forgotten.

The old alignment of Route 66 that I'd followed tempted me to continue west but I had read that not far beyond the Trading Post, the bridge over Dead Wash had been removed, making the road impassable. So I turned around and headed back to the freeway, content with my visit to this somewhat hidden vintage of the past.

By noon the wind had shifted to my favor and was blowing hard out of the west. When I reached the tiny town of Sanders, I was tired, it was lunchtime and I wanted to stop and eat in a Valentine Diner, one of roughly 2200 that had been built in Wichita, Kansas between 1938 and 1974. Before leaving on my trip, I had read that the diner in Sanders was the last one on Route 66. These self-contained, eight-stool, 10x25-foot restaurants had been trucked all over the United States on flat-bed trailers, sold to anyone who was interested in opening their own restaurant and had $3,300 to buy one.

Blowing dust and tumbleweeds escorted me to the building named *Diner*. As I got closer I saw its similarity to the abandoned diner in Twin Arrows and also the one for sale in Winslow. This one, however, was trimmed in pink and had a pink Route 66 sign with black numbers painted on the white front wall. The pink seemed garish in this environment of earth tones. I grasped the pink handrail, walked up the two wooden steps, opened the pink door and entered, my arrival announced by a screeching buzzer that lasted for several seconds. The seven pink stools at the counter – the eighth one had been removed to make room on the counter for the cash register – were occupied by Navajo men. Conversations stopped and all eyes were on me. My nods were not returned as I walked to the back where a room had been added, complete with four pink chairs at every table. Unlike yesterday in Winslow, today I had a room to myself. The wooden floor creaked as I walked to a table where I could keep an eye on my bike outside. Waiting for the waitress, I smelled old grease, intermingled with a vague memory of bleach.

With a scarcity of conversation, my waitress took my order. In shorter time than I'd anticipated, I was enjoying a ham and cheese sandwich, a bowl of straight-out-of-the-can Campbell's chicken and rice soup, chips and lots of iced tea. As I ate I could hear the wind whipping the flags outside and the tumbleweeds brushing along the outside wall as they headed to barren land where they scattered their seeds. I looked over my final Arizona route card, and perused the walls, barren except for three full-page newspaper advertisements that had been converted into posters. Each one extolled cars from the 1940s, including the 1949 Ford, "built for the road ahead."

I had finished my meal and was catching up in my journal when my waitress gave me my bill. Before she left to get my change, I asked her, "Is the owner here?"

The way she hesitated to answer led me to believe that she thought I wanted to complain about something. Assured there was nothing wrong, she said, "I'll get her for you." While I waited, I wondered if the Diner was owned by a Navajo. A few minutes later my answer walked up to my table. She had brown hair (every Navajo I'd ever seen had black hair), and was dressed in blue jeans, and wearing an apron. Sara introduced herself and I did likewise. I told her I'd ridden my bicycle all the way from California just to eat lunch in her Valentine Diner, an attempt at levity that didn't provoke her to smile. I had the feeling that, like at the Bagdad Café in the Mojave Desert, people came here from all over the world, even on bikes every now and then. But unlike at the Bagdad, there was no guest register and visitors like me weren't fawned over.

Sara looked like she was busy as the cook, (I guessed,) so I cut the chit-chat and moved on to the reason I wanted to talk to her. "I've seen two Valentine Diners other than yours on Route 66. The one in Twin Arrows is forlorn, closed and disintegrating and the one in Winslow is all spruced up and ready for sale. Do you know of any others?" I asked.

"I think there's one in Holbrook but I'm not sure."

"You've expanded your diner."

"Yeah. We added onto it awhile back. We needed the extra space if we were gonna serve all the people who come here to eat." With only myself and seven others here for lunch, I wondered, even with the addition, if she had enough business to stay in business.

I thanked her for taking the time to talk to me and asked her to sign my journal. She wrote, "Good luck on your journey. Sara Middleton."

Recharged and with the wind still at my back, I streaked the final sixteen miles to New Mexico. Along the way I passed an accident, the first I'd seen. A pickup had overturned, the cargo in the bed now scattered in the middle divider and across the two east-bound lanes. The driver was sitting on the ground, talking with people around him, his truck nearby on its side, totaled. A Highway Patrol officer had stopped traffic so the wreckage could be cleared but he waved me through. Every now and then riding a bicycle had its privilege. Until the traffic started flowing again, I had the east bound freeway lanes all to myself.

Several miles before the New Mexico border, I exited I-40 onto the Route 66 frontage road, following it first on the south side of the freeway and then the north. Nearing the border I looked toward the far side of the freeway and saw a large yellow sign with one red and one green chili pepper and the words, *Welcome to New Mexico, The Land of Enchantment*. Ahead of me, the welcome on the frontage road was less enthusiastic – a small generic green sign with the white letters, *New Mexico State Line*.

As I passed the sign, I sat up straight, thrust my arms into the air like I'd just won a stage in the Tour de France, hollered "alright!" and coasted to a stop. I was in the state of my birth, my mind awash with joyful memories and the anticipation of being with family in two days.

17

Adversity 101: The Mid-term Test

Before leaving the New Mexico border and headed to Gallup, I set my watch ahead one hour to Mountain Daylight Time. I was hungry and welcomed dinner coming one hour earlier. Next came the ritual of affixing the Arizona Route 66 sticker next to the one for California, visual evidence of my progress and for anyone who might be interested. Busy with these little chores, I thought about the many times I'd been at this border over the years, the wing vents of my '62 Falcon wide open, its 4/60 air conditioning cooling my perspiring body.

But today was different from all those previous times. Absent speed, I focused on the graceful contours of the red sandstone bluffs on my left and right. I smelled the earth recently watered by the fractured clouds drifting above, the ravens a reflection of the peacefulness I felt. Images in the past had been fleeting and blurred but today my senses delivered detail. I was alive and felt blessed to be here.

As Robert Persig had penned in his book, *Zen and the Art of Motorcycle Maintenance*:

"In a car you're always in a compartment, and because you're used to it you don't realize that through that car window everything you see is just more TV. You're a passive observer and it is all moving by you boringly in a frame. On a (motor) cycle *(parentheses mine)*, the frame is gone. You're completely in contact with it all. You're in the scene, not just watching it anymore. And the sense of presence is overwhelming."

I agreed with Pirsig, but it was Wendell Berry who went a step farther in his piece, *An Entrance to the Woods*:

"The faster one goes, the more strain there is on the senses, the more they fail to take in, the more confusion they must tolerate or gloss over – and the longer it takes to bring the mind to a stop in the presence of anything."

Borrowing from both authors, I knew it was the absence of speed that was enabling me to make the most of my experience. So far, everywhere I'd gone, even those infrequent places where I'd been before, I felt like I was there for the first time, on my first date with Route 66, not unlike my first date with Donna. In the patience of moving slowly, my senses working overtime, I'd inhaled her sweetness, admired her vibrant glow, and hung onto her every touch, just like I was doing with the Mother Road.

Moving east, Arizona slipped behind. Continuing to accompany me was the roadside advertising that coaxed tourists to stop and buy curios of the southwest. Past the border, I saw a fort, built in 1950 for *The Big Carnival*, a movie starring Kirk Douglas. Clearly visible from the freeway were large yellow letters on the fort wall. They spelled the name of the trading post owner next door – Chief Yellowhorse.

The title of Chief given to Juan Yellowhorse was one of honor (and maybe also part of his marketing strategy) and not based on any elected responsibility he held within the Navajo Nation. He had renamed the old Miller Trading Post after himself and operated it until he died in 1999. Since the Navajo government is led by an elected President, it would have been more realistic and honest if Juan had named his business President Yellowhorse. In the long history of the Navajo Nation, only Barboncito and Narbona were referred to as "Chief" while the equally important leader, Manuelito, wasn't.

Adding to Yellowhorse's advertising diorama were Plains' Indian tepees perched on the high cliff overlooking the trading post. The traditional housing of American Indians along Route 66 in Arizona and New Mexico varies from the six or eight-sided, log and earth hogans of the Navajos to the masonry stone and adobe of the Pueblos. A tepee on either reservation is as common as a three-legged horse. As a generic form of advertising, it leaves Route 66 travelers with the erroneous impression that American Indians in the southwest live in tepees.

Twenty miles from the state line I reached Gallup, elevation 6506 feet. Cycling through town, I passed the El Rancho Motel, built in 1937. Spencer Tracy, Katharine Hepburn, Kirk Douglas, Humphrey Bogart, Jack Benny, and Ronald Reagan stayed here and each of them has a room named after them. A short distance beyond the El Rancho was my destination for the day, the El Capitan, built in 1955.

Before going to my room, I asked the motel clerk if he could recommend a good place for dinner. He suggested two – a Chinese restaurant and a steakhouse. He also mentioned, but didn't recommend, a Spanish restaurant. As it turned out, that's where I went to eat. I just couldn't pass up enjoying New Mexico cuisine, this time enchiladas layered with New Mexico red chile accompanied by Spanish rice, whole pinto beans, and sopaipillas.

While the entire meal was scrumptious, it was the sopaipillas that caused my salivary glands to work overtime. Each sopaipilla started out as a small piece of dough which was deep fried. During this process it puffed up into the shape of a hollow pillow roughly the size of a softball. Two sopaipillas came with my dinner but since they weren't enough to satisfy my craving, I ordered a third. I dressed each bite with either a liberal drizzle of honey or a dab of butter and then hurried to get everything into my mouth before it ran all over my hand, down my chin, or dripped onto my plate. Such gastronomic fun.

I had an extra skip in my step as I returned to my motel room. I was in New Mexico, my home state, my energy restored with a delicious dinner, and I felt great physically. My call home to Donna started with her telling me that it was raining in Davis, somewhat unusual for May but welcomed.

> *Today Dug traveled ninety-seven miles and made it to Gallup, New Mexico. That's two days in a row over ninety miles. Only one more town, Grants, before he gets to Albuquerque. Dug thanks the Masons (old friends living in Illinois) for their contribution to Yolo Habitat. It means a lot to him. Some trivia from Dug: I never see snakes run over on the freeway but I do on secondary roads. I spooked a cottontail today and clocked it at 14½-mph as it hopped down the road in front of me. He asks us all, "Does anyone know how to get hold of Lance Armstrong? If*

they do, tell him it's not too late for him to join me...but he has to carry his own gear." Love, Donna

Absent a wake-up call the next morning, I woke up late. My internal clock had failed to compensate for the fact the sun had come up earlier and I'd lost an hour changing time zones. I hustled to nearby Earl's Restaurant, a Route 66 establishment since 1947. The waitress took my order and five minutes later, on the dot, she brought my eggs, hash browns and toast. On the side was a small dish of complimentary red chili salsa, proof positive that I was in New Mexico.

Unlike my normal 6:30 start time, I didn't begin pedaling until well after 7:00. Route 66 left Gallup as it had entered – a frontage road paralleling the interstate. I was back in a piñon-juniper forest with red sandstone bluffs far to my left. Like in Arizona, the piñons were dying here too. It made no difference to the beetles that they were killing the state tree of New Mexico. I rode by the entrance to Red Rock State Park, the site of the Gallup Intertribal Ceremonial every year, a four-day late summer gathering (pow wow) of American Indians from all over the United States and Canada. In 1940, parts of *The Grapes of Wrath* were filmed in this area.

Sixteen miles east of Gallup the frontage road ended, leaving me with no alternative but to pedal up the I-40 on-ramp into a gentle breeze out of the southeast, not a good sign this early in the morning. I hoped for a change in the direction and intensity of the breeze but instead it picked up. The frequent semis helped some, parting the oncoming air and then pulling me along in their wake for a short distance. This went on for the next eleven miles until I reached The Continental Divide, the highest point on Route 66 in New Mexico at 7263 feet. Less than a mile beyond the Continental Divide, the frontage road reappeared. I exited the freeway, thankful that for the next twenty-four hours I would be on a two-lane alignment of Route 66 that had not been covered by I-40 concrete.

The frontage road skirted the small town of Thoreau, named for Henry David and pronounced "thru" by its residents. Next came Prewitt and it was here that the frontage road took a deliberate turn to the south, forcing me to ride head-on into the wind, which was now blowing harder. I had come just over thirty miles from Gallup and was ready for another break. I stopped, leaned the bike against a highway sign, sat down on the shoulder and snacked. The freeway was just far enough away that the traffic noise was reduced to a soft whooshing. In the midst of this soothing sound, a loud boom startled me. I looked toward the freeway and saw a veil of blue smoke curling upward behind a passing semi. I finally realized that a tire on that semi had blown out, leaving rubber scattered in its wake behind it.

Over the four-hundred miles from Santa Monica, I'd seen abundant evidence of exploded truck tires but until now had never given any thought to what it would be like if a truck tire blew out as it passed me just over an arm's length away. Being smacked by a flying slab of rubber would certainly cause me to lose control and more than likely end my day in a hospital.

Somewhat rested, I resumed riding, trying to accept the wind, now blowing steadily at an estimated 25 mph. I watched the smoke rising from a smokestack to my left, staring at it intently as if in so doing I could bend the wind and the direction of the smoke 180-degrees to my favor, a tailwind. It was a vain hope as the headwind grew stronger. A farmer up ahead was plowing his parched field, creating in the process a towering cloud of dust. I put my head down and plunged into the choking, blinding blast. When I emerged on the other side, my eyelids worked overtime to clear the dust from my eyes while saliva did the same with the grit in my mouth.

The computer on my handlebar bore the discouraging evidence of my minimal forward progress – 4 mph. I tried to improve my aerodynamics by hunching over the handlebars. This position didn't work, since the configuration of the handlebars on my mountain bike made it impossible for me to steer while leaning that far forward over my front wheel. Sitting upright increased the wind resistance as did my four loaded panniers. Short of taking them off and throwing them into a ditch, I would just have to adjust…somehow.

While my breaks became more frequent, so too did my railing at the wind. I wondered why California and Arizona had pleasured me with a tailwind and now, here in my home state where I expected everything to go right, I was being treated so unjustly. The wind had become a personal affront, punishment I didn't deserve. As the tumbleweeds and litter barreled toward me, dodging them became an extracurricular and energy consuming task that caused me to swerve all over the road.

By noon I was only two-thirds of the way to Grants and still had twenty miles to go. At the rate I was going, I would be lucky to arrive there by dark. Sixty miles in one day would be pitiful but more important, I wanted to assure my arrival in Albuquerque tomorrow by cycling beyond Grants today.

But the wind didn't care about all this. Over and over gusts slammed into me, abruptly shoving me out of control, sometimes several feet onto the shoulder and other times into the thankfully empty traffic lane. This was particularly dangerous since the headwind prevented me from hearing the noise of any vehicle coming up from behind. The gusts had become erratic blasts and trying to anticipate them was futile. My forward progress was so pathetic that I decided I could go faster if I walked the bike for one mile and then rode it for one, or until my anger and exhaustion reached the point I couldn't take it anymore. Then I would walk again. During one of my baby-step interludes, the first verse of the song *Mariah* popped into my head:

> *Away out here they have a name, for wind and rain and fire.*
> *The rain is Tess, the fire's Joe, and they call the wind Mariah.*

I shouted the words in each line, too angry to sing them. When I came to the word Mariah, I renamed the wind, using every word I could think of to convey how furious I was. Expressing my frustration helped me to momentarily regain a sense of emotional balance.

As I worked my way along, I tried to get my mind off the wind by thinking of other things. While doing this I remembered the bicyclists I'd seen two days ago, walking their bikes west into the wind. They were unwilling to even wave at me while I pedaled effortlessly in the opposite direction. The wind, created by the arbitrary interplay between high and low pressure areas, had brought them agony and me pleasure. Now twenty-four hours later, I was in their shoes and had a deeper understanding of the narrow difference between a curse and a blessing.

Wind, hills, and narrow roads with heavy traffic were my three biggest biking challenges. Hills bothered me the least since I could usually tell where I would top out and reap the pleasure of the downhill coast on the other side. Narrow roads eventually got wider. What made wind so difficult to deal with was not knowing when it would end. Back home in Davis, I'd seen the wind blow all day, calm down somewhat at night, and at the first sign of the sun, start up all over again, continuing this routine for several days.

Up ahead the small town of Milan came into view. With sheer persistence I willed myself there, knowing that Grants was only a few miles beyond it. Entering Milan I saw the Grants State Bank on my right. My outward intent in stopping was to cash a traveler's check but what I really wanted was an excuse to get out of the wind and into a place where I might find some sympathy. In the bank I got all three. I was the only customer (who in their right mind would be out in that howling wind?). While cashing my check, the tellers all got involved in finding out what I was doing and where I was headed. They were the shot in the arm that I needed. Before wishing me good luck, they filled one of my water bottles and insisted I help myself to their stash of window candies.

Within half-an-hour I reached Grants. In the 1930s it was called "The Carrot Capital of the United States," thanks to its volcanic soil and abundant water for irrigation. In 1950 uranium was discovered nearby and Grants' population swelled from 1,200 to 12,000. The uranium industry prospered, mining this raw material used in nuclear reactors and atomic bombs. In the early 1980s the boom ended when the recession forced the mines to close.

As I rode through town, I welcomed the buildings as they interrupted the wind. At the far end of town I found a pay phone on the windward side of a liquor store and called Donna. She listened sympathetically while I spilled the story of my struggle and how it had taken me nine hours to go sixty flat miles.

When she finished with the pep talk I needed, we hung up and I entered a nearby Pizza Hut. I immediately headed to the bathroom where I washed the accumulation of grit from my face and hands. For dinner I ordered a small pizza and made myself a huge salad smothered with blue cheese dressing. I sat eating, gathering my scattered thoughts like a gambler would his chips. Outside the wind was still blowing. Maybe it was my imagination but it didn't seem as hard. By the time I'd finished eating, my sense of optimism had returned. Instead of checking into a nearby motel, I decided to meander down the highway. I'd go as far as it felt comfortable and if I couldn't find a motel, then I'd gamble on finding a safe place to camp out.

18

Them Ain't Mean

Before leaving the comfort of my restaurant booth in Grants, I looked over my route cards and saw a note I'd written months before, reminding me when I got south of Grants, to look for a Pony Truss Bridge built on Route 66 in 1936. Anticipating this attraction would help take my mind off the wind that was still blowing, but much less aggressively.

About half-an-hour later the narrow bridge, barely wide enough for two cars going in opposite directions to pass, came into view. Immediately I was drawn to its simplicity. On each side alternating steel trusses formed Vs. The high end of each truss was riveted to a steel plate giving the bridge strength. The Pony Truss design was distinctive, not only because of the low arches on each side of the bridge but also because of the absence of any cross bracing over the roadway.

Beyond the bridge I followed the road through a massive lava flow, ancient violence long since cooled. I picked up one of the rocks, black as subterranean darkness, and was surprised at its heaviness despite the many holes that riddled it. I was tempted to climb around in the lava but what sounded like rattlesnake rattles echoing around me, changed my mind. Whether this was my imagination or not, my fear of snakes was provoking me to get out of there and not tempt any rattler, seen or unseen, to uncoil and sink its venom-filled fangs into one of my calves.

What wasn't my imagination was the wind. It had stopped. Without its resistance, twelve miles-per-hour felt like flying as I rode through McCartys and San Fidel, towns in name only. Four miles beyond San Fidel I came to the road leading to the Sky City Casino and Hotel, an Acoma Pueblo enterprise. This was likely my last chance to sleep indoors for tonight but since the sun still hung above the horizon, I decided to continue making up time.

Down the road I stopped and took a picture of the Mount Taylor Motel, built in 1946 and now in ruins. I checked behind the motel to see if I might find a hidden place to sleep but thought better about moving on after seeing all the empty alcohol bottles and shattered glass left behind by previous transients. Further on I came to the Villa de Cubero Trading Post and saw the *No Vacancy* sign shining. My fantasy had once been to rent a room here where Ernest Hemingway had stayed for two weeks when writing *The Old Man and the Sea*. With that dream dashed, I was resigned to picture him writing, surrounded by lots of New Mexico sand and the ocean to go with it at least two days to the west.

I passed Budville and Paraje, two more towns in name only. My difficulty in finding a secluded place to hide for the night was starting to worry me. With the sun slipping behind the mountains in the Cibola National Forest to the west, memories of my fourteen-day solo bicycle ride seven years ago came to mind. On that adventure from Davis to Santa Fe I had camped out every night. One night I tried unsuccessfully to find a spot hidden from the highway where the upper half of my body would be in Nevada and my legs in Utah. Another night I bedded down behind a large boulder in the Hurricane, Utah city park, only to be awakened by loud hissing followed by cold water hitting me in the chest at 2:00 am when the automatic sprinklers came on.

My most memorable search for a place to sleep on that trip occurred on the outskirts of Centerville, Nevada. It was nearing sundown when up ahead I saw a bar and a lawn next to it. I decided to see if someone in the bar would give me permission to sleep on the grass. After a quick call to Donna from the pay phone outside, I entered the bar and walked up to the bartender. If he was surprised with my garb – bike helmet, shorts and t-shirt – he stifled his laughter and said, "Howdy. What'll ya' have?"

"Well, I'm not really interested in a drink but I do have a question. I'm just passing through on my bicycle and was wondering if tonight I could throw my sleeping bag on the grass under that Christmas tree outside."

"Nope, 'fraid not," he said. "The owner won't let nobody sleep the night there." In an effort to be helpful, however, he hollered at a patron, "Hey Sam, you know where this guy could spend the night? He's on a bike and just wants a place to roll out his sleeping bag."

Sam sat hunched over and alone, staring at the beer stains on his table while communing with his drink. He either didn't hear the question or was ignoring it. But it seemed that everyone else had heard as the void created by Sam's non-response was quickly filled by their desire to help me.

The first to emerge out of this pool of bar patrons was Mabel. She wore jeans she had been poured into and with her blouse unbuttoned more than just enough, her cleavage was receiving abundant attention from the males in the room. Immediately I felt she was more on-the-make than serious about wanting to help me.

She took a healthy swallow of her drink and said, "You're on a bike, honey?" I started to answer but she interrupted, "Is it a Harley?" Before I could answer, she waived all intent of having a formal conversation when she asked, "Ya' wanna beer?" Not waiting for my polite refusal, she continued, "Where ya' from?"

Finally getting a chance to answer, I told her, "The Sacramento area." I decided not to be more specific since she probably didn't know where Davis was, at least not in her present condition.

"An' ya' rode a bike all the way here?"

I thought about telling her, "No, I pushed it," which was partially true since I had pushed the bike five miles through snow three feet deep where the lightly traveled Sierra highway hadn't been plowed open yet. But instead I said, "Sure did, all the way, and I'm riding a bicycle, not a Harley."

"Well I'll be damned," she summarized, intent on intoxicating me with her breath as she moved closer.

Outside it was getting darker and I wasn't making any progress in finding a place to spend the night. Observing Mabel's inability to resolve my dilemma, the bartender intervened and told her, "He doesn't need a drink right now Mabel, just a place to sleep tonight."

Seeing this opening created by the bartender, another besotted rescuer moved in. "Hi there friend; how ya' doin'?" He draped his arm over my shoulders and said, "You can...shtay at my place."

"Henry, you don't have room for him in your trailer," said his drinking buddy watching the drama from his stool at the bar. "And besides, your ole lady will kill you if you bring home another stranger without her knowin'."

"The…hell…she…will," Henry directed to no one in particular as everyone burst into laughter.

I was now surrounded by a rotating group of five or six Sunday night inebriates, all exchanging loud and unreliable solutions to my accommodation dilemma.

It was the bartender who again interceded. "Say Tony, could this guy stay at your place?"

Tony tipped his cowboy hat backward, and said, "No reason why not. But I'm not ready to go yet. Maybe in half-an-hour."

By now I was looking for any excuse to get out of the bar and this was it. With his invitation on the table, I suggested to Tony, "How 'bout if I start pedaling to your place now, before it gets completely dark, and I'll meet you there?"

"Sounds right by me," said Tony. Pointing toward the door, he directed me to, "Just go down the road out front. You'll see a barn. Turn left and go to the yellow house at the end. That's my place. Oh yeah," he added. "Ignore the dogs. Them ain't mean."

I waved to everyone and left the bar with no intention of ever seeing any of them again. I pedaled as fast as I could down the road in the darkness, worried that one of my recent acquaintances, Tony included, would drive up from behind, fail to see me since I didn't have a rear light, and in their state of intoxication knock me into oblivion.

As I rode along, looking for somewhere to hide for the night, I saw two huge mounds of earth looming on my right. There was no road to them so I pushed the bike off the highway and using my flashlight, found a hidden spot between them where I spread out my sleeping bag. Surrounded by wildflowers and a brilliant sky overflowing with stars, I fell asleep.

With memories of this and other searches for camping spots accompanying me, I continued to look for a place where I could bed down tucked away from Route 66. In the twilight, I saw a dirt road heading toward some bushes several hundred yards away. My tires left an easy-to-follow trail in the dust but there was no evidence that anyone had been down that path recently. When I got to where I knew I couldn't be seen from the nearby houses or vehicles on the highway, I laid out the ground cover, put the bedroll over that, and skipped unrolling the cushion pad since the ground was soft enough.

Looking at my computer one more time I calculated I'd ridden twenty-five miles past Grants for a total of eighty-seven miles today. Despite the wind, the day had ended successfully and Albuquerque was within reach by tomorrow afternoon.

Before falling asleep I looked to the east and saw 11,301-foot Mount Taylor, the Southern sacred Navajo peak. Riding through Flagstaff, Arizona several days before, I'd passed the San Francisco Peaks, the sacred peaks to the west. The other two sacred peaks were Blanca to the East and Hesperus Mountain, to the North. All four marked the boundary of the traditional homeland of the Navajo Nation, the Dinetah. I was blessed as I fell asleep, surrounded by holy ground.

San Francisco Peaks, northern Arizona.

19

Home for Mother's Day

The crowing of roosters at nearby houses, my bedroll damp from the overnight dew, and the ice crystals crackling under my ground cover all convinced me it was time to get up and get moving. The sun wasn't up yet at 6:15 a.m. but the colors in the high cirrus signaled its impending arrival over the mesa to the east. After being spoiled every night by having to make a simple turn of a thermostat dial to adjust the temperature in my motel room, waking up outdoors was taking some effort to get going.

I was already wearing all my cold weather clothes except for my fingerless riding gloves, head and ear covers and windbreaker. I put them on and packed the bike, hoping when I got to the highway and started pedaling, I would warm up. But it was a vain hope as the wind chill created by my forward movement turned my nose into a dripping faucet and my fingers and toes into twenty painful appendages.

Within half-an-hour relief appeared in the form of a picnic table on the sunny south side of a gas station/mini-mart. Before unpacking my granola I went inside and bought a quart of milk and pint of orange juice. I would have to go without a banana and the donut I craved since the store stocked neither.

The sun felt so good, so warm in fact that I took off my sweatshirt while eating. I wrote in my journal and watched customers enter and depart the store. One man, wearing a cowboy hat, turquoise watchband and necklace, and driving a mud-spattered Ford pickup missing the left headlight, came out and instead of returning to his truck, detoured to say hello. He had seen my bicycle and it had piqued his curiosity. With the, where did you start? and where are you going? questions and answers out of the way, he pointed toward the hills a short distance behind him and explained, "I live over there in Laguna Pueblo. Every Easter I ride my bicycle to Jemez Pueblo and back. I don't take any food, just water. It's my annual pilgrimage."

"That's about one hundred miles from here, isn't it?"

"Yeah. It takes me two days to make the round trip."

I wanted to ask him about his bike, if he carried any tire patching equipment, extra clothes and first aid but he needed to get to work. As we shook hands goodbye, I had the feeling that if we had met here last evening he would have offered me a place to sleep. After he left I made one last trip into the store, this time to use the restroom and then buy a ham and cheese sandwich for lunch.

Moving again on my favorite highway, I meandered downhill into a red rock canyon on the Laguna Indian Reservation and around a curve named Dead Man. It wasn't hard to imagine the accidents that must have occurred at this abrupt right turn when this was Route 66. I passed over a Route 66 black and white shield painted on the roadway and a few miles later the road ended. For the first time in twenty-four hours I was back on I-40.

Seventeen miles from Albuquerque, bicycles were no longer allowed on the freeway so I took the off-ramp that led me to a Through Truss Bridge. Route 66 traffic once used it to cross the Rio Puerco (Pig River). Built in 1933 by the Kansas City Structural Steel Company, the bridge was closed permanently to motor vehicles in 1999, restored, and then reopened for exclusive use by pedestrians and bicyclists. Much bigger than the Pony Truss Bridge I'd ridden over yesterday, the sides on this bridge were four stories high and had steel bracing over the roadway. Before riding across its 250-foot length, I checked the load limit – fifteen tons. It would support me and the load on my bike, which sometimes felt like it weighed that much when I climbed a hill.

The traffic on adjacent I-40 kept me company as I alternated between riding and walking out of the Rio Puerco Valley on the long, uphill frontage road. When I topped out I was on Nine-Mile Mesa overlooking the Rio Grande Valley and Albuquerque. The view ahead was dominated by 10,678-foot Sandia (watermelon) Mountain. Nearly 5,000 feet higher than Albuquerque, its humpbacked bulk rose majestically into the azure sky.

It Only Hurts When I Sit Down

Everything seemed unreal, like it had a week ago at the Colorado River. Was I really here? I wanted to linger, to revel in this time and place so I decided to stop and eat the sandwich I had bought earlier. I pushed the bike thirty feet off the frontage road, propped it against the barbed wire fence that kept nearby livestock from wandering onto the roadway, and sat down with my back against a fence post. I watched sparrows flit from awn to awn, seeming frantic in their search for seeds. Cumulus clouds appeared out of nowhere overhead but when I looked for them five minutes later, they were gone. With my arrival in Albuquerque would come the end of the first third of my journey and the welcome from my brother, Kim, and his wife, Sheila. The more I thought about the scene awaiting me the more joyful I felt.

I finished eating, writing and dreaming, retraced my path through the roadside vegetation to the asphalt, and resumed riding. Within a mile a high pitched hissing startled me. Like back in the lava field outside Grants, my immediate thought was that a rattlesnake was shaking its rattles, an insistent warning before striking. I looked toward the shoulder and instead of seeing a rattlesnake, I saw a cold, wet erratic stream of green goo spurting out of a small hole in my front tire before

The Rio Puerco Bridge near Albuquerque.

hitting my right calf. In seconds the inner tube deflated, the air taking with it the green slime intended to plug small punctures. This was my second flat but unlike the first one in Rancho Cucamonga, California, there was no bicycle shop nearby to help me this time. That fact and the time it would take me to patch the tube threw an immediate damper over the euphoria I had felt only seconds before.

I started my repair by taking off the two front panniers and then unstrapped everything – bedroll, ground cover, tent, cushion pad and dirty clothes bag – from the back rack. I removed the computer and trip cards from the handlebars and placed them with my helmet and prescription dark glasses on the ground several yards away. Only the two rear panniers remained attached to the bike when I turned it over.

After I took the tire off, I used the two plastic levers in my patch kit to pry one side of the tire over the rim, making it possible to pull the deflated inner tube from inside the tire. With the tube out, I used my pump to inflate it until I saw what was left of the green slime oozing from a miniscule hole.

From my repair kit I removed a small patch and a capsule of vulcanizing fluid. I squeezed the capsule but nothing came out. To my surprise it was completely empty. I was disgusted, knowing I had failed to check this out before I left on my trip. There was no way for the patch to seal the hole without the fluid. So I went to Plan B and replaced the tube with the new one I carried.

I wasn't sure what had punctured my tube but I guessed it was a goathead, a seed from a prolific weed called Puncturevine. It originated in the Mediterranean and is now found worldwide. Each seed is roughly one-quarter of an inch long and has several hard, stout spines long enough to penetrate a bicycle tire and have just enough length left to pierce a tube. Other names given to this multi-spined pest are Texas sandbur, bullhead and tackweed.

If a goathead was the culprit, it had probably stabbed my tire when I wheeled my bike through the weeds at lunchtime. I should have left the bike just off the highway or upright against a highway sign, but with my arrival at my brother's home only an hour away, I had gotten careless in my hunger and excitement. Taking my bike off the roadway where this ubiquitous weed multiplied with abandon was something I should never have done.

Before installing the new tube, I checked the tire, feeling inside and out, for goathead spines that might have broken off and were still available for future puncturing. I didn't find any but I did see a quarter-inch long slit in the tire tread that might have been caused by a piece of glass. There was so much broken glass on the roadway that it was impossible to avoid running over some of it. I didn't carry a spare tire so I just ignored the slit and then forgot all about it.

With the tire reassembled and back on the bike, I inflated it, and then turned the bike over. I needed something to keep the bike stationary while I reloaded all my gear. Since there was nothing to lean the bike against, I settled for the only choice I had, my waist.

I succeeded in keeping the bike from moving more than a few inches as I used the wide belt I carried to strap my camping gear to the rear rack. Moving on to the front panniers, I knew they would be more difficult because I'd have to steady the bike while leaning over it. I was almost finished hooking the first pannier when the front wheel pivoted to the right and the bike started rolling away from me. As if guided by some demonic force, before I could stop it the bike rolled straight toward and then over my dark glasses. Of course, the tire missed the helmet, route cards, and computer, all of which could have withstood an impact with the bike tire. I picked up the glasses and saw that the frame was broken. One lens had popped out and was lying on the ground, streaked with scratches. After all the miles I'd traveled relatively problem free, because of my carelessness, everything was suddenly going wrong.

An hour later, around two p.m., I arrived at Kim and Sheila's. A sense of relief overcame me. After ten days and 865 miles, I was ready for a day of rest, to regroup, wash clothes, enjoy home-cooked meals, and spend Mother's Day in Santa Fe.

Sheila fixed me a tall glass of iced tea and the three of us talked. The specifics of our conversation are lost but I remember how comfortable I was, how wonderful it felt to be with family. Sheila provoked me to smile when she said, "You sure don't look like you've been riding a bike for ten days." For whatever reason, I did feel great, aside from craving a nap and taking care of my bike and dark glasses problems. Kim took me to a nearby bike shop where I bought a new slime-filled inner tube and, to patch future flats that I had no intention of having,

Together on Mother's Day, Santa Fe. Left to right: Shane (nephew), and his son, Rise, Mom, Dad, Kim Alderwick (niece), Kim (brother), Lynn (sister).

a full tube of vulcanizing fluid. I should have replaced the front tire but I'd forgotten about the slit and wouldn't remember it until two days later when I was well beyond Albuquerque.

In the evening after Sheila's delicious fish dinner, I washed a load of dirty clothes and while we talked, Kim spent over an hour patiently polishing the lens until all the scratches were gone. With that finished, he used epoxy to repair the cracked frame. In the midst of this activity, Ryan called. He and his wife, Julie, wanted to say hi and make sure that the letter and four Clif bars he had sent to Kim's house had arrived. They had and after we hung up I read his note. "I'm thinking of you all the time, Dad. Keep yourself safe, enjoy the journey and I'll see you soon," his last comment in reference to my eventual arrival on Route 66 in Springfield, Illinois where they lived.

And then Donna called. Among several things, she wanted me to know that Stu Bresnick, the director of Yolo Habitat for Humanity, had told her, "Over $1,000 has been donated so far in honor of Dug's ride." My spontaneous tears of joy flowed unimpeded.

> *Dug made it to Albuquerque this afternoon. His many experiences of vulnerability on this trip have put him back in touch with how important it is to have a loving family to come home to. Tomorrow is a day off. He and his brother will drive up to Santa Fe to celebrate Mother's Day with their mom, dad and sister, Lynn. He'll leave Albuquerque to continue his sojourn across New Mexico on Monday. Love, Donna.*

I had one special thing I wanted Kim to do before I went to bed. Since he wouldn't be with me when I exited New Mexico in a few days, I wanted him to put the New Mexico Route 66 sticker on the crossbar of my bike. He obliged and I now had five stickers to go.

Sunday, May 8th, was Mother's Day. My day of rest started with two cats waking me as they played hide-and-seek and then attack-the-toes I was moving under the covers. I felt welcomed.

Kim and I enjoyed coffee along with his homemade breakfast cereal and around mid-morning we drove north on I-25 to La Ciudad de Santa Fe, The City of the Holy Faith. My visit was supposed to be a surprise on Mother's Day but I had forgotten about the letter I'd written to Mom before starting my trip, telling her about my possible visit. I had ruined my own surprise.

The welcome from my parents, both now in their 90s, was nonetheless joyous. It was good to be home, in the house where I grew up, if only for a few hours. My sister joined us and after another round of hugs we all went out to eat lunch at the Blue Corn Café. I had looked forward to this, another chance to enjoy New Mexican cuisine.

There is a tendency to think that the food of the southwest is all the same. But New Mexican cuisine is distinct from what is called Tex-Mex or Mexican. In New Mexico there is a unique blending of the foods contributed by the Spanish (who colonized New Mexico in the 17th century), American Indian, European, and Mexican cultures. It is our nation's oldest culinary heritage, with its roots coming from the ancient ones, the ancestors of today's Pueblo Indians.

At the Café, for our appetizer we used warm corn chips to scoop hearty helpings of guacamole. I followed that with my meal of enchiladas, generously draped with mild red chile sauce and accompanied with whole pinto beans, rice and three honey-laden sopaipillas. As I looked around at all of us enjoying our food and each other, I was thankful I had a family to be with on this Mother's Day. Only my brother, Chris, who lived in Owasso, Oklahoma, was absent.

After lunch we returned home and sat visiting in gastronomic contentment. Lynn informed me she was making a donation of $19.39 to Habitat for Humanity, the amount in reference to the year I was born. Clever. My nephew, his wife and their six-year-old son joined us, and the afternoon went fast. Dad made popcorn and Lynn cut us each a piece of her chocolate cake. Before Kim and I left I asked my family to write in my journal. My nephew wrote, "Not only do you gather great stories to tell but your trip becomes a great story for us to tell." Mom and Dad wished me a good trip and to be careful. I was moved by my sister's words, "To my dearest older brother. I'm totally amazed at what you are doing and very proud of you."

It was hard to leave my family but I still had things to do to get the bike and myself ready to rejoin my adventure tomorrow. Back in Albuquerque, I lubricated my chain and repacked my panniers. I lightened my load by leaving behind my 3½ pound tent and several shirts I wouldn't need. To my load I added Ryan's Clif bars and the traveler's checks I had mailed ahead. After a good night's rest, I would be ready to cycle on.

I fell asleep wondering what the road ahead would bring. I had never been on Route 66 east of Albuquerque. Everything would be new from here to Chicago. Gone would be the familiar terrain, towns, and services I knew from a lifetime of travelling on this highway between Santa Monica, California and Albuquerque. I was leaving the West where I was comfortable. From here on I would have to embrace, not only new experiences but also the uncertainty and apprehension of not knowing what to anticipate as the miles rushed up to greet me.

20

Bring on the New

Two days of nourishing meals, nights of noiseless sleep and the joy of being with family left me invigorated, ready to rejoin my adventure. At breakfast I thanked Kim for repairing my glasses, playing taxi driver, and recharging my sense of optimism. After one last check to make sure I'd packed everything, we hugged and I was on my way. Feeling strong and excited, my confidence left no room for thoughts of failure or danger ahead.

Route 66 originally went northeast from Albuquerque, climbing 2,000 feet to Santa Fe. From there it turned southeast until, when nearing Las Vegas (the cottonwoods), it bent deliberately south. In 1937, all this changing of direction was eliminated in the process of straightening the road between Albuquerque and Santa Rosa, my destination for today. Since I was following the 1939 alignment, the one in use the year I was born, my path to Santa Rosa from Albuquerque would be a day shorter and instead of a 2,000-foot climb, an overall drop of 700 feet. What an invigorating way to hit the road.

The Mother Road in Albuquerque doubled as Central Avenue. I was accompanied at varying times by impatient drivers hurrying to work, a street sweeper gathering debris, delivery vans blocking the right hand lane, and public transit buses doing likewise. The commotion and congestion reminded me of Santa Monica Boulevard. I cycled past the Armed Forces Induction Center where forty-four years ago I stood at attention with forty-six other naïve inductees, raised my right hand, repeated the pledge, and began my three-year enlistment in the Army as a trained killer. Today I gave a perfunctory salute at the building in memory of that life changing moment and pedaled on.

Central Avenue climbed steadily east out of the Rio Grande Valley and fifteen minutes from downtown I stopped at the front entrance to Presbyterian Hospital. It was here, sixty-six years ago, that my life began. My parents had driven all night from the tiny town of Reserve to Albuquerque, much of it on dirt roads, ending their seven hour, one-flat-tire, 200-mile trip with three hours to spare. Maybe my birth wasn't any more remarkable than most but I felt an overwhelming need to share it. So I interrupted the only person available, the custodian who was washing the glass entrance doors to the hospital, and told him, "I was born here 66 years ago." Caught by surprise and not quite sure how to respond, he lowered his squeegee, summoned a huge smile, and while extending a vigorous handshake said, "Well, congratulations."

Beyond the hospital I passed the University of New Mexico, my home during my freshman year in college. Opposite the University was the twenty-four hour Frontier Restaurant, opened in 1971, and until his death in 2008, the favorite haunt of author Tony Hillerman. His affection for the Frontier hickory-flame burger had started when he was a student at UNM and continued during the years he was a journalism professor.

On the eastern outskirt of Albuquerque, Route 66 paralleled I-40 and entered Tijeras (scissors) Canyon at the southern shoulder of Sandia Mountain. Cyclists commuting to Albuquerque waved, leaving me with the comfortable feeling of being among friends. One of them, seeing me studying my route card, stopped to assure me I was on the right road.

Much of the southwest, including the territory around Albuquerque, was explored by Vasquez de Coronado from 1540 to 1542. Forty-six years later, Don Juan de Oñate, New Mexico's first Governor, claimed the territory of New Mexico in the name of King Philip II of Spain. On April 20, 1769, Antonio Sedillo, a lawyer and also an officer in the Spanish Army, was given a land grant by the King of Spain. It encompassed 86,249,600 acres and included all of present day Albuquerque.

I meandered up Tijeras Canyon and found the Sedillo sign that marked the turnoff to the town site where Antonio had built his hacienda. I had promised my next-door neighbor in Davis, Daniel

Sedillo, a direct descendant of Antonio, that I would take a picture of this sign. Had the United States government not appropriated Antonio's land grant, Daniel might be living here instead of in California.

Nearing the east end of the Canyon, I had a choice of routes. I decided to avoid busy I-40 and instead climb Sedillo Hill. The road was peaceful and as I neared the top, the views west to the nearby summit of Sandia Peak and sixty miles north to the snow-covered Sangre de Cristo (Blood of Christ) Mountains behind Santa Fe were spectacular. Jutting upward were Lake Peak, 12,000 foot Santa Fe Baldy and the Truchas (trout) Peaks, North Truchas at 13,275 feet the highest peak in New Mexico.

Beyond Tijeras Canyon the plains of New Mexico sprawled before me. I stopped to take a picture, foolish enough to believe that this was where the hills ended, the flat grassland began and the rest of the way to Chicago would be either level or downhill. I picked up speed, a light tailwind pushing me along as Route 66 paralleled I-40 once again. Despite everything seeming to go my way, I was in fact ignoring two problems. Several links in my chain were binding again, causing them to jump over the teeth in the pedal sprocket like they had back in California on my second day. And if that wasn't bad enough, I thought I saw a chard of glass imbedded in my front tire.

I finally decided I was flirting with a spill by not stopping to rectify both problems. I took off the front panniers and everything on the rear rack. When I had the bike turned over, I probed the slit with my small screwdriver and could tell the shine was due to color in the tire tread and not a sliver of glass. It was the same shiny slit I'd seen before I got to Albuquerque, only the cut had gotten another eighth of an inch longer just from the pressure exerted by the air in the tube. I berated myself for not replacing the tire in Albuquerque but the fact was, I had forgotten all about it. In the bicycle shop my intention had been to buy patching fluid, a spare tube, and then be on my way. If the air pressure in the tube forced the front tire to split open now, I had no spare tire. Not good. My next chance of finding a bicycle shop where I could replace the tire would be in Amarillo, Texas, three days east. Or, I could turn around and go back to Albuquerque. I decided to stop playing the woulda-coulda-shoulda game and act on an idea I had to at least temporarily repair the tire.

In my tool kit I had several 2"x3" patches. I removed the tube and placed a patch inside the tire with the adhesive side toward the tread and over the slit. When I inflated the tube I hoped the patch would diminish the pressure of the tube on the slit, preventing it from lengthening any further.

Next I went to work on the chain. I had no tool to replace links so I used my small screwdriver this time to force the binding links a fraction apart, hopeful I wouldn't break a link in the process. Turning the pedals while lubricating the links, they now rolled smoothly over the teeth on the sprocket. Only time would tell if I had solved both problems.

Ten miles later, everything was going fine mechanically so I decided to give myself a pat on the back and stop for lunch in the small town of Moriarty, its self-anointed title The Pinto Bean Capital of the World. I was several bites into my turkey-breast and ham sub when a man came up to my table, said hi, introduced himself as Gary Sullivan and readily accepted my invitation to join me. Gary's questions were the same as others and after we worked our way through them, it was my turn to get to know him. He told me he was from Nambe, about fifty miles north of Moriarty, and had come here to soar. The wind that was pushing me along had given him an incredible morning in his glider. Before we parted, he signed my journal: "Great to see you try something that the rest of us think about but never try." I didn't tell Gary but, with my fear of flying, I could have written the same thing in his journal, if he had had one.

East of Moriarty, Route 66 and I-40 were one. From here to Santa Rosa, roughly seventy-six miles, I would have no choice but to ride on the freeway shoulder. Twenty miles down the road I broke the monotony and took a short detour into Clines Corners, founded by Roy Cline in 1934. Highway 285, a major north-south highway, crossed Route 66 here and Roy had decided way back then that this would be a fine place to build a gas station and raise his family. It was his son, Roy Jr., who named the town.

Back on I-40, I stopped to take a picture of a colorful abutment supporting an overpass that crossed the freeway. The concrete had been engraved with two fifteen-foot-long Roadrunners, the New Mexico state bird; a Yucca plant, the state flower painted green; and the Zia Sun symbol.

It Only Hurts When I Sit Down

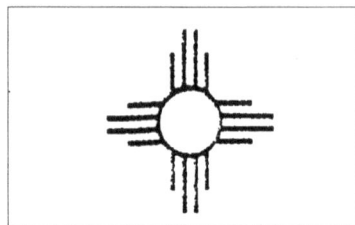

Roughly thirty miles north of Albuquerque is the Zia Pueblo and the Zia symbol belongs to them. The red circle on a yellow background represents the sun and is found on the New Mexico state flag. Projecting from the circle are sixteen short red lines. The Zia nation believes that the giver of all good gave them gifts in groups of four. These gifts include the seasons, directions, parts of the day and phases of life.

Around five o'clock I stopped for dinner at my only choice, a Dairy Queen at an impossible-to-miss off-ramp in the middle of the eastern New Mexico plain. The day had gone fast and I was still twenty-five miles from my hoped for destination of Santa Rosa. If I averaged a reasonable twelve miles-per-hour, it would take me two hours to get there. But at that speed, I would have to bike on the freeway after dark, something I knew was dangerous to do. With a full stomach and rested, I decided to push it and if I didn't make it, I'd just sleep outdoors.

Pronghorn antelope and prairie dogs ignored me as I rode down the freeway, the gentle up and down of the hills not slowing me. The tailwind continued and I flew along, motivated by the setting sun behind me. I took the first I-40 exit into Santa Rosa, crossed the Pecos River, and as darkness settled around me, checked into a motel. After showering, I logged my day's progress into my journal, as I did every day. The numbers on my computer bore evidence of how terrific this day had been, in spite of my tire and chain problems:

Total miles – 122
Average speed – 13.3mph
Maximum speed – 37mph

These three measures would be the highest on any day during my trip, made possible in large part by my rest in Albuquerque that had rejuvenated my strength.

Before falling asleep I made two phone calls, the first to Rudy Sandoval. His sister, Mamye, had been a co-worker in the Sacramento City School District, and I had promised her I would contact her brother when I got to Santa Rosa. She had told him I was coming and that I would welcome a tour of his town. Rudy's answering machine took my call and I told him I would try to reach him early tomorrow morning. The second call was to Donna.

> *Dug called late. His weather has been beautiful all day. He wants to send the following message to Margie Shunk, a friend he claims has a genetic defect that causes her to prefer chocolate ice cream over vanilla: "My non-biased survey has shown that nine out of ten people on Route 66 prefer vanilla milkshakes to chocolate. The margin of error for my survey is +/- .24536904." KOVR TV, the CBS affiliate in Sacramento, contacted me and wants to do a story on Dug and his ride. Not sure how we'll arrange that. Thanks everyone for your support. Love, Donna.*

The following morning I ate breakfast and then called Rudy around seven. He answered after two rings and we arranged to meet for coffee at the restaurant across from my motel.

Neither Rudy or I had described what we looked like but I had a feeling he was the driver of the blue 1956 Ford pickup that pulled up in front of the restaurant less than ten minutes later. I stood by my table and watched this man, dressed in a gray blazer, red polo shirt and blue jeans, his upper lip sporting a neatly trimmed moustache, walk in, grip my hand, and say, "Hi Doug, I'm Rudy." With this introduction, I knew that our visit was going to be special. He ordered coffee with his breakfast, and we launched into getting to know each other. He had lived most of his life in Santa Rosa and in addition to being on the City Council, is the owner and projectionist of the only movie theater in town. Our conversation progressed with constant interruptions. Everyone who walked by our table stopped to say hi to Rudy. This was followed by him introducing me like I was a long lost brother. In this small town of less than 2,700 people, everyone was family.

Rudy said he wanted to show me around Santa Rosa, The City of Natural Lakes. Our first stop was at The Blue Hole, an eighty-one foot deep artesian pool. Scuba divers from New Mexico and Texas come to this city treasure to train and be certified. I looked into its depths, the deep blue encouraging me to come for a swim. A small school of large fish did likewise as they meandered past me near the surface in this serene setting.

The Blue Hole, a diver's mecca.

Rudy showed me other lakes, Perch, Hidden, Twin and Park to name a few. While driving between two of them he stopped, pointed ahead and said, "See that opening there in the piñons?" I turned my head to look, and he continued. "That's where the original alignment of Route 66 went."

If Rudy hadn't pointed out this obscure dirt path I would never have guessed this was scant evidence of the old road disappearing into the countryside. He then pointed out some words fading from the side of a nearby boulder. It looked like graffiti. "The paint on that rock is an old advertisement for a business in Santa Rosa," he said. It was the first and last time I would see a Route 66 boulder billboard.

The final stop on our tour was at the Santa Rosa Visitor's Center. Rudy introduced me to the director, Richard, who was the President of the New Mexico Route 66 Association. We talked for awhile and as Rudy and I were leaving, a bicyclist rode up. I overheard him tell

Richard he was heading east and needed some directions.

With my tour over, Rudy brought me back to the motel. I introduced him to my two-wheeled, still unnamed friend and asked him to sign my journal. He wrote, "Have a safe trip on old and new '66'." It was nearly ten o'clock when we said goodbye.

When Rudy and I met at the cafe, he had mentioned that after showing me around, he had to attend a Homeland Security meeting that started at 8:00 a.m. I had stifled the temptation to suggest to him that the threat of terrorist activity in Santa Rosa was just as preposterous as me sprouting wings and flying to Chicago. As he headed to his meeting, I hoped al-Qaida wouldn't take advantage of his being two hours late.

Despite my later than usual start, my plan for today was to ride eighty-five miles to the town of San Jon (Hoe-n). If I ran out of daylight, ambition or energy, I could stop in Tucumcari, sixty miles away, where, unlike in San Jon, I was guaranteed to find an abundance of motels and restaurants.

I rode out of Santa Rosa on Will Rogers Boulevard looking for a county maintained dirt road that was an old alignment of Route 66. Rudy had assured me it would be easy to find…but it wasn't. Since I was running late, I didn't feel like I had time to wander around looking for it. So I settled for following the I-40 frontage road.

Around noon I stopped at a gas station/deli in what was left of Newkirk and bought a sandwich and a cold bottle of V-8 juice. Sitting on a highway guard rail eating his lunch near the front door was the bicyclist I'd seen back in Santa Rosa. I was eager for conversation and curious about his story so I joined him. As it turned out, he was the only bicyclist I would see heading east from Santa Monica to Chicago.

John introduced himself, his distinctive accent immediately identifying him as being from England. He was a head taller than me and had thick bushy hair. I was intrigued by the obvious differences between us. He had no helmet, side-view mirror, or front panniers, wore a short sleeved shirt, and had the tops of his socks pulled up over the bottom of his long pants.

As we talked I found out that he was four years younger than I and his three children were in their 30s, about the ages of my son and daughter. He had flown to San Francisco and ridden down the

San Joaquin (he pronounced it Joe-a-queen) Valley where he had been stopped twice by Highway Patrol officers. He couldn't tell me the exact route he had followed to here but he gave me the impression that from San Francisco he had gotten on his bike and just followed freeways whether it was legal for him to be on them or not.

John mentioned he had met some people from Oklahoma City several days before and had accepted their invitation to spend time with them before he flew back to England. All he had to do was safely negotiate his remaining four hundred miles.

I told him how impressed I was that he had come from a foreign country, successfully ridden out of the congested Bay Area, down to and through the punishment of the Mojave Desert, across Arizona and now almost all of New Mexico. His constant smile gave evidence to the fun he was having.

While we talked I thought about suggesting we ride together. I eventually decided not to bring the subject up. I knew that John was riding faster than me, mainly because his load was lighter. This didn't have to be a problem since we could arrange to meet ahead. What convinced me not to ride with him was knowing he wasn't following Route 66 and liked to stay on the freeway whether legal or not. Being from England, he might be able to get away with this but I doubted a police officer would overlook me riding on the freeway knowing I knew the rules here in my own country. Before John and I parted, he signed my journal: "Thanks for a most pleasant lunch time conversation sitting on the metal barrier. John Dobson, Manchester, England."

Even now I wonder if I made the right decision. Had I been in England I would have welcomed his advice and companionship. I continued on down the frontage road and saw John pass me on the freeway later on. Before I reached Tucumcari, I saw him resting on the freeway while I passed by on the frontage road. We waved and after that I never saw him again.

Tucumcari is twice the size of Santa Rosa. It was once named Liberty and then Six-shooter Siding. The name Tucumcari is a Comanche word that means "to lie in wait," a name also given to a mountain south of town. People traveling east or west on I-40 know that Tucumcari "lies in wait" hundreds of miles before they get there, thanks to the many impossible-to-ignore billboards that read, "Tucumcari Tonight – 2000 rooms."

I entered town just after four p.m. and stopped at a monument built in 1997. Honoring Route 66 and the golden age of the automobile was a ten-foot long chrome tail fin and three round, protruding, red tail lights, mounted one above the other. On top of the fin was the celebrated number, sixty-six.

I was exhausted after only sixty miles so I stopped at a restaurant and had a roast beef sandwich. Like so many times before, filling my stomach and resting for awhile restored my energy and buoyed my attitude, leaving me with what I hoped would be my last decision for today: where to spend the night.

In planning my trip I had considered staying at the Blue Swallow Motel in Tucumcari.

The *Smithsonian Magazine* once declared, "The Blue Swallow may be the last, best and friendliest of the old time motels." Built in 1948, it is listed on the National Register of Historic Places. Unfortunately, while searching earlier for a restaurant, I had ridden by The Blue Swallow and noticed that the "No Vacancy" sign was already lighted. I would have to be content seeing the blue swallows in motionless mid-dive over the carports.

Before leaving the restaurant I decided to cycle twenty-five more miles and spend the night in San Jon. What I needed was some assurance that the only motel was still there. After an abundance of spirited conversation, the restaurant patrons and staff all finally agreed: Yes, there is a small motel in San Jon. If they were wrong, I was resigned to camping out… someplace.

I followed Route 66 and at 7:15 arrived at the San Jon Motel. I checked into one of the three rooms still vacant and within ten minutes, the last two were taken. Soon thereafter the wind began to blow from the east. I used a bathroom towel to plug the gap under the door but that, together with the draft tossing the curtains around, only added more dust to provoke my sneezing.

There was no in-room phone but the pay phone outside the office worked. Donna answered my call and we were together again across the miles. She told me that a friend of ours, Peter Carey, had e-mailed the following, "A Cautionary Tale for Bike Riders."

A man decided that he was going to ride his 10-speed bike from Phoenix to Flagstaff. He got as far as Black Canyon City before the mountains just became too much and he could go no farther.

He stuck his thumb out, but after three hours hadn't gotten a single person to stop. Finally, a guy in a Corvette pulled over and offered him a ride. Of course the bike wouldn't fit in his car. The owner of the Corvette found a piece of rope lying by the highway and tied it to his bumper. He tied the other end to the bike and told the man that if he was going too fast, to honk the horn on his bike and he would slow down.

Everything went fine for the first thirty miles. Suddenly, another Corvette blew past them. Not to be outdone, the Corvette pulling the bike took off after the other. A short distance down the road, the Corvettes, both going well over 120 mph roared through a speed trap.

The police officer noted their speeds with his radar gun and radioed the officer ahead that he had two Corvettes headed his way at over 120 mph. Then he added, "…and you're not going to believe this, but there's a guy on a 10-speed bike honking to pass."

Dug is now about seventeen miles from Texas and has gone over 1,000 miles! He saw lots of rabbits today which provoked him to ask me," What do you get when you cross a rabbit with a lollipop? A sucker born every minute." Looks like he hasn't lost his sense of humor. As he rode along today he noticed that swallows were building their nests on the west side of overpasses. Dug wants to know if any of us knows why. Love, Donna.

After our laughter-filled conversation, I went to the motel office and asked the owner about the head wind blowing from Texas. He assured me, "That wind'll die down by mownin." I could only hope. If it didn't I might have to start looking for a Corvette and a piece of rope.

Too lazy to use my ear plugs, I heard the high pitched singing of the wind as it raced all night through the power lines and rattled the air conditioner outside. Not to be outdone, the branches of the bushes kept pace, slapping against the motel wall and window. I slept fitfully, consumed by the dread of having to buck another Grants-type headwind tomorrow. When I stepped outside my motel room at first light, the wind was still howling but had shifted from the east to the southwest. Heading to Texas I would have an oblique tailwind and for the time being, still no storm clouds.

The twenty-four hour Phillips 66 truck stop was only two blocks away. Breakfast was the usual – two buttered slices of wheat toast, two eggs over hard, hash browns, watered-down-pulp-free orange juice, everything served on Styrofoam. I ate using plastic utensils while listening to unintelligible country western lyrics coming from the speakers on the walls. Even the truckers scattered around the room were speaking what sounded like a different language. It had a melodious twang complete with elongated vowels, especially the letter "a," as in, "Aah kaain't come tonaaht," or "yaaa'll taaayk keh naa." My education in southernese was off to a rugged start.

21

The Geo-Mathematical Center and Beyond

An abiding sense of contentment accompanied me as I pedaled away from the San Jon truck stop. My reservoir of calories was replenished and the bike was doing its part, the chain issuing quiet as it engaged the cogs. The oft troublesome front tire showed no sign of depletion and as I neared Route 66 just ahead, the traffic was minimal.

But as much as I wanted everything to be light and fluffy, the obvious decay of San Jon jerked me back to reality. When I-40 had been built and this little town bypassed, the population, as if on command, had begun its inexorable plummet. In the year 2000, 306 people called San Jon home and twelve years later it was down to 210. Supporting this numerical evidence were abandoned homes and businesses. People were well into giving up and moving on, opting for a fresh start. It was "Grapes of Wrath" all over again.

Growing up in Santa Fe I often felt a similar pull of the highways leading out of town to Taos, Albuquerque, and Las Vegas. This desire wasn't provoked by poverty but rather by my juvenile wanderlust. One morning I acted on that magnetism, got on my one-speed Sears J. C. Higgins and rode south toward Albuquerque, my first bike trip beyond the Santa Fe city limit. Fifteen miles from Santa Fe, I turned around at the Turquoise Post, an attraction long since paved over by I-25. I ate my sandwich, watched the clouds scurry in the firmament above and then headed back home, not because I was bored or my taste of the road was satiated, but because Mom had told me to be back home by mid-afternoon. She had given me enough time to scratch the lure of elsewhere on that dangerous, undulating, two lane road. And now here I was, fifty years later, my Route 66 adventure in full blossom.

The frontage road leaving San Jon paralleled I-40 until they joined four miles from the Texas state line. My 388 miles on The Mother Road in New Mexico, the most in any state, were coming to an end. I would miss the beauty of The Land of Enchantment but also its roads with the smooth, wide shoulders. A standard for safety and the overall accommodation of bicycles had been set, a standard I hoped would continue.

The first sign that greeted me after I crossed the border into the Lone Star State carried the uninspiring but accurate words, Texas State Line. A short distance further, a much larger sign spoke more directly to me. Along its top edge I read, "Welcome to Texas." The state flag occupied the middle section and along the bottom edge was the admonition to, "Drive Friendly – The Texas Way."

I stopped near the larger sign to snack and reset my watch ahead one hour to the Central Daylight Time Zone. Losing that one hour meant reducing, by at least twelve, the number of miles I'd cycle today. I had entered my fourth state, started my third week on the road, and by noon I hoped to be halfway between Santa Monica and Chicago, joyous milestones all crowded into the same day.

Entering a new state was like starting a new year, but with no fireworks. America's Main Street would cut due east across the upper panhandle of Texas and in 185 miles I'd be knocking on the door to Oklahoma.

For the first twenty-three miles in Texas, every driver "drove friendly." And then, up ahead on a long, straight stretch, I saw a car pulled over, blocking the shoulder lane, my lane. I was always leery when this happened before, my vulnerability on high alert. As I got closer, the balding driver stepped out, walked around to the rear of his car, and waited for me with his arms crossed. When I got close enough, I began memorizing the three numbers and three letters on his Wisconsin license plate. Whether it would work or not, I decided to speak first, giving him the message that I was in charge here.

"Hi, what's up?" I said as I rolled to a stop.

"I'm an avid bike rider and just wanted to ask you, doesn't the traffic bother you?"

Most avid bike riders I know have a bicycle clamped to the roof of their car or hanging off the back, but he had neither. Despite the absence of this equipment, especially a bike, I decided to back my fear of physical harm down a few notches.

"Well, I just got onto the freeway before the border back there and yes, the traffic does bother me from time to time. But the truckers drive safely and the shoulder is wide," I said. I wanted to continue, explaining that narrow country roads and city streets were actually more dangerous but as I finished answering what turned out to be his first and only question, he abruptly turned around and without another word, got back into his car and drove off. Straddling my bike, I watched him speed into the distance and could only wonder, what was that all about? He hadn't even offered me a PowerBar, a bottle of water, or wished me good luck, common courtesies for "avid bike riders."

It was 11:30 when I stopped for lunch in Adrian. High on the outside wall over the café entrance was a Route 66 Roadside Attraction sign that read: *Midpoint Café, located at the exact geo-mathematical center of Route 66*. On each side of this sign were four highway shields, one for each of the eight states Route 66 went through. I was now 1139

Half way to my destination.

miles from both Santa Monica and Chicago.

Inside the café, I was the only customer. I had anticipated some sort of welcome, maybe even congratulations for making it half-way. Waitresses all along had, without exception, been very interested in what I was doing but not the one here. She was very businesslike, tight-lipped and aloof. I had the feeling that her curiosity wouldn't have been sparked even if I'd ridden in naked from the moon with a two-headed jackrabbit sitting on my shoulder.

She brought me my lunch just about the time her mother arrived unexpectedly. While eating, I eavesdropped on their loud conversation two booths away – their beauty shop appointments, their plans for dinner ("yaaa'll steeel comin over fuh dinna tuhnaaat?") and how the grandkids were doing getting over their colds. I feigned studying my route cards and Texas map, and wrote in my journal while eating. Before leaving I wandered through the small curio shop, picked up a free mid-point bumper sticker, paid my bill, and demonstrating my growing grasp of the language said, "Bye ya-all."

Outside I put on my armor – gloves, helmet, side view mirror and dark glasses. As I was hooking the side view mirror to the frame of my dark glasses the frame snapped in two and the right lens hit the ground. This time my brother Kim wasn't around to help but I figured all I needed was some Krazy Glue to fix the frame. I walked back into the café and explained my predicament to my waitress. She told me she would check with the cook. A few minutes later she returned and handed me an unused tube of Krazy Glue.

I sat out of the way on the stool at the end of the counter and while I repaired my glasses, the waitress and I had the conversation I'd longed to have when I first came in. She was busy now with customers at several tables but every time she picked up an order, refilled her water pitcher or removed a piece of pie from the display case, she would check on my progress. It was during one of these interludes that she inquired about my trip and became more and more fascinated with my adventure. When I walked out of the café the second time, my glasses were repaired and my impression of Texas hospitality had taken a leap, definitely higher than that of Wisconsin.

While I was in the café, the wind had increased, blowing strong from my right out of the southwest. I rode east through Vega, Wilderado, and with only 130 people, Bushland, the last town before Amarillo. William Henry Bush, from Chicago and no relation to the White House Bushes, had given some of his land here for a town site as well as a right-of-way for the Chicago, Rock Island and Gulf Railway. The town was dedicated in July 1908 and the following January, William's brother, Charles, opened a post office.

Gradually the high-rises in Amarillo, my destination for today, emerged on the horizon. At about the same time, on my right I saw Cadillac Ranch, created in 1972 and dedicated in 1974 by Ant Farm, a counter-culture art collective under the patronage of Stanley Marsh III. He owned the property where the ten Cadillacs, all lined up and facing west, were impaled in concrete at a 70-degree angle.

I pushed my bike through the turnstile and followed the one-hundred-yard path through a bumpy, fallow corn field to the unusual public art - a representation of the tail-fin era in car design from 1948-1964. Nobody was painting graffiti on the Cadillacs, something that is encouraged. In fact, I had anticipated a can of spray paint being available so I could make my contribution, but there was none. A fellow visitor told me that every so often the Cadillacs are repainted so people

Impaled Cadillacs, an artistic statement.

have an unblemished surface to write "whatever they jolly-well want."

As I was leaving, near the turnstile I met a woman and her two little girls. The wind was whipping their long hair, making it difficult for me to see their faces. She was very interested in my trip but the girls wanted to see the cars. Before we parted I asked her if she would recommend motels where I might stay in Amarillo. She named several and then wished me "good luck."

Amarillo's original name was Oneida, a word with American Indian ties. This was changed to the Spanish word for yellow, Amarillo (ah-ma-ree-yo; trill the "r" if you will), the color to match that of the homes built on the dry lake bed. I followed Business Loop 40 into and through the city, my intent, as always, to find a place to stay on the east side of whatever town was my destination. What I didn't want to do when I started pedaling every morning was to risk being hit by a driver coming up from behind me, blinded by the rising sun. If I started out from the east side of town, I knew I'd be safer with the heavy morning commute coming toward me into town, the sun behind them.

Amarillo, population 174,000, was slipping by and motels were becoming scarce. I finally stopped at one, picking it because I was desperate and it had "Route 66" in its name. I should have questioned this choice when I entered the front office and walked up to the counter.

But I was tired of the wind, hungry, and felt it would be embarrassing to walk in, look around, and walk back out, knowing that if this was my last choice I'd have to come back. Furthermore, I reminded myself that my intent all along was to support independently owned motels, like this one.

The person in charge was seated behind what looked like a bullet-proof glass barrier. The lights were off in the office and it was difficult to see him. We talked through the slot in the bottom of the glass, the same one used to pass transactions. His voice was soft and I had to say "What?" several times before he got the hint and spoke louder. He asked for my ID so I pushed my driver's license through the slot and watched as he talked in a foreign language with a woman I guessed to be his wife. They agreed on a room that was right behind the office. The price was $38.00 even. I paid my bill, he returned my ID and gave me my key and the motel's business card. On the card I noticed that his motel had "nice and clean rooms."

I pushed my bike to the room and struggled to unlock and open the door while two groups of people gathered above me, leaning over the railing and watching from the second floor walkway. At the same time, a woman started walking toward me from the far side of the motel, her full intent, I guessed, being to check me out. As she walked by me, she said "hi" and thankfully, kept going. I finally solved the pull-twist-push-lift combination of the doorknob, stubborn key, lock, and jammed door and hurriedly wheeled my bike inside where I felt only slightly safer.

The argument being screamed in the adjoining room seemed louder than when I'd heard it outside my door. I wondered if someone was about to lose their life or just be battered. I tried to pull the curtains closed so people wouldn't be able to look inside my room. But they hung askew, hooks either missing or ripped from the fabric at the top and the draw cord torn in two and tied half-open.

I had requested a non-smoking room but as I walked around, I saw cigarette burn holes in the bedspread and fraying carpet. In both the bedroom and the bathroom I found dark brown and black burn marks lined up on the edge of the night stand, chest of drawers, bathroom sink and tub enclosure. I smelled the sheets and bedspread and was thankful they harbored only a faint reminder of burning cigarettes.

Sitting on the bed, it was then I recalled the short conversation I had with the woman and her two little girls as I was leaving Cadillac Ranch. I had asked her for motel recommendations in Amarillo and she had told me, "Stay away from the north side. It's not a good area." And now, here I was, in a motel in north Amarillo.

After two weeks, I was beginning to understand about motels. The chains tended to cluster at or near freeway on and off-ramps. Meanwhile, Route 66 went through older and poorer parts of towns and while accessing those motels by bicycle was easier, the choices weren't always safer. Many of the old motels that used to serve Route 66 travelers are now closed, boarded up, have been torn down, harbor prostitutes and drug users, or have been turned into low-cost apartments, which was the direction I guessed this motel I had chosen was headed.

I washed up, unpacked a few things, and then walked to a Chinese Restaurant I had been told was three blocks down the street. On my way I walked past a prosperous looking motel, its fresh paint gleaming in the setting sun. On the wall facing the street, the large marquee advertised the rate for a single at $28 per night, plus tax. I had ended my search for a motel just a little too soon but it was too late to change my choice.

After stuffing myself with chicken fried rice, I walked briskly back to my room, fought the key, lock, and doorknob battle to get in again and when inside, would have bolted the door but there was no bolt. Security would be the lock in the door handle, easy to pick or kick in if anyone wanted. I tried unsuccessfully to swat the irritating flies buzzing around the room. I was equally unsuccessful in latching the window in the bathroom. Anyone familiar with the security weaknesses in this room, would only have to climb through the bathroom window if they wanted to get in. I decided there was no point in worrying about all the deficiencies. I had a roof over my head, the rooms on either side were quiet now, and my room phone made it easy to call my family.

I started with Ryan. I was running out of slide film so he said he'd find some for me and mail it to my brother, Chris, in Tulsa.

I was still five days from Tulsa but I called Chris anyway. I told him I was getting closer and to think about a place where we could link up.

And then I called Donna. After our chat, her daily email went out.

Dug told me that regular unleaded gas is $2.02/gallon in Amarillo compared to $2.45/gallon here in Davis. Remember his question last night about the swallows: Why do they build their nests on the west side of overpasses and not the east? Three theories have been emailed to me.

From Kim, Dug's brother: So they can poop on you when they see you coming.

From Dick, Dug's cousin: So they can sleep in and not be awakened too early by the sun.

From Matt, a friend: Swallows don't eat worms so they don't need the sun to wake them up to be early birds.

Dug thanks you for your support and humor. Love Donna.

The evening passed without further drama and the next morning, my first in the Central Time Zone, I made the same mistake I'd made back in New Mexico after entering the Mountain Time Zone. The sun came up later and, without an alarm clock, I overslept. I dressed in a hurry, packed the bike, left the key in the office and headed to the Cattlemen's Club and Cafe for breakfast. A whisper of wind was blowing, out of the north for the first time since I'd started my journey. The thought crossed my mind that the overcast looked like rain. But I was just guessing. I didn't have the slightest idea what was happening with the Texas weather but I was soon to find out.

22

Facing My Fear

Travel authors have an intimate understanding of what plunging into unfamiliar places is all about. Pico Ayer put it this way in his piece, "When Worlds Collude": "Travel is, as much as anything…a challenge of one's trust because we're naked and somewhat undefended when we're in a foreign place. Travel asks you, how much are you going to surrender to the unknown?"

My unknown began in earnest east of Albuquerque where I'd never been on Route 66. Leaving the urban sprawl of New Mexico's largest city, I raised my internal white flag as feelings of being in control disappeared almost completely. I was a self-conscious, wandering immigrant, trying to pretend I knew what I was doing. Eventually I would come to fully understand that the success of my trek would depend on the distant support of Donna, my family, friends, and well-meaning strangers, like one in the Amarillo restaurant this morning.

Lingering over breakfast, I was having trouble making sense of the directions on my next route card and map. I was all mixed up trying to figure out how to follow 6th Ave. to Buchanan Street, then Business Loop 40/Amarillo Blvd to Hwy 60, and somewhere down the road link up with Route 66. Directions I'd written down back home were complicated by the absence of street names and mileage markers. On her last excursion, this time to give me my bill, I asked my waitress for directions. Without thinking twice, she told me, "I'll get Terry to hep you. He knows all 'bout this area." A few minutes later, a customer who had been eating alone headed in my direction, his coffee cup in hand and his ample belly burying his belt buckle.

"So where ya' headed?" Terry asked, dispensing with any formal greeting. He declined my offer to sit down, sending the message that he intended on keeping short this interruption in his morning reverie. So I showed him my incomplete map of Amarillo and explained, "I'm riding a bicycle, following Route 66. I'm just not sure how to get from here to the Route 66 frontage road."

Terry scratched the stubble on his right cheek, squinted at my map in a way that made me think he needed glasses, and suggested, "If I's you, I'd get back on the freeway. Just turn at the next lat."

"But you see, bicycles aren't allowed on the freeway. If you can show me on the map the street that connects Business 40 with the Route 66 frontage road, I can take it from there.

Terry took a swig of his coffee, sloshed it from one side of his mouth to the other, swallowed, set the cup down, removed his sweat-stained Texas Rangers hat, wiped the perspiration from his brow with his left wrist, smoothed back what little hair he had left on his balding pate, and slowly shook his head, all the while ignoring my map. He was stalling. I guessed he knew perfectly well how to get around on these neighborhood streets but had never bothered to learn their names, let alone read a map. Bowing out gracefully, he said, "I'm sorry. I doughn' know wha'chee talkn' 'bout."

I thanked Terry for trying to help me, paid my bill and left. After an hour of serious wandering, guessing that every turn I made was the right one, I finally found my way to the elusive frontage road.

It was already 9:00 a.m. but I still hoped to make it to Groom by lunch. Other than that, I had no set destination for the day. Shamrock was ninety-four miles away, a doubtful distance considering I'd gotten up late and dilly-dallied over breakfast. McLean was only seventy-five miles away, a reasonable possibility.

The rolling ranchland made for comfortable, if somewhat boring, riding. I played with the functions on my computer, thought about Donna getting ready for work, and hoped the donations to Habitat back home were continuing to grow. Terry crossed my mind and I wondered why people, almost without exception, had so much trouble giving directions. They seldom used east, west, north or south, left, right, or street names. They'd tell me to go up, down or past some hidden or demolished structure. The most inaccurate directions usually started with the words, "It's only a few more miles," or "You can't miss it," throw-away comments that assured what I was looking for was nowhere near and if it was, I'd be sure to miss it. On the rare occasion of being given specific directions or precise distances, I wanted to hug that person, even do a dance.

My entertainment this morning also included guessing how far away the next overpass was after it came into view. The last overpass had loomed into view less than half-a-mile away, a full mile shorter from the one before it. The breeze had stopped and I was, except for the hum of my tires on the asphalt, enveloped in an eerie quiet. Above me was a chalky sky, the overcast bloated and ominous.

Sweating profusely, I stopped under the next overpass to snack on trail mix and drink water. A few minutes later an electrical company truck pulled up, the driver stopping on the wrong side of the deserted frontage road right next to me. "How ya' doin?" he asked.

"Fine."

"Where ya'all comin' from?"

"Amarillo today. I started in California two weeks ago."

"Well," he frowned, "You sure picked a bad day to do this."

I wondered what he meant but instead of asking him point blank, I told him, "I didn't pick this day as much as it picked me." My response sounded profound but it didn't make any sense. Before I could make an attempt to bring sense to my half of our conversation, his two-way radio came to life, squawking his call numbers. When he finished talking, he told me that dispatch was sending him to another electrical outage. He wished me good luck, his final words, "Be careful." As he drove off I knew if I was in California I'd be in harmless fog that was getting thicker. But here in west Texas, all I had was an uncomfortable feeling and a vague warning from a stranger. Maybe it was going to rain a little. If it did, how big a deal could that be?

Just beyond the overpass I saw a large barn on my right, semicircular in shape. I considered continuing my snack break inside while taking the time to repack the contents of my panniers into the waterproof plastic bags I'd brought along. But I wasn't hungry anymore and there didn't seem to be any urgency to repack. Leaving the sanctuary of the overpass, I decided if the weather fell apart, I'd sprint to the next unseen overpass or turn around and come back to the one I'd just left.

Just over one mile later, the first rumble of thunder came with no warning. It roamed the sky above me following the path of the unseen lightning before it. Accompanying the next boom were large rain drops. Each successive thunderclap came louder and then I saw the first lightning bolt. I counted the seconds between the flash and the sound of the thunder. There were six. The strike was just over one mile away behind me, somewhere near the barn whose safety I'd abandoned. The lightning seemed to be shredding the clouds. The torrential downpour intensified, now mixed with hail one-half inch in diameter. The lightning strikes were moving closer and I knew if I turned around and sprinted back to the safety of the barn, I'd be going into the danger. With my panic button fully depressed, I looked for shelter.

To my left was a short row of thirty-foot tall evergreens lined up next to each other in the shallow ditch between the frontage road and the freeway. As I thought of cowering under them, I heard Dad's words, said every time we went fishing in the Sangre de Cristos above Santa Fe. "Never get under a tree on a ridge or the tallest anything when you're in a lightning storm. The highest point – you – will attract the lightning."

In contradiction to everything I knew about lightning storms, I decided the trees were my only shelter. If I stayed on the road I'd be a perfect lightning rod but in the trees, maybe lightning would hit a tree I wasn't under. So I pushed the bike into the ditch, leaned it against two trees, unpacked my orange poncho and draped it over the bike to keep my sleeping bag and the gear in my panniers from getting any wetter. I put on my rain pants and jacket over my wet clothes, crouched down and pulled a corner of the poncho over me. When the next flash of lightning came, the number of seconds between it and the following boom was down to two, the lightning almost on top of me and creeping nearer. I watched the engorged raindrops plummet, the most intense rainstorm I'd ever seen. Waves of water scudded across the road, filling the ditch and soaking my feet. I huddled next to the metal bike, realizing it was, in tandem with the trees, an obvious attraction for a bolt of lightning.

As my demise neared, my mind flashed back to my boss in the Forest Service one summer fifty years ago. Jose had been on a two-week leave with the New Mexico National Guard at Fort Bliss in Texas when he and another soldier were killed by lightning that struck the tent they were in. Thinking about Jose's fate, I pondered mine. I wondered if my last sensation would be feeling my hair stand up. Would I die quickly? How long would it take before I'd be found in this mucky ditch, my bright yellow rain gear fused to my skin? I thought of my friends and family, all of them left to wonder how I could have been so stupid to get caught out in the open like this. They knew I knew better.

When the next bolt of lightning flashed, I closed my eyes and counted to one before the thunder shook everything around me. The storm was on top of me, the clouds and rain so thick I couldn't see more than twenty feet. The next strike would either hit the trees or be past me.

It was ironic, but despite the violence, I was comfortable. I wasn't cold despite my clothes and feet being wet. The display of nature uncontrolled by human intervention was beautiful. This was weather that nourished the fields and would eventually result in crops being harvested. I struggled to emphasize my privilege of witnessing this event up close while at the same time trying to deemphasize its threat to my existence.

When the next flash of lightning came, it was past me, three seconds before the thunder came. The rain was starting to ease as I pushed the bike out of the ditch and raced back to the barn and safety.

Ten minutes later, I was in the semi-dark and empty barn, two pigeons keeping me company. Their droppings were everywhere and I accidentally sat or stepped into them several times. But I didn't care. I dried off and repacked the clothes that were still dry into the plastic, waterproof sacks. I cooed to the pigeons, welcoming their presence as they flew around inside. Outside the barn the rain fell gently and the thunder moved out of hearing range. My peanut butter on Wheat Thins tasted good. I was thankful to be alive and had learned a lesson about taking shelter when it was available.

Back on the frontage road, I splashed through puddles, my legs and feet soaking. I wondered what surprises the completely overcast sky still had in store for me. Every ranch house, barn, overpass, pump house or other structure that I passed became a potential shelter. My apprehension built when I ventured beyond each one without immediately seeing another up ahead to take its place.

My incessant search for shelter was relieved, at least for the time being, when Groom loomed. From a distance, on the west side of town I saw the Cross of Our Lord Jesus Christ, at 190 feet tall, only eighteen feet shorter than one like it in St. Augustine, Florida. In town I stopped at the *Groom/McLean News* and bought a newspaper for my collection. They offered to mail it to me, at their expense, so I took them up on their generosity. In the bank I cashed a traveler's check and then mailed two postcards at the post office. Written last night, both had somehow emerged dry after this morning's deluge. At the small but well-stocked grocery store I bought a banana, a bag of salted sunflower seeds and a package of cantaloupe pieces. On the bench in front of the store I enjoyed my picnic, exchanging hellos with passersby as I kept watch on the milky overcast.

When I left town, I was rested and, unlike when leaving Amarillo, I knew that the weather could turn against me without warning. East of Groom, I saw in the distance a water tower that had been built with a ten-degree lean, making it look like it was about to fall over. It was an attraction for the now-closed Brittan truck stop and restaurant. Pedaling along on the Route 66 frontage road, the many dips and rough surface made for slow going. Risking a traffic ticket, I moved onto the smoother, more level I-40 shoulder where the familiar draft of the semis pulled me along.

Thirty miles from Groom I arrived in McLean, ticket and raindrop free. I decided to eat dinner first and then make up my mind on whether to cycle, as I often did, another twenty miles, this time to Shamrock. I stopped a pedestrian to ask for places to eat and he suggested a hamburger joint and the Red River Steakhouse. In an effort to plan ahead, I also asked, "Are there any motels in Shamrock?"

"Yes, but I wouldn't advise you go there tonight. They've been dealing with hailstorms and heavy rain all day," he warned. "And this is tornado season now, you know." Finally I'd heard the "t" word. I wasn't really surprised, having seen the inky sky and heard the thunder ahead of me as I'd ridden into McLean.

As we parted, I contemplated shortening my distance for today. I recalled Donna's advice on the phone last night. Due to my penchant for testing others' wisdom, as if accidentally proving them wrong made me right, she had said, "I hope you'll pay attention to what people tell you. Enjoy the adventure and don't hurry it along." There was no good reason to go another twenty miles today and I didn't want to risk my life in another storm, equal in intensity, or even worse, to the one this morning. It was time to be sensible and take care of myself.

McLean's population of 830, and dropping, is doing its part to maintain the lore of The Mother Road. I rode by the first Phillips 66 service station built outside of Oklahoma. The narrow building with its steep pitched red roof and two red gas pumps had been restored in immaculate detail. I found the Devil's Rope Museum, which is also the headquarters of the Texas Route 66 Association. Because it was closed I couldn't pick up any information about Route 66 or see the displays featuring the history of barbed wire. I was also too late to try and find the remains of the WWII German POW camp that was outside McLean.

My exploration over, I headed to the hamburger place for dinner. My preprocessed chicken patty sandwich was accompanied by French-fries oozing grease into a deepening pool on the waxed paper that held them. I was the only customer so the young waitress had little to do in between spurts of order-taking at the drive-up window. When a boyfriend showed up, they settled into a booth where they pawed, nibbled, argued, reconciled and made plans for a future rendezvous, acting all along as though I wasn't even there. I interrupted their sexual teasing several times, encouraging her to momentarily unclench by waving my empty water glass, my last greasy napkin, or pantomiming my need for more catsup to squirt on my glistening fries.

Having had enough of my food and the cavorting that passed for waitressing, I retraced my path back to the west side of McLean and leaned my bike against the office wall of the independently owned Cactus Inn Motel. The only motel in town, here was my opportunity to again support the resolve and entrepreneurial spirit of another Route 66 business.

In the motel office the owner agreed with the pedestrian's advice. "He gave you the right advice to stay here in McLean tonight. The weather in Shamrock is very dangerous, especially for someone on a bicycle." I filled out the guest registration, and paid my $38.75 bill with traveler's checks. While completing this process, she went through her litany of information: the location of the ice machine, checkout time, how to make a long distance call on the room phone – Dial 9 and then your calling card number – and an unsolicited recommendation to eat breakfast at the hamburger place I already knew too well. Her posture ramrod straight and her gaze caring and direct, she handed me my key and insisted, "If you need anything, you let me know right away."

There was one need I didn't have and that was to look over my shoulder tonight to see who was watching me as I turned the key smoothly in the lock and pushed my bike into the room. On the wall behind the headboard, the first thing I saw was a large painting of galloping horses. In addition to the furniture found in most motels, my room had a table with two chairs and a plush easy chair. Light from ceiling and wall fixtures, floor lamps, and the lamps on the two nightstands made it possible to read from anywhere in the room without a shadow on the page. There was an alarm clock, hair drier, coffee pot, and tissue dispenser, and a basket filled with soap, shampoo, moisturizer, and other comfort items. But what really surprised me was in the bathroom. Hanging from the towel racks were light green wash cloths, hand towels and bath towels, the patterns all matching. I was unable to recall ever seeing anything but white towels in any motel where I'd stayed.

My motel room tour completed, I rigged a simple clothesline over the heater using a length of cord I carried. I unpacked my panniers and hung the damp clothes over the warm breeze from the heater fan. Within an hour, everything was dry and repacked into the waterproof bags in my panniers.

My domestic chores completed, I called Donna, skipping my threating confrontation with the lightning storm. After our conversation, she sent out her daily e-mail.

> *Dug's a little discouraged tonight; he rode only 72 miles today due to thunderstorms. He feels an urgency to make it to Chicago by the start of Memorial Day weekend. I urged him to relax and appreciate an extra couple of hours of rest.*
>
> *He knows for sure he's in Texas now since he saw his first road-killed Armadillo. He's noticed that the towns he rides through are filled with birds, especially mockingbirds and killdeer.*

Another e-mail arrived in answer to Dug's question on why swallows build their nests on the western side of overpasses. It came from Art Mills, a good friend of Dugs: I'm surprised no one has picked up on the actual reason for the swallows nesting habits. The reason is so they will get a good nights sleep and wake up well wested.

Dug regrets to report that today he saw swallows nesting on the eastern side of an overpass. Maybe Texas swallows are different from New Mexico swallows.

Dug sends his thanks to our friend Marie Reil for her Route 66 fold out maps from the National Historic Route 66 Federation.

Thanks everyone for checking in. Love, Donna

The next morning I extended my time in the comfortable motel by eating my granola and banana breakfast, along with dark-black coffee, in the room. By 7:00 a.m. I was on the road. Two hours later I arrived in Shamrock, the last Route 66 town in Texas. I dodged pothole puddles from yesterday's storm while riding up to a pay phone. Staying seated in my two-wheeled office, I used one hand to dial Donna and the other to hang onto the pay phone. Today was May 13th and when she answered I wished her, "Happy Birthday." I was glad to hear that the roses I'd ordered had arrived. Talking with her in the morning for a change gave us both a charge to the start of our day. After we hung up, I made a spur-of-the-moment (somehow very appropriate in Texas) decision to eat a second breakfast. The pancakes and ham tasted great and while I didn't know it at the time, this meal was going to have to last me until dinner, sixty-two miles from here.

Beyond Shamrock, thirteen miles on the I-40 frontage road were all that remained between me and Oklahoma. The sky looked just like it did yesterday, the fog again reducing my visibility to less than half-a-mile. I was uncomfortable with the cool breeze blowing against me from the northeast so for warmth I put my windbreaker on over my long-sleeved polyester shirt.

While enjoying the last of Texas, I passed a farmhouse with several outbuildings. On the west side of the home, I caught sight of something unusual in the grass. Curious, I went back, leaned the bike against a tree and walked over to what looked like a child's playhouse, all but several inches of its roof and a circular aluminum vent buried in the ground. The approximately nine-foot square, rusted corrugated metal roof rose to a slight pitch in the middle. Near the southeast corner was a wooden door lying flat, hinged to a separate concrete foundation. It finally dawned on me that I was looking at an underground storm shelter.

Safe underground in Texas.

I walked around it, completely oblivious to the fact I was trespassing. I tried to imagine living here, our family fleeing in the dark, shouting directions to each other as the wind howled, propelling debris through the pouring rain and lightning. When we got the wooden door unlocked and lifted open, we would follow our flashlight beams down the steps into the shelter, praying the approaching devastation would miss us. This was definitely not a place where I cared to live.

A short distance later, I left Texas. It had been an eventful 185 miles and I felt thankful to be alive.

23

Music in the Old Meat Market

Not counting California, so far I'd crossed the borders of three states and at each one there had been no police presence ordering me to turn around and go back home, a threat found at many borders around the world. What I had encountered instead were large welcome signs, multi-colored in Arizona and New Mexico, and black and white in Texas. Each in its own way had given evidence to my forward progress and the opportunity for artists to demonstrate their creativity.

Now at the Oklahoma border I coasted up to the state sign, its beauty achieving a new high. Resting on a massive oval red cement slab was a sign that had two distinct sections. The bottom portion was a twenty-five foot long, three foot high and two foot wide rectangular block of concrete covered with rough-contoured white plaster. On top of this base was a similar sized beige colored block of granite which had the word *Oklahoma* inscribed in 2 ½-foot tall letters on both sides. Taking the place of the second letter "O" was a circular American Indian shield with feathers, in honor of Oklahoma's American Indians, among them the Cherokee, Chickasaw, Choctaw and Osage Nations.

I leaned back against the "K," snacked, drank water, closed my eyes and welcomed the quiet that surrounded me. I put away my Texas route cards and pulled out the first few for Oklahoma. Knowing that Oklahoma had saved 90% of historic Route 66 stirred my anticipation. I affixed the Texas Route 66 sticker to my crossbar, adding it to the other three states before making sure my load was tied securely.

Eight cloudy, comfortable but warming miles beyond the border, I rode into Erick, population 1,023. Erick is where songwriter Roger

Miller grew up. In 1964, he won a Grammy for Best Country Song, *Dang Me*, and also for Best Country and Western Album. His recording of *King of the Road* in 1965 earned him the award of Best Country and Western Recording Vocal Performance, Male. He died in 1992 and in tribute to him, Route 66 through town was named The Roger Miller Memorial Highway. Another songwriter from Erick was Sheb Wooly who wrote *Purple People Eater* in 1958. Sheb Wooly Avenue was named after him.

    I rode along Roger and Sheb's streets, frustrated in my unsuccessful search for a restaurant. Resigned to the fact that lunch would be, like yesterday, peanut butter on Wheat Thins, an orange, and trail mix for dessert, I changed my search to finding a shaded patch of grass for my picnic. About then I saw a bearded man up ahead hollering something about Route 66. I stopped riding and watched as he shuffled up to me, out of breath. He threw his arm around my shoulder and told me his name was Harley. Between gasping breaths, he insisted I stop and visit with him and his wife, Annabelle. "We're the owners of the SandHills Curiosity Shop, and you hafta see our place if you're followin' Route 66," a fact he had figured out after sizing up my four loaded panniers and my lengthening line of state Route 66 stickers. As we talked it was clear that his enthusiasm didn't really leave me any choice in this matter, hungry or not.

We walked the block to their shop on Sheb Wooly Avenue, a place that had once been the City Meat Market. Harley, speaking as though I was severely hard-of-hearing, made enough noise to alert Annabelle to our nearing presence. She met us on the porch and gave me a hug, warm evidence that the label "stranger" was inappropriate here. Inside, Harley steered me to a chair where, as he put it, "You relax now and take a load off." As I sat down he was quick to point out, continuing in his rich southern drawl, "That there char has a natchral notch in front that'll accommodate your masculeen anatomy." Annabelle laughed in agreement, having heard Harley's explanation so many times that she had no reason to be embarrassed. But I was. Glancing down at my crotch I could see the deep indentation where a large knot had once grown. We raced through introductions and when I brought up my failure in finding a place to eat lunch in Erick, Harley assured me, "We'll give ya' somethin' ta eat afore ya'll leaves."

Harley's face was framed by his long brown hair combed straight back and his frizzy ten-inch beard. Somewhere along the way he had lost a couple of front teeth which now served, along with his blue eyes, wrinkles, and high forehead, to define his character. Meanwhile, Annabelle's long gray hair fell onto her shoulders, her broad smile and laugh soft in complement to Harley's more boisterous, extroverted, personality.

Harley had taken up a position in front of me directing the show, asking questions, and telling jokes while Annabelle, quieter, played his straight. Both of them were dressed alike, wearing long-sleeved, yellow pullover shirts with blue and white striped overalls. I later found out they have matching red and white striped overalls that were bought by Harley's mom from a University of Oklahoma football fan for one-dollar apiece. Harley calls that outfit, "*Our redneck tuxedos,*" which fits with his calling Erick, "*The Redneck Capital of the World.*"

The inside of their shop, really more like a museum, was filled with books, records, and musical instruments. Among them was Harley's first guitar, given to him in 1958 by Roger Miller when Harley, who grew up in Erick, was twelve. Harley told me he plays it when he sings *King of the Road.* Surrounding me were antiques, including a pool

The Annabelle and Harley concert.

table, bearskin rug, Mickey Mouse poster, and signs. One area had pictures, letters and post cards, all written by people who had visited them, from Australia, France, Japan, Ireland, Sweden, and all over the United States. Annabelle managed to squeeze a word in, telling me she once lived in northern California and is both a songwriter and an artist. She explained that the only thing for sale in their shop is her art.

But I sat conflicted. While this maelstrom of enthusiasm swirled around me, inside a voice was telling me that I needed to move on, that I was wasting time, and definitely needed to eat. Gradually I got a grip on my compulsive need to get going, realizing that it was unplanned experiences like this I had hoped to have when I began my trip. And I had accidentally stumbled into this one. I also knew that when I was hungry, I became impatient and found it difficult to go along with whatever was going on, regardless of how interesting.

Harley and Annabelle decided it was time for them to serenade me. They call themselves The Mediocre Music Makers so my expectations were far from high. It wasn't until later that I read about Harley having spent twenty-two years as a touring musician, playing guitar and accompanying Charley Pride, Dottie West and Jan Howard, all Country and Western singers who have won numerous awards. Ten uninterrupted minutes later, they finished their concert and I sat slack-jawed. I had been mesmerized by their harmony and Harley's fingers moving effortlessly up and down his guitar frets, stretching to create chords and a melody that transported me to a peaceful and contented center within. I could only think that it was too bad their voices and guitar-playing had an audience of only one.

Following their concert, Harley pointed out the five original Route 66 signs they had hanging on the walls. They took down three of them and Harley had me stand on a short ladder holding one of the signs. With Annabelle standing next to me and holding the other two signs, he took our picture. I wanted a picture of them so we went outside and they held the same signs, leaned their shoulders into each other and flashed cheekbone-to-cheekbone grins that said, "We are having big-time fun." I then asked them both to sign my journal. Harley wrote, "Rock on Doug," and Annabelle, "Get your kicks on Route 66! Have a great trip Doug."

Before I left, Annabelle gave me two post cards, one a drawing she did in 1994 of the Old Meat Market. She also gave me a flyer that advertised their shop and several newspaper reprints of articles that had been written about them. At the bottom of one was the following information: *Hours – we open when we wake up and close when we pass out!*

As I prepared to leave I asked Harley, "Do many bicyclists visit you?"

"Oh yes." He then told me about Vasile Stoica, a Romanian with congenital paraplegia. He had come through here in 2003 using a specially designed manual wheelchair. He completed the entire length of Route 66 in sixty-six days. Knowing what I had already been through – the narrow highways, hills, extreme weather and the long distances between towns – I marveled at his accomplishment and wished I could have met him.

Harley and Annabelle gave me a final hug and as I rode away, a car pulled up in front and their next audience piled out. These visitors were in for an experience they would never forget. Cycling out of town,

I hummed the song Harley and Annabelle had sung to me. I couldn't remember the exact words but I thought they were:

Put your head on my shoulder
And pretend that you love me
One more time
For the last time.

Unsure of both the title and lyrics, I decided when my trip was over, I would call them and ask.

Doug and Annabelle, of the Mediocre Music Makers, in the Sandhills Curiosity Shop, Erick, Oklahoma.

24

Violent Weather Stalks Me…Again

Route 66 out of Erick is a four-lane, divided highway. While enjoying the wide shoulder, the absence of traffic, and the afterglow of my conversation and concert with Annabelle and Harley, it dawned on me that Harley hadn't offered me anything for lunch as he said he would. But it wasn't as though I was starving. To keep my hunger pangs in remission I'd just ration the dwindling snacks in my food pannier, hoping they would sate my appetite until I got to the nearest Elk City restaurants, by my estimation only four hours away in bicycle riding time.

Five minutes beyond Erick a car pulled alongside. The woman driver leaned over and somehow managed to avoid veering to the right and hitting me as she both downshifted and cranked the passenger window open. "Hi," she hollered. "I saw you ride into Erick earlier. Where ya' headed?"

I kept riding and told her, "To Chicago. I'm more than half way there."

"That's amazing. Are you doing this for a cause or anything?" Many people had wanted to know why I was making this trip but this was only the second time someone had asked me if it involved raising money for a charity.

"We're getting ready to build three Habitat for Humanity homes back in California where I'm from."

"I know about Habitat. Jimmy Carter's involved in that. I'd like to contribute."

I hadn't been actively soliciting donations as I went along, and told her, "That's nice of you but…"

"No, I want to donate. I think this is a great cause and you're an inspiration doing what you're doing."

With her insistent affirmation hugging me, we both pulled onto the shoulder and stopped. She pulled her wallet out of her purse and told me she was on her way to Elk City, headed to the bank and then to buy a part for her well pump. She handed me the only money in her wallet, six one-dollar bills, and apologized for not having more. I thanked her for her donation and taking the time to stop and talk. I gave her a receipt and before we parted she graciously signed my journal, writing, "Good luck. Jacque Francis. Erick, OK," and then drew a small smiley face.

As the miles from Erick increased, the overcast thinned and gradually disappeared. By the time I rode into Elk City, a town whose original name was Busch, named after Adolphus, the St. Louis beer baron, it was dinnertime. Thanks to the oppressive humidity, my hunger and the interminable rolling of the terrain, I was worn out and famished.

While looking for a place to eat, for the second time this afternoon a vehicle pulled alongside. The teenage passenger, missing most of his front teeth, rolled down his window and yelled, "Where ya' goin?"

The noise coming from a hole in the pickup's muffler prevented me from hearing what he had said, so I yelled back, "What?"

"WHERE….YA'….GOIN?"

"Chicago."

"On *that*?"

His response, with its sarcastic emphasis on the word "that," took me by surprise. Up to now, nearly everyone had been interested in my equipment and was gracious in wishing me a safe trip. But now, with one word, this teenager, in serious need of dental work, had questioned the ability of my bike to carry me the length of Route 66.

"Well, I've already come this far from Santa Monica," I said, trying to mount a subtle defense. And then, aware that he probably didn't know where Santa Monica was, it was my turn to emphasize the word "that," adding, "*That's* in California." And *that* was the end of *that*. The driver and his passenger, having had enough of this stimulating conversation, roared away, spewing noxious dark gray gas fumes in his wake. I had been in Oklahoma less than one day and more people had already initiated conversations with me than in all of Texas.

Just ahead on my right was a pizzeria. It had been eight long hours since my two breakfasts and my caloric status was deep into deprivation. Two college-aged women greeted me inside at the hostess stand. They looked downright perky wearing the company approved attire – blue jeans, white blouse and a red and white checked apron. The one with Judy on her nameplate looked at me and said, "Boy, you need some air!" I wasn't sure what she meant but I guessed my exhaustion was showing. Surprised by her candor, I laughed as she led me to a booth. Before sitting down, I put my helmet, journal, gloves and dark glasses on the table and detoured to the restroom to rinse my tired sweaty face with cold water.

For dinner I started with a large, self-serve salad smothered with bleu cheese dressing. Next came a small Canadian bacon/olive pizza, a second mound of salad, and three glasses of iced tea. While working my way through the second half of my pizza, a woman and her teenage daughter walked up to my table. "Excuse us for interrupting your dinner. We saw your bicycle outside and were wondering, where are you headed?"

"I'm on my way to Chicago."

My answer was followed by the usual questions, answers, and then the wish for "good luck." As they walked away, I heard the woman say to her daughter, "See, I told you he was following Route 66."

Dinner never failed to recharge me. Only eight miles away was Canute, named for a King of Denmark. Bypassed by I-40 in 1970, Canute's population had dwindled to just over 500. I wanted to spend the night there but doubted the town was large enough to have a motel.

Not willing to take a chance, I asked Judy, "Is there a motel in Canute?"

"Yes, I think so," she said, giving me a conflicting answer.

"I need to know for sure since I don't want to camp out with my bike if there isn't one."

She suggested that Betty, the other waitress on duty, might know so she left to get her. They both walked up to my table and Betty got right down to business. "What was it you wanted to know?" she asked.

"Is there a motel in Canute?"

"Gee, it's been a long time since I've been there. I always go by on the freeway; don't go through town; no need to. I think there might be," she concluded, and we were back to page one where I'd started with Judy. Mixed messages seemed to be the specialty here.

"Well, I'm on a bicycle and before I head there, I really need to know if there's a place to spend the night," gently pushing my point.

It was then that Judy had a second brain flash. "I just remembered. Our dishwasher, Fred, has parents who live in Canute. I bet he'll know," and off she went to get Fred.

Participation in the convention at my table increased to three when Judy returned with Fred, leaving Phil, the cook, the only employee on duty not involved in discussing my urgent need for lodging. I told Fred what I was trying to find out to which he told us, "There used to be a motel in Canute but I don't know if it's there anymore." This wasn't the information I wanted to hear but like everyone else, Fred was just trying to be helpful.

Meanwhile, sitting across the room, quietly enjoying their pizza was an elderly couple. They had overheard the circuitous conversations at my table and were ready to take advantage of the impasse. He turned around, raised his voice to be heard, and said, "There's a motel in Canute. It's just off Route 66 in town. Can't miss it."

Bingo! Ask and ye shall receive…eventually. We thanked him, everyone returned to their duty stations, I paid my bill and stepped outside, surprised how much cooler it felt than before dinner.

Looking to the east, the direction I was heading, I saw nothing but unobstructed blue sky. In contrast, to the west several miles was a massive black cloud. The sun was no longer visible and the wind had stiffened making it hard to pedal and stay upright. I could see it was moving slowly in my direction but decided if necessary I could outrun it to Canute, only eight miles away.

As the streets of Elk City merged into rolling hills, I pedaled along as if I had nary a care. It wasn't until I glanced back that my attitude changed. This vicious storm, larger than the one from two days before, was about to teach me another lesson, one I might not survive. As the darkness increased so did the wind. Motorists driving both directions were putting on their headlights, wipers, and some stopping on the shoulder. A few minutes later I watched this massive cloud catch and then overtake me. I could no longer deny that another hail, rain and lightning storm was about to unleash its fury on me out in the open. But something more terrifying had been added to this threat. From a short distance to my left I could see three to six black fingers that looked like juvenile funnel clouds, dancing toward the earth from below the mother cloud. I'd never seen a tornado form but this was close enough to how I imagined it must look. I had to find shelter.

I put the bike into the highest gear I could handle, stood up to pedal, ignored the slate-black sky and raced to Canute. Ten minutes later, out of breath and my legs screaming pain, the whipping tailwind blew me into Canute. Ahead I saw the two-story motel one block off Route 66. I pushed the bike into the lobby, thankful that the entrances to the rooms were from an interior hallway and I wouldn't have to go outside unless the fury leveled the motel.

The clerk was matter-of-fact about the maelstrom I'd exited, to the point of putting me in a room on the side of the motel that would take the brunt of whatever disaster was headed my way. I tried to accept his nonchalance as his way of building my confidence but it was impossible. With my key in hand, I went to my first floor room, opened the curtain, and pulled a chair up to the window (not the most brilliant place from which to watch the heavens unload). I sat mesmerized by the dancing black fingers, now less than one mile away. They would spiral without rhythm, down and up erratically, all the while trying unsuccessfully to kiss the ground like the lightning. They would either disintegrate or retreat into the hostile blackness that gave them birth, only to be replaced by others that were more successful in their downward growth. As the lightning and thunder moved over the motel, the sheets of rain obscured the developing funnels and turned the parking lot outside my window into a lake.

As the deluge raged, I decided that being mere inches away from the window pane was the wrong place to be if a tornado was about to touch down. So I closed the curtain half-way and called Donna on the room phone while sitting on the floor. I touched lightly on the storm outside, knowing how horrified and helpless she would be if she heard me scream as a tornado obliterated the motel while we were talking.

Good evening everybody. When I answered the phone tonight, Dug's first words were, "I'm safe," which he repeated several times. He made it to his motel just ahead of a storm. Throughout our conversation, Dug interspersed his comments with, "It's pouring out there! The parking lot is a lake! It's just pouring! It's amazing. I hope I can get out of here in the morning." I guess these kinds of rain storms are common place in Oklahoma but they're a bit much for this New Mexican transplanted California boy. Dug felt happy having ridden eighty-six miles today.

Bill Owens, a friend of our son Ryan, has weighed in on the question, Why do swallows nest on the west side of overpasses? "Birds don't plan ahead worrying about tomorrow's sunrise; rather they live for the moment, seizing every opportunity of the day they are in. Just like Dug, they enjoy life as they live it and watch the sun as it sets in the West. Carpe Diem."

The lowest gas price Dug has seen so far was in Sayre, OK. – $1.999 for unleaded regular at a Shell station. Dug encourages us to come to Oklahoma if we want cheap gas.

Thank you everyone for reading and for thinking of Dug.

Love, Donna.

Tired, scared, and wondering if today, Friday the 13th of May, would be my last, I jammed my earplugs into my ears, turned out the lights and buried my head under the covers. My full bladder awoke me around 4:00 a.m. The rain had stopped as had the thunder and wind. After relieving myself, I fell asleep again. But not for long. From the room next to mine came the noise of a cavorting couple. Their vigor shook the shared wall, while their bed, with its creeks and squeaks, accompanied their groans, moans, and heavy panting.

When their coupling was over, the man in that room answered his first cell phone call, his voice loud and gruff. I covered my head with my pillow but it did no good. It was 5:30 when I gave up trying to go back to sleep and instead got up, dressed, ate my portable breakfast, and stifled the temptation to pound on the door of the now quiet room next to mine as I left the motel.

The last two days of foul weather had put me in a doubting, apprehensive mood this morning. I was thinking less about the joy of my adventure and more about the interminable questions – How far would I get today? What direction would the wind blow? Will I make it to Chicago? What mechanical problems lie ahead? and on and on. The fact that I had so little control continued to test me regularly.

Unlike the last two days, the sky this morning was cloudless. The water from last night's storm was gone and the parking lot dry. The sun coming over the horizon, the air sweet-smelling and invigorating, birds darting about, farm animals grazing, and the attraction of an old highway stretching before me, broke through my pessimism. All the spontaneous experiences I was having with nature, people, and interesting places were bringing me joy, fascination and inspiration. Realizing this, I knew my adventure so far had been everything I hoped it would be.

Route 66 from Canute continued separate from the freeway. It crossed an old concrete bridge, the abutments at either end chest high and as solid as the day they were built. If a car hit one, it would be no contest. Here, in the early morning with no traffic, seemed like a good time to do something I had wanted to do for quite awhile – use my bike to measure the width of America's Main Street.

My bike is just over five feet long. Two bike lengths completed the distance from the shoulder to the center stripe, much narrower than I expected. I took a picture of my bike jutting into the traffic lane, repacked my camera and before leaving, practiced my "moo," saying good morning and goodbye to the small herd of curious Angus that had ambled over to watch me from the nearby fence.

Twenty-eight miles later, I reached Clinton, population 9,000. Clinton's original name had been Washita Junction, but in 1902, the postal service had refused, for a reason I had been unable to find, to accept its original name. So it was renamed after a Judge, Clinton Irwin. I passed a Conoco gas station, the advertised price for regular unleaded gasoline the lowest I had seen so far, $1.959 per gallon. It was mid-morning and like yesterday, I was hungry already. So, also like yesterday, I stopped and ate a second breakfast, this time at the Cherokee Trading Post and Truck Stop east of Clinton. I had no doubt that my body was telling me I was falling behind in my consumption of calories.

It Only Hurts When I Sit Down

Original "66" was often a tight squeeze.

Clinton used to be the site of Pop Hicks Restaurant. Before it burned down in 1999, it had the distinction of being in business longer than any other restaurant on Route 66. The first state-sponsored Route 66 Museum is in Clinton and across from it is a Best Western Inn that was frequented by Elvis. I thought about stopping to go through the museum but I wanted to take advantage of the improved weather and cycle some serious miles today.

It was 11:30 a.m. when I arrived in Weatherford. Proud of being the birthplace of astronaut Thomas Stafford, there is a museum in town honoring him. I rode by the Route 66 Drive-in Theater, the first of two with this name that I would see on my trip. Riding through town I was entertained for several blocks by music from loudspeakers positioned on the sides of buildings. Since leaving New Mexico I had endured a steady diet of Country-and-Western music, mostly in restaurants. So I was surprised the music here on the streets of Weatherford was jazz. Hungry again, a booth at a Quiznos Sub fulfilled my need for a place to rest and eat lunch.

Leaving town I was on the north frontage road, still riding on old Route 66 concrete, when, for the third time in the last two days, a vehicle pulled alongside, this time a pickup with a shell. The passenger hollered, "Are you following Route 66?"

"Yes, since Santa Monica."

"So are we, but we're driving it."

For the next two minutes our conversation continued, the driver and his passenger both firing questions at me as we went along at twelve mph. We heard a horn honk and when I glanced back I saw five cars backed up behind them, impatient because they couldn't pass. Not wanting to irritate a motorist and cause an accident, we decided to pull over and continue our visit on the shoulder.

Jack Patten, 62, and Tom Fitch, 68, had been neighbors in Iowa until 1972 when Tom moved to Las Vegas, Nevada. Determined to keep their friendship alive, they decided to get together every year and go someplace. This year, Jack flew to Las Vegas where Tom picked him up and they started their Route 66 drive in Victorville, California. Jack said, "We didn't want to get in all that mess in Los Angeles so we decided not to start there."

Our rapid-fire conversation about our respective adventures was motivated by knowing we had only a short time to talk. Tom asked, "Did you see the shoes in the trees in Amboy?" I had no idea what he was talking about.

"No, I missed that I guess."

"We miss a lot too," said Jack. He was the navigator, and was using the *Route 66 Travelers Guide*, written by Tom Snyder, to guide them. He waved it at me and joked, "We spend more time going back to things we've missed than we do going forward."

Both men were retired and having the time of their lives. They asked me if I was riding for a cause. I told them, "Yes," and pointed to the laminated Habitat for Humanity decal I had affixed to the front of my handlebar bag. It was remarkable that whenever I mentioned Habitat, people would invariably say something like, "President Carter is involved in that, isn't he?" And so it was with Jack and Tom. Tom pulled his wallet out and gave me $20 which he insisted on donating. My donation pouch now had over $60 in it.

Before we parted we took each other's picture. Mine of them was the last on my roll. Unless my luck changed and I found a roll of slide film to buy, I would be out for the next two days until I got to my Brother Chris's house north of Tulsa in Owasso. I asked them both to sign my journal. Later I would read: "Hi Doug. This is Thomas Fitch, Las Vegas, Nevada," and, "Good Luck Doug, Jack Patten, Des Moines, Iowa.".

Leaning out the window before they drove away, Jack told me, "I ride my bike in the seven-day, 500-mile *Ride across Iowa* every summer. You should come join us." As they left, Jack waved and his final words to me were, "God Bless You."

My visit with them inspired me. They joined the growing number of people who, just by being themselves, were helping me to see my trip as a fascinating adventure. I was slowly moving beyond the need to control everything.

25

Hillbillies' Only Gots White

Forty-six miles beyond Weatherford, the old highway, after skirting the towns of Hydro and Bridgeport, finally appeared in El Reno, named for Major General Reno, a Union officer killed in the Civil War. Too hungry to wander around testing my theory that reputable restaurants were those with their parking lots filled with cars, I stopped at the first place I came to, a Mexican restaurant. The waiter, without any delay, brought me a menu, a glass of ice water, a large basket of dinner chips and two small bowls, one filled with hot-sauce and the other a mild cheese sauce. Not sure what to expect gastronomically, I hesitantly dipped a corn chip into the warm cheese first and then another into the hot-sauce. They were so delicious that, if I hadn't been so hungry, I might have made a meal of just the chips and dips alone.

I ordered my usual two enchilada dinner, this time adding a tortilla to sop up the sauce embracing the enchiladas. Starting somewhere in Texas, after ordering iced tea I had been asked, "Sweetened or non-sweetened?" From that meal on, I always ordered sweetened.

Settled into my booth, I thought about my day, dominated by Route 66's unending undulations. They were in stark contrast to the path of adjacent I-40 with its gradual up and down terrain as it bullied its way through the tree-covered hills and filled-in valleys. After a day of gaining and then losing elevation over and over, I felt like I'd started from near sea level in California's Sacramento Valley and climbed to the top of 8300-foot Carson Pass. But unlike in California, here in Oklahoma I had no stunning geographical view to show for my effort. Despite all my climbing, I was roughly at the same elevation where I started fifty miles ago. The hills had beaten me up and my body felt it. I had been tempted many times to move onto the freeway but the feeling that I'd be cheating if I didn't stay on old Route 66, as well as the threat of getting a traffic ticket, kept me from switching.

Energized again after eating a hearty dinner, I gave thought to staying in the Motel 8 in El Reno, maybe in Room 17 where the bathtub scene in the movie *Rainman* was filmed. But Yukon was only twelve up-and-down miles away so I gathered my renewed energy and headed there to spend the night. It was a push but when I made it to Yukon, Country and Western singer Garth Brook's hometown, I was easily within two days of Owasso where I'd enjoy a much needed day of rest and the company of my brother, Chris.

My first call from my motel room was to my son, Ryan. He had found slide film and shipped it along with some other surprises to Chris. Next I called Donna. It was double the fun because our daughter, Darlene, was visiting and they were celebrating her nearing 30th birthday. I was sorry not to be home with them. After we hung-up, I walked to a nearby Sonic and ordered a vanilla ice-cream cone, joining in their celebration as I walked back to the motel alone.

Dear Ones, Dug began his 18th day at 6:30 a.m. Because Oklahoma has saved 90% of its share of the original road, he has been riding on the original alignment most of the day.

Wildlife and road-kill: Dug saw lots of wild turkeys, redwing blackbirds, and run over armadillos, turtles and one porcupine, all on minimally traveled Route 66.

About the swallows (Are you tired of this topic yet?), Dug said he went under an overpass and the swallows and their nests were thick on both the east and west sides.

Stay tuned for Day 19. Love, Donna.

One of my chores every evening was to find a restaurant for breakfast. It had to open by 6:00 a.m. and preferably not be out of my way. Last night the motel owner told me the Waffle House was open twenty-four hours and only one mile from Route 66. Hunger trumped distance as I rode there this morning, passing five deer that ignored me as they grazed on the greenbelt nearby. I also noticed that the wind was blowing from the east. After eating I would resume my down-up, love-hate affair with the hills, now complicated by an unwelcome headwind.

Twelve miles from Yukon I rolled into Oklahoma City, the capitol of Oklahoma. It was Sunday so I had the streets almost to myself in this city of half-a-million, the largest city in Oklahoma. I followed Route 66 through town and up to the impressive Capitol. Its original architectural drawings had allowed for adding a dome which was completed in 2002. On top of the dome was the statue of an American Indian holding a staff. As I circled the capitol it seemed as if he was slowly turning, watching me to ensure my safe passage.

I didn't have time to detour and see the Oklahoma City National Memorial that honored the 168 people who died on April 19, 1995 when the Murrrah Federal Building was bombed. So I added it to my list of places to see with Donna sometime in the future.

I-40, my concrete companion since Barstow, Arizona, left me in Oklahoma City and continued due east. From here to St. Louis, Route 66 and I would veer northeast, accompanied by I-44, the fourth of five freeways, replacing the Mother Road.

One hour later, the large sign at an EZ Stop gas station heralded the lowest price yet on Route 66 for a gallon of regular unleaded gas, $1.909. I felt a freedom being unchained from the necessity of having to fill a gas tank. I pedaled on into Edmond, the final resting place of Wiley Post. He had died with Will Rogers in a 1935 plane crash in Alaska. Among Wiley's many accomplishments were his discovery of the jet stream and being the first aviator to fly alone around the world. Edmond also made tragic headlines in 1986 when a postal employee killed fourteen co-workers here before taking his own life.

East of Edmond, the highway turned dangerous. Drivers not wanting to pay the toll on I-44, the Turner Turnpike from Edmond to Tulsa, were joining me on adjacent Route 66. The increased traffic, absence of a shoulder, narrow traffic lanes, and reduced visibility due to the hills all improved my chances of being hit. Most drivers were careful and considerate but some demonstrated their impatience and possessiveness by revving their engines or intentionally driving near me as they sped by. One lady in a black Mercedes blared her horn and with deliberate intent to force me off the road, swerved toward me as she passed. I watched as she pulled into a Sonic Drive-in up ahead.

As I neared her, my anger heightened my intention to confront her. But just before I reached her, I changed my mind, concluding that people with aggressive and violent tendencies weren't only to be found in postal facilities. Some were here on the road with me. Knowing how vulnerable I was on my bicycle, I didn't want to provoke this woman more than I seemed to be doing while minding my own business.

It was noon when I arrived in Arcadia. I'd ridden thirty-eight miles in five hours, the going slow and miserable, thanks to the hills and the headwind. I felt like I was back in western New Mexico, pleading and yelling my case about the injustice of the resistance. Particularly exasperating was the wind on the hills. It was invariably calm when I coasted downhill but when I started to climb the other side, the headwind always picked up, taunting me.

Arcadia is home to the Round Barn, built in 1898, recently restored, and now on the National Register of Historic Places. I decided to eat lunch first and if I had time afterward, I'd visit it.

I walked into the café named *Hillbillies* and seated myself at a table next to a window where I could keep an eye on my unlocked bike outside. As my eyes adjusted to the darkness inside, I saw that only three tables were occupied. Five minutes after sitting down, I still hadn't been brought water or a menu. I decided I was wasting time so I gathered my helmet, journal, and dark glasses and just as I got up to leave, the young waitress finally showed up. To save time, I decided to order something that I was reasonably sure was on the menu – a roast beef sandwich, soup and iced tea.

"I'm sorry, we ain't got no roast beef," she informed me, her voice perky and with a hint of pride in her knowledge of the menu. If her tardiness in arriving at my table the first time was any indication of what her future behavior would be, I decided against taking a chance on her returning promptly if I took the menu and studied it. So I moved to Plan B.

"Then can I have a ham and cheese sandwich with fries but no soup? And I'd like the sandwich on whole wheat."

The words, "whole wheat" were just leaving my lips when she told me, "We don't have no whole wheat. We only gots white!" Her tone of voice was such that I felt fully chastised for my foolishness, ordering something other than white bread in a restaurant named Hillbillies. I was out of Plans now so with resignation and subdued compliance I said, "Okay."

With my order grasped in her hand, my waitress skipped off to the kitchen. Every few minutes she would emerge, flitting like a hummingbird from table to table, talking loudly, giggling often, and then retreating to her kitchen sanctuary where she would sing loud and off-key, just a few lines of whatever tune was in her head, and there were many.

While I waited hopefully for my order and endured the "music", two couples came in and sat down at the table next to me. They had been riding motorcycles, the evidence their black leather pants and jackets. One woman took off her jacket and while doing so, I glimpsed the letters, "Calif" on the back. But I couldn't read the name of the city above it. I was getting ready to say "hello" and ask the woman if she was from California when all four people lit cigarettes. At that point my curiosity clashed with my aversion to tobacco smoke. Finding out her hometown just didn't seem all that important anymore.

When my lunch finally arrived, I peered into the plastic red basket and saw my sandwich perspiring grease. The French fries were equally drenched. Had I known the cook's effort was going to result in what was now in front of me, I could have saved us both a lot of time and effort by just ordering half a cup of lukewarm oil to sip at my leisure. When she made her next pass in my general vicinity, I asked my waitress for a handful of napkins, every one of which I used to sop up the fatty puddles and pat down the weeping fries.

To help take my mind off what was slithering its way to my stomach, I wrote in my journal. As I thought about the wind and rolling topography awaiting me outside, I remembered something my daughter and son-in-law had told me before I left on my trip. "Attitude is the difference between adventure and ordeal, Dad." This reminder and words of encouragement were what I needed.

Lunch had taken too much time so I decided the Round Barn would have to wait until another time. Beyond Arcadia I buckled down and whipped through the small towns of Luther, Wellston, Warwick and Chandler, the latter known as the Pecan Capital of the World. I entertained myself looking unsuccessfully for Oklahoma's state animal, the American Bison, and its state tree, the Eastern Redbud. My maps kept me headed in the correct direction and my snacks nourished. After Chandler came Davenport and by 6:00 p.m., I checked into the Sooner Motel in Stroud. I washed up and walked across the street to enjoy a chicken and olive pizza, a mound of undressed salad, and multiple glasses of sweetened iced tea.

Returning to the motel, I stopped at the office to talk with the owner. I mentioned I was headed to Tulsa where I planned to link up with my brother. He told me I was within fifty miles of my destination, my only complication being a 30% chance of rain tomorrow. I knew the restaurant across the street opened at 5:00 a.m. so I didn't have to ask him for a restaurant suggestion for breakfast.

One thing I did want to know was the meaning of the word "Sooner." Since this was the name of his motel, I figured I had come to a knowledgeable source. I had no idea what it meant, beyond its attachment to the students at the University of Oklahoma. "Originally, it was used to describe someone who staked a homesteading claim in the Oklahoma Territory before it was legal to do so," he said. "Today it refers to residents of Oklahoma."

Back in my room I felt like I was falling apart. Maybe it was a psychological letdown since I was nearing the comfort of being with my brother. The bike was complaining, the chain squeaking and the gears stiff when I shifted. Everything needed lubricating and I had been ignoring this daily maintenance despite the fact it was simple and not time consuming. My body was complaining too, the reason a pulled muscle in my right leg. When I walked, it didn't bother me, but on the bike the ache refused to go away. The hills, wind and dangerous highway were taking their toll and I was ready for a day of rest.

Outside my motel room I oiled the chain until the squeaks stopped and the gears shifted smoothly. Next I worked the Bio-freeze roll-on over my sore leg. It felt cold at first and then a few minutes later, warm. I set out my clothes for tomorrow, repacked my panniers, wrote in my journal and then took care of a little task that had been unplanned before I started my trip.

Within the first mile back in Santa Monica, I had seen money in the street. I ignored it the first few times until at a stop light in Beverly Hills I looked down and saw two pennies. With nothing to do until the light changed, I picked them up and put them into my handlebar bag. They were followed by other pennies, nickels, dimes and quarters. No bills…yet. Of the twenty days since starting, today was a bonanza. Leaving the Waffle House this morning I found two quarters lying in the gutter. In Oklahoma City, at intersections and the entrances of many roadside businesses, there was so much money on the ground that if I had tried to pick it all up I would never have made it to Stroud by nightfall.

Sitting in my motel room, I guessed I had found over $1.00 today. I counted it out and my guess was close – ninety-seven cents. It all went into the bulging plastic baggie in the handlebar bag where it joined the three cash donations to Habitat that had been given to me. My plan was to give it all to Stu, the Executive Director of Habitat in Yolo County, when I returned home. The look of surprise on his face would be worth the effort spent picking it all up.

After counting my loot and before taking my shower, I called Donna. She told me the TV had stopped working. Amateur electrician that I am, I suggested several solutions and hit on one. The TV was unplugged. Most of our conversation was spent with me sitting on my pity-pot. She listened without complaint, giving me the chance to dump my worries and struggles. Just being able to talk to her about how I was feeling seemed to lighten my load. I was thankful for her patience and empathy.

> *Good evening everyone. Dug is in Stroud, Oklahoma tonight. He's covered about 1500 miles now with around 800 more to go. He's a little discouraged tonight. He has decided that if God hadn't rested on that seventh day, he would have finished the job and smoothed out Oklahoma. In an attempt to maintain some perspective, he's thought about the early explorers. The hills of Oklahoma must have driven them crazy, along with not knowing where to find food and water.*
>
> *We are grateful for and very much appreciate your support, positive thoughts and prayers. Love, Donna.*

If there was one thing I could count on to disturb my rest at night, it was worrying that I would oversleep. As a hedge against this happening, every night I pulled the curtain open eight to ten inches before getting into bed. The next morning, the light at dawn would always awaken me. This night, groggy and not sure what was happening, I mistook the glare from street lights to be the nearing sunrise. I got up, dressed, put on my glasses and looked at my watch. It was only 2:56 a.m., way too early to get up. So I went back to bed, too lazy to get undressed. Three hours later, the noise from the increased traffic outside, as well as the real dawn visible through the parted curtains, did their job. I didn't need my watch to confirm it was time to get up.

I ate and was on the road by 7:00 a.m., blessed with no headwind and a thin overcast. Gradually Route 66 turned to the northeast and the breeze blew from the southwest. While the wind stayed consistent, I couldn't say the same for the highway. I had a wide shoulder to ride on the first ten miles from Stroud to Depew. But the next seven miles to Bristow were shoulderless, the traffic lanes narrow and the speed limit sixty-five, a perfect recipe for disaster.

In Bristow I saw a pay phone up ahead. The thought came that a surprise call to Donna would be fun. It was about 7:00 a.m. her time when she answered. "So why are you calling?" she asked with apprehension. Since starting my trip, I had only called her once in the morning and that was on her birthday. So I was certain her question was provoked by the thought that I had a problem.

"I was thinking about you a lot this morning. I'm excited about getting to Chris' place this afternoon and just wanted to tell you I love you and hope you have a good day." As she shared her support, concern and love for me, I could hear the worry in her voice slip away.

From Bristow to Sapulpa I had the gift of a wide shoulder, a joy to ride on. I came to two short early alignments of Route 66 and took the bumpy detours to ride on them. They wandered through forests thick with deciduous trees and low lying bushes. The pervasive quiet reminded me of hiking with Donna in the Redwoods in Northern California. I stopped, snacked and took advantage of the peacefulness, thankful for the privilege of having this adventure.

Somewhere on the outskirts of Kellyville, the next town, I passed The Cease Fire Full Gospel Church. The same denomination had one more church, this one on the outskirts of Tulsa. I wondered what the story was behind that name but didn't stop to find out. Oklahoma's worst train accident occurred in Kellyville in 1917. Twenty-three people were killed when two trains met head-on. Beyond Kellyville I crossed an old steel truss bridge. With its original brick surface still in place, it was different from all the other steel bridges I had been on. Not having any film to take a picture was frustrating.

It was lunchtime when I arrived in Sapulpa. This town was named for Chief Sapulpa, a Lower Creek American Indian who started a trading post in this area in 1850. Tulsa wasn't far away now so I lingered at lunch in the very busy downtown Route 66 Café. I sat at a corner table, ordered a salad and taco soup, the latter something I couldn't remember ever having eaten. I watched people come and go and enjoyed my soup, spicy and delicious, thick with hamburger, kidney beans, hominy and onions. Every spoonful contained ample capsicum that provoked my eyes to tear.

Leaving Sapulpa I rode by the Frankoma Pottery Plant. It was founded in 1933 by John Frank who moved his business to Sapulpa in 1938. Famous for its many clay creations, I planned to stop and purchase a pitcher, vase, or some type of dish that I would mail home to have as a visible memory of my trip after I got back. The hours posted on the door said it was open today, a Monday, but the store was closed.

Tulsa, a town of nearly 400,000, had its beginning as a Creek Indian community. At a later time, it was called The Oil Capitol of the World. My thoughts about Tulsa wandered to its being the hometown of Cyrus Avery, The Father of Route 66.

Cyrus was a member of the 1924 National Association of State Highway Officials. They pushed for a national highway system of numbered interstate routes. Credit is given to Cyrus for establishing the Chicago to Los Angeles route and designating it Route 66. He was responsible for over 400 miles of this highway running through Oklahoma and its two largest cities, Tulsa and Oklahoma City. It was no coincidence that it also went right in front of his gas station, tourist court and restaurant in Tulsa.

I hoped that the 5x8-inch handlebar cards I had prepared before I began my trip would guide me on Route 66 through Tulsa. I had spent months using multiple sources to make them as accurate as I could but they were still a work in progress, as evidenced by the many times

I had crossed out incorrect directions. Using the directions below that I'd typed on two route cards, I hoped to make it from Sapulpa through Tulsa without getting lost.

> *Thru Sapulpa on 66/Dewey to 66/Mission, lft*
> *66 1 mi to X144 on old Sapulpa Rd or Frankoma Rd*
> *Lft to Frankoma Pot*
> *Frankoma Rd becomes SW Blvd over Ark Riv to 12th St, rt*
> *12th becomes 11th after over expresswy*
> *11th becomes 10th at Boulder*
> *10th to Elgin, curve rt*
> *Bear lft at Warhse Mkt where 10th becomes 11th*
> *11th to 193rd Ave*

These directions, which covered about twenty-two miles, turned out to be accurate. The difficult part of following Route 66 through Tulsa was the roughness of the pavement and the fact that the streets made no accommodation for bicycles. I slammed into bumps, potholes, and cracked pavement in the traffic lane and gutter. Each collision tested the bike's frame, and also my patience. Up to now, I had been adamantly opposed to riding on sidewalks. I had a legal right to be in the street but as my frustration grew, I gave up on the street and got onto the sidewalk. But it was worse. There were no curb cuts at each intersection so I had to dismount at the abrupt drop-off at every street as well as deal with the uneven concrete caused by tree roots. I was just thankful the streets were not crowded with commuters going home.

Chris and I had arranged by pay phone to meet on the east side of Tulsa. Our plan was for me to find the last restaurant on 11th street and then wait there for him until he got off work. There were no restaurants past 129th Avenue so I stopped at a Taco Bueno. While I waited, my emotion welled. He had lived in Owasso, north of Tulsa, for twenty-three years and this was my first visit to see him. And I was on a bike of all things.

Our reunion an hour later was joyous. It was great to be with family again. When we arrived home his two cats, Lacey and Holly, graced me with their presence by jumping onto my lap and purring. It was good to just sit and feel the tension slip away as Chris and I talked. Before dinner, he gave me the things Ryan had sent: three rolls of slide film and three one-pound bags of nuts, raisins and M&Ms. With my snack supply now replenished, I had enough to keep me nourished on the road for several days. My son was looking out for his dad.

> *Hi everyone. Things went tons better for Dug today. A lovely sunny day with a tailwind and gentle hills. The road continued to be littered with dead armadillos, turtles and possums. After eight days of riding from Albuquerque, he is now in Tulsa for a day of rest with his brother Chris.*
>
> *Dug's friend, Art Mills, emailed this thought about Oklahoma hills: "I've read excerpts from the journals of folks in the 1800s who were traveling through those hills. They said it was incredibly easy to get lost from one another because if you wandered a few hundred yards away, you lost sight of your traveling companions."*
>
> *Another theory on swallow nesting has arrived from Dug's former boss, Mike Yount. According to him, "The swallows in Texas nest on the east side of bridges because they are a different variety called Swallamos." Dug is beginning to wish he had never brought this swallows subject up.*
>
> *Tomorrow we all get a respite. The next update will be in two days. As always, your love and support mean much to us. Blessings to you. Donna.*

26

Life or Death – A Matter of Inches

Force of habit woke me early the next morning. Chris and I had breakfast together and after he left for work, I did a wash, wrote postcards to family, Stu at Habitat, and Julie Rooney, the reporter who had written the *Davis Enterprise* piece about me. By 10:00 a.m. I could no longer ignore how tired I was. The last thing I remembered was Lacey and Holly cuddled up on the couch, purring beside me.

Following my morning nap I put a serious dent in the lunch stash that Chris had bought for me. While eating I reorganized and repacked my panniers, adding Ryan's packages of trail mix, M&Ms, and three rolls of slide film. The handlebar trip cards I would no longer need went into an envelope to be mailed home. I replaced them with the ones I'd need for tomorrow's miles and then lubed the chain, adjusted the brakes, tightened several loose nuts and lowered the seat a fraction. All this activity provoked another wave of lethargy. I thought I could ward it off by sitting down and thumbing through *Love Languages*, a book Chris had on his coffee table. But before I knew it I was asleep again, this nap lasting longer than the one I'd taken in the morning.

When I awoke, I had no idea where my energy had gone but knew it needed to show up soon. With at least 750 miles to go from Owasso to Chicago, it was way too soon to have a let-down. In an attempt to shake my lethargy, I took a walk around the neighborhood. When I got back, my ambition was still in the gutter. During my walk the wind had blown a gale from the west, forcing every flag I saw to blow without slackening. I could only hope that by morning it wouldn't change direction and become a headwind.

Shortly after Chris came home from work, his daughter Melissa, son-in-law Matt and their son Dillon, along with several neighbors, came over for dinner. I tried to hide my malaise and be sociable. From time to time the conversation would turn to my adventure and when it did I felt the excitement coming back.

After everyone left, Chris and I talked, covering a myriad of subjects. One thing he wanted to know was if I talked with any truckers. I told him about the one in the Ludlow restaurant but most of my communication with truckers was non-verbal, when they honked "hello" or I waved to thank them for pulling over to pass. Chris' purpose in bringing this up was to suggest they were looking out for me, talking on their CBs to alert each other of my presence, something I hadn't thought about.

Before I went to bed I asked Chris to do two things. Even though I wasn't out of Oklahoma yet, I wanted him to put the Oklahoma Route 66 decal on the crossbar of my bike. And then he signed my journal, writing, "Thanks for including me in your trip. I know you can make it. Many people along the way, including me, are praying for you. Love, Chris. Your young 56-year-old brother."

My final activity for the day was to call Donna. All was well at home. She told me about several e-mails she received today. My former co-workers in the Special Education program in the Sacramento City Unified School District wrote to say they had contributed to Habitat as had our daughter's mother-in-law. As I thought of the many people contributing to Habitat and sending me e-mails through Donna, I felt my enthusiasm returning.

When I planned this adventure, I broke it up into three roughly comparable distances: Santa Monica to Albuquerque, Albuquerque to Owasso and Owasso to Chicago. In between each break I would stop to rest where one of my two brothers, or my son and his wife, lived on Route 66. These breaks were proving to be very crucial and before heading to bed I thanked Chris for giving me the time to recharge my physical, mental and emotional batteries.

The next morning Chris and I were up by 6:00 a.m. After breakfast, his neighbor came over to help load my bike into Chris' truck. Half an hour later we hugged and said goodbye at 11th Street and 129th Avenue in Tulsa. I was cycling by 7:30, heading northeast, feeling invigorated by the calm, cloudless morning.

Nine miles from Tulsa is Catoosa, a name with Cherokee roots. Most references say it means "on the hill," which refers to Catoosa Hill west of town. Four hundred forty-five miles from Catoosa is the Gulf of Mexico, linked by the Arkansas and Mississippi Rivers, thus making Catoosa the United States' farthest inland seaport.

Before leaving Catoosa I found the post office, mailed my post cards and the completed handlebar direction cards along with several souvenirs I'd collected. Since I was the only customer in the post office, the postal clerk took advantage of her temporary down time and asked me lots of questions about my trip. After our short but enjoyable visit, she told me, "You have a safe journey. There's lots of crazy people out there." Yet another stranger was expressing their concern and wishing me well.

Just north of Catoosa I looked for the Blue Whale, a long-time Route 66 attraction. Afraid I'd missed it, I walked the bike up to a fence and waved at the man using a riding mower to cut the grass in his huge yard. He rode over to the fence, turned off the motor, and I apologized for interrupting his work. "It's no bother," he said. "What can I do for you?"

"I'm looking for the Blue Whale." The immediate grin that creased his face told me he would have no problem giving me the answer I wanted. He pointed the direction I was headed and said, "Over there, by that flag, is what you're looking for." About two hundred yards beyond where we stood, I saw, partially hidden behind some trees, the object of my search. Before I could say "thank you," he asked, "Where ya' from?"

"California."

"Well I'll be damned."

"I must have taken a wrong turn in Los Angeles," I joshed.

"I'll say you did. So this is how you spend your vacation?" he asked.

"I'm retired so every day is like a vacation anymore."

"Well, I hope you have a nice trip," he concluded.

I thanked him and as I rode away I realized he was the first person I'd talked to who hadn't asked me where I was headed.

Like every other roadside attraction on America's Main Street, the

Blue Whale has a story. Before it became a famous swimming hole, it was a place where people came to see the small zoo, including the alligators. Its owner, Hugh Davis, knowing his wife collected ceramic whales, decided in the early 1970s to build a giant whale. With the help of his friend, Harold Thomas, they constructed the whale, using wood, pipe and concrete, painted it blue, and planted it in the now alligator-less pond. Hugh gave the whale to his wife Zelta as a wedding anniversary present. The whale, with its smiling mouth wide open, reposed in what became a popular swimming and picnicking attraction. Children would jump into the pond from the whale's jaw or use the slide protruding over the water from the back of its throat. Some would enter the open mouth, run through the eighty-foot long whale and up the path to the top of its tail from where they would jump or dive into the eight-foot deep water.

Time for a picnic.

In 1988, Davis closed the Blue Whale. He died two years later and until recently visitors were warned by signs on the fence to stay away from this Route 66 attraction. As I stood at the fence, it was obvious that the repair and restoration efforts of Catoosa's citizens and the employees of Hampton/Hilton Hotels Corporation had been successful. The early morning sun glinted off the whale's light blue paint as it seemingly floated on top of the water. Its smiling mouth was edged with red paint and its huge red eye with a black pupil looked at me with joy and happiness. No swimming is allowed but picnicking must be since the grounds were mowed and new picnic tables were visible inside the fence.

From Catoosa I pedaled on, reveling in history. The next town of Claremore was named for an Osage American Indian chief. Claremore is rightly proud to be the hometown of Will Rogers and that pride extends to Route 66 which, among many names, is called The Will Rogers Highway. Other tributes to Will Rogers include Will Rogers Blvd., Rogers State University, Will Rogers Hotel and the Will Rogers Memorial and Museum.

Two other famous people hail from Claremore. Lynn Riggs wrote *Green Grow the Lilacs*, a book that became the musical *Oklahoma*. Clara Fowler, at the age of 18, was the featured singer on a fifteen minute radio program sponsored by Page Milk Co. Her success led to her new name, Patti Page, The Singing Rage. Several of her songs became hits in my youth: *The Tennessee Waltz,* and *Mockin' Bird Hill* in 1951, and "*How Much is that Doggie in the Window?*" in 1953.

Before leaving Claremore I found a gas station pay phone and called Darlene. Thirty years ago today, May 18th, I was in the delivery room when she was born. She has grown to be a confident, beautiful and talented woman. I wished her happy birthday, thankful we could be connected over the miles by phone.

Riding out of Claremore, I saw a bank up ahead. I was low on cash so I decided to cash a traveler's check, a process that had been as simple as sneezing…until now. Inside the bank I was greeted by three tellers. I went to the one in the middle. "Yes, I can cash a $50.00 traveler's check," she said, "but I need to have it approved by the branch manager first."

I waited at her window and watched her disappear to my right. Five minutes later I was still waiting. During this time the other two tellers talked with me. They had no customers and their interest in my adventure had been aroused by my bike helmet, gloves and riding shorts, all seldom worn in this area.

As we chatted, my frustration grew in tandem with my wait. I told them I needed to be moving on and that I was wasting precious time. They sympathized with me and then the teller to my right said, in a whisper, "We have a new manager and she won't let us complete a transaction like yours without her approval."

Not sure what to do next, I turned around and saw my teller leaving one office and entering another, my traveler's check in her hand. I turned around and told one of the tellers, "Maybe I should just ask for my check back."

"Well, we certainly wouldn't blame you," said the teller on my left. "It's hard for us to do our jobs under these conditions," unloading her complaint.

About the time I decided to track down my teller, she reappeared at my window. She apologized for the delay, and explained, "I need you to print your name on the 'Pay to the Order of' line, endorse the check on the back, and then show me your identification."

Fifteen minutes after entering the bank, I left with fifty dollars in cash. Since that experience with the little Oklahoma bank, I have had trouble cashing traveler's checks in other banks but never in businesses. The reason (forgery) given to me by bank personnel always seems to border on not wanting to be bothered unless, of course, one is a customer of that bank.

An hour beyond Claremore was Foyil, home of native son, Andy Payne, and the marker commemorating his achievement. Part Cherokee and a runner in high school, he had participated in what became known as The Bunion Derby, a footrace in 1928 from Los Angeles to Chicago and then on to New York. This race was intended, in part, to bring attention to two-year-old Route 66. Andy ended up winning the eighty-four day race in 573 hours, 4 minutes and 34 seconds. For his effort he received $25,000. He later served in the U.S. Army, earned a law degree and was the Clerk of the Oklahoma State Supreme Court for thirty-six years.

Now three weeks into my journey, I was at peace with my progress and thankful I hadn't had any accidents, especially falling off my bike. I feared falling, having once done so on a training ride. While riding through a creek that flowed over a mountain road, the front wheel had slipped on some moss, dumping me, left side first, into the water. Except for being cold and soaking wet, my only injury was to my dignity. On another training ride I wasn't watching where I was going, rode off the shoulder and crashed down an embankment, bloodying my knees and hands. Never, however, had I fallen while riding my fully loaded bike. Now that was about to change.

Vinita, the next town, was my destination for lunch. I'd gotten used to Oklahoma highways where the grass grew right up to the narrow white line that marked the right edge of the pavement. It was commonplace to see highway department tractor-mowers keeping the grass short on both sides of the highway. Nature had landscaped the highways but having only a white line for a shoulder to ride on left precious little space between me and passing vehicles.

When cars coming from both directions showed every intent of meeting alongside me, my routine was to ride off the highway into the grass and maintain my forward momentum. When the immediate danger from a passing car subsided, I would continue pedaling through the grass and then back onto the highway.

Nearing Vinita, the peacefulness of the windless morning was interrupted by a car coming toward me and two others approaching from behind. At our respective rates of speed, I judged we would all meet just a short distance up ahead. I wanted to make room for these three cars to pass me safely so just before they got to me, I rode off the highway into the unmown grass. What I couldn't see under the grass were shallow ruts. When my front wheel hit the first rut, the one closest to the highway, it immediately twisted abruptly to the right, jerking the bike out from under me and throwing me toward the highway. I instinctively closed my eyes as I fell, my left shoulder and hand slamming into the ground. When I opened my eyes, I saw the right rear wheel of one of the cars behind me pass mere inches away. Everything happened so fast, I had no time to be scared.

Lying sprawled in the grass, I watched the two cars disappear up ahead, both with no intention of stopping. As I got up, my left wrist felt like I had sprained it in breaking my collision with the ground. My left knee hurt a little but everything else felt okay. When I stood the bike up, I saw that the chain had come off the pedal sprocket but other than that, the bike was undamaged. I was surprised that my side-view mirror, attached to and protruding from the left side of my dark glasses, hadn't jammed into the ground and shattered and that the panniers and other gear were still firmly attached to the bike.

As I stood leaning on the bike, a car sped past me and I could see how, if I'd been a few inches closer to the highway when I fell, I would have been hit. It was then I started shivering. It took several minutes to pull myself together and by the time I did, I knew I had learned a lesson. From now on, when it was necessary to go onto any shoulder I would reduce my speed, stop, and then push my bike off the road. When the danger passed I'd return to the highway and remount. This would be time consuming but would improve my chances of not falling as well as not getting run over.

I finally arrived in Vinita around 1:00 p.m. I was famished. In a small café I ordered a bowl of spicy tortilla bean soup and a salad. The salad was a mound of lettuce topped with two small tomato slices. I ate everything including the full basket of Saltine crackers.

Vinita is the second oldest town in Oklahoma. Founded as Downingville in 1871, the name was later changed to Vinita, in honor of the sculptress Vinnie Ream. It was she who created the life-sized statue of Abraham Lincoln seen in our nation's capital. When she died she was honored with burial in Arlington National Cemetery.

Beyond Vinita I took advantage of the nice weather and rode steadily on. Between the towns of Afton and Miami I passed up an opportunity to ride on the Sidewalk Highway, an early alignment of old Route 66 that was only nine feet wide. It had been built this narrow due to a shortage of funds. When two cars met on this stretch of old highway, both had to steer their right side wheels onto the shoulder to keep from crashing into each other.

In this area I had to cross a narrow, shoulder-less, two-lane-bridge. When confronted with this situation on previous bridges, knowing many people had little patience for bicycles impeding their progress, I always waited to cross until there were no vehicles following me. Since no traffic was coming from either direction on this bridge, I started across. But while on the bridge, a semi suddenly appeared, coming up from behind. I had nowhere to go to get out of the way so I kept moving. The driver slowed to the 10 mph I was going and didn't pass me until I was off the bridge. I thanked him with an appreciative wave.

Miami, pronounced "my-am-ah," has its share of history. T-ball, baseball for the youngest players, started here. Jim Thorpe, the great American Indian athlete, was from Miami. I rode through town on Steve Owens Blvd. He too grew up in Miami and went on to the University of Oklahoma where he played football and won the Heisman Trophy in 1969.

Mickey Mantle Blvd. led me into the next town, Mickey's home town of Commerce. I stopped for dinner at the "Lil Café." They had no soup and I had no desire for any of the fried food on the menu. For the second time today I ordered a salad, this one filled with ham chunks and unlike my lunch salad, an abundance of tomato slices.

Five miles beyond Commerce I said goodbye to the 394 miles of Route 66 in Oklahoma. I had crossed the state without once having to ride on a freeway. The number of miles in this state had barely surpassed the 388 in New Mexico and the 374 in Arizona. And now I was entering the state with the least Route 66 miles.

Kansas Route 66: Blink and You'll Miss It

Route 66 almost misses Kansas as it cuts a fourteen-mile rectangular path out of the southeast corner. When I crossed the border into the Sunflower State, I was greeted by yet another beautiful sign, this one filled with a huge sunflower and the words, *Welcome to Kansas*.

Not far beyond the border I stopped at a grocery store in Baxter Springs. I was considering biking ten more miles to Galena and getting a motel there. In response to my question about nearby motels, a store clerk changed my mind when he told me, "Construction workers have taken all the rooms in the only Galena motel. If I was you, I'd get a room here at the Baxter Inn 4 Less."

A short time later I parted with $42.80, the most I'd spent to date for a motel room. Feeling momentarily deceived by its name, I wondered which motel it was "less than" as I walked across the street for a Big Mac, fries, diet soda and vanilla cone.

As I ate and checked my computer, my progress for the day took my mind off the cost of my room. Not only had I ridden 104 miles from Tulsa but I had averaged twelve mph, the third highest average daily speed since starting in California. Today felt similar to the day I left Albuquerque. In both cases a day of rest had restored my energy and I'd zipped right along.

> *Hi Everyone! Dug's in Baxter Springs, Kansas tonight, just over the border from Oklahoma. The weather was good – scattered clouds, slight humidity, 80s, and a southeast wind which was behind him most of the way. And most of the road was wide with a good shoulder. He did have a crash today but he's alright.*

The e-mails about swallow nesting habits refuse to end. Dug's niece-in-law, Kim, has submitted a theory about swallow nesting behavior. "In these politically charged times it may not be a matter of West or East side but a matter of Right or Left. In Texas, the birds on the West side might be interpreted as Right, Texas swallows being more conservative. The East side swallows would be, of course, Left. We need to know where swallows in Massachusetts nest before we can draw any confident conclusions."

With that I'll say "good-night." Many thanks to you all for keeping up with these updates. Love, Donna.

After a restful night's sleep, I headed to breakfast in downtown Baxter Springs at Murphey's Restaurant. The sky was filled with patchy clouds, the air already warm with a hint of humidity. The restaurant used to be The Baxter National Bank and speculation still exists on whether or not the bank was robbed by Jesse James and Cole Younger in 1876. The old checks under the table glass were fun to read as I waited for my order. One check written to the bank had no date but the amount was obvious – $1.00. Another check dated May 28, 1902 had the word "dollars" crossed out. It had been written to a B.A. Smith for sixty cents.

I was savoring my eggs, hash browns and toast, when a customer walked in. He paused at a wall rack where his and others coffee mugs hung from wooden pegs. He found his, took it with him to a counter stool and sat down. I'd never been in a diner where they kept your coffee cup clean and ready to be used every time you dropped in for your favorite cup of "Joe."

Following breakfast my friendly, prompt waitress, a wisp of a woman with a hacking cough, gave me my bill. We chatted about my trip and she asked a question no one had asked until now. "Are you riding your bike back to California or flying?"

"Neither," I said. "I'm not fond of flying and have no desire to pedal back to California bucking the prevailing headwinds. I'm looking forward to my wife flying out to meet me and after we spend a few days with our son and daughter-in-law in Springfield we plan to let the California Zephyr take us back to Davis from Chicago."

Before she left my table she concluded our conversation by lightly tapping me repeatedly on the shoulder with her right index finger, and telling me, "Have a safe trip, you hear?"

Route 66 out of Baxter Springs was North Willow Avenue. I followed the signs with a yellow sunflower and the black number 66 in the middle and within four miles came to the one-lane, 130-foot-long, Marsh Arch Bridge. It was built in 1923 and has been on the National Register of Historic Places since 1983.

Designed by James Marsh, it is the only remaining Marsh Arch Bridge on Route 66. It is also one of the few remaining steel-reinforced concrete truss bridges, also called a through-arch bridge. It was scheduled for demolition in the 1990s but in 1994, a joint project of Cherokee County and the Kansas Historic Route 66 Association saved the bridge. Since then, rehabilitation grants from the National Park Service Route 66 Corridor Preservation Program have helped with needed maintenance.

Before riding over the bridge, I walked around admiring it. Its brilliant white paint gleaming in the early morning sunlight, added to its contrast with the blue sky and fully leaved trees. Both sides of the bridge were supported by a graceful seventy-foot-long white concrete arch. Extending from the bridge surface to the top of each arch were eleven vertical concrete supports varying from short at the ends of the bridge to longest in the middle. The gracefulness of both arches and their supports spoke of a time when simplicity and function joined to serve the designer, builder, and motorist well. Riding over the bridge in the early morning quiet, I enjoyed another simple experience that added to the fulfillment of my dreams about this adventure.

Kansas bridge saved.

28

Mizuree or Mizurah?

Had I been asked the derivation of the word Kansas, I would never have guessed it came from a Sioux Indian word meaning "the people of the south wind." The same was true for Missouri, its name meaning "the town of the large canoes." Wind and water were important, not just to a bicyclist like me but so much more to the American Indians that settled here.

As in previous states, I looked for another colorful state sign but on this secondary road there was none to welcome me to the Show Me State. Beyond where I guessed the unmarked border to be, I stopped to snack and affix the Kansas Route 66 sticker to the crossbar of my bike. I had crossed six states and had two to go.

The first town I came to in Missouri was Joplin, population around 50,000. Rev. Harris Joplin founded the first Methodist church in this area in the mid-1800s and it was from him the town got its name. Bobby Troop included the names of twelve cities in his song, *Get Your Kicks on Route 66*, Joplin being the third after Chicago and St. Louis. Writer, poet and playwright Langston Hughes (1902-1967) and actor Dennis Weaver are from Joplin and Harry Truman, our 33rd President, was born in Lamar, a short distance north of here.

Webb City, a smaller town of 10,000, was six miles beyond Joplin. I followed the multiple rights and lefts on my handlebar cards until I came to a blocked street. I changed direction and wandered around lost. Up ahead I saw a woman flip her cigarette butt into a nearby puddle. Figuring she was a native Webb Cityite and could help me, I headed toward her. Just as she reached for the door handle I hollered,

"Excuse me. I'm lost."

She turned around, took one look at me, put her hands on her hips and said, "Well that's just great! I'm a dumb blond and you're lost. Now we're both in trouble."

When I finally stopped laughing, I told her, "Well, I'm sorry but that's one prejudice I don't have."

A smile wrinkled her heavy makeup as she asked, "Okay, whatcha lookin for?"

"Broadway."

"That's easy. It's the next street over. You just continue on this street you're on and in another block it'll merge with Broadway."

"I really appreciate your help," I told her.

"You have a safe trip and be careful."

Carterville, population around 2,000, was next. It would be the third and last town I'd go through that shared the surname of a past or current president. And yet none of these cities had been named for any of them – Carter, Bush, or Clinton. I passed a used car lot with a For Sale sign in the front window of a 1960s-vintage Greyhound bus. Four of the nine windows on one side had been covered over in the process of converting it into a motor home. Visible in the destination window above the front windshield were the words "Lost in Time." Seeing this old bus brought back memories of riding in one like it from Santa Fe to Philadelphia in 1962, on the way to my Army assignment in Hanau, Germany. If given a choice now between riding a bus for thirty-eight hours or my bike for thirty days, I'd take the bike without hesitating.

Half-an-hour later I came to the 66 Drive-in Theatre on the outskirts of Carthage. Opened in 1946, it had closed sometime later, was turned into a salvage yard, and then reopened as a theatre in 1998. It was the second outdoor theatre I'd seen named for the fabled highway.

The expanse of grass at the entrance was being mowed by a woman riding on a blue tractor-mower. I wanted a picture of the marquee and decided including the woman and her mower would add interest to the shot. Gradually she mowed toward the marquee where I was waiting. When she saw me focusing my camera, she stopped. I smiled and motioned for her to continue moving but she refused. When I repositioned myself to include her, she backed her mower until she thought she was hidden behind a low hedge. I snapped the picture

Drive-in theaters still exist.

before she realized she wasn't. As I left I waved but she didn't reciprocate.

Highway 96, a narrow dangerous road without a shoulder, doubled as Route 66 east of Carthage. The towns ahead for the next forty miles had dwindled in population, suffering the same negative economic impact as so many other towns that had been bypassed by the freeway.

After Carthage came Avilla, population 137. The next two towns, Plew and Rescue, were so small they weren't on the Missouri state map but they were shown on my official Kansas-Missouri Route 66 map. I passed a mailbox and the street name on it caught my eye – Old 66. I'd seen this back in California where people along this historic road proudly included it in their address. The welded structure that held the mailbox also supported the silhouettes of three iron owls painted blue. On the largest owl the owner had stenciled his surname.

In the vicinity of Phelps, a town that was on my Missouri map but with no listed population, I stopped at a gas station-deli and bought a stale, mass-produced ham sandwich, and a carton of milk. In the absence of any restaurants, this would have to do for lunch. In the shade of a nearby tree, I leaned against the gnarled trunk and thought about all the inoperable equipment I'd seen in the yards of so many homes this morning. Junked cars, large appliances, tractors,

RV's, boats, scrap metal and lumber often made it difficult to see the house where the homeowner lived. I decided that having your own accumulation of junk was the way resourceful and self-sufficient people could be assured of having the parts to repair things when they broke down.

Beyond Phelps the wide spots in the road were all unincorporated and went by the names of Albatross, Heatonville, and Spencer. Leaving Spencer I took a planned detour onto an older Route 66 alignment and crossed Johnson Creek on a 100-foot steel, thru-truss-bridge built in 1926. I was sweating profusely, the heat taking a toll on my stamina. The creek and its shaded bank looked inviting so I decided to treat myself to an unplanned break. I leaned the bike against the bridge railing and eased my way down the steep embankment, surprised at how unsteady I was. At the creek I took off my shoes and socks and immersed my legs to mid-calf in the cool water. It felt good to spread my toes and let the water course between them. I peeled off my sweat-soaked shirt and using the bandana I carried, I washed the grime off my upper body and legs. To increase the amount of water I could distribute over my body, I cupped my hands in the creek and then tossed each hand-held pool of water over my head, refreshing me as it trickled down my chest and back.

I was considering how to get comfortable enough to take a nap when I noticed fingerling fish in the pool to my left. Every so often one would part the surface to gulp an insect that was floating by unaware of the danger beneath it. To my right I saw more fish, these a little bigger. They were content to idle gracefully in the slow current, some nibbling on my toes while others wasted no energy waiting underwater for the food to come to them.

Sitting by the creek, my mind wandered to an observation made by author Robert Pirsig in his book, *Zen and the Art of Motorcycle Maintenance*. He had made the comparison between traveling in a car or on a motorcycle, comments that seemed applicable to me on a bicycle. What Pirsig found important when traveling was being in the scene, something he couldn't do as a passive observer in an air conditioned car where everything raced past framed by a closed window. Even though he hadn't said so, I wondered if Pirsig ever elevated bicycling, or even hiking, to that of motorcycling, all three means of travel providing

Creeks are so refreshing!

their own special opportunities to be part of the scene.

Leaving the tranquil creek, the road climbed a hill and led me east through Paris Springs on roads variously numbered Route 66, Highway 96 and 266. I stopped somewhere along the way at another gas station-deli, bought a bottle of tomato juice and poured it into a Styrofoam cup I'd filled with ice. Before I left I refilled the cup with ice and water and took it with me. My right hand, while performing the duties of braking and steering, also held the cup. I had done this several times on my trip and as a consequence, I was getting better at not spilling the cup's contents while avoiding objects on the road. Drinking the water and sucking on the ice both helped to hydrate me and also made the heat and humidity more tolerable.

It was late afternoon when I rode into Springfield, Missouri, The Queen City of the Ozarks and the generally accepted birthplace of Route 66. It started innocently enough in 1923 when Cyrus Avery, a Tulsa businessman, was appointed to the Oklahoma State Highway Commission. Two years later the Secretary of Agriculture appointed him to the Joint Board of Interstate Highways, its responsibility being to designate and mark the new federal highways.

Congress wanted a highway from Virginia Beach, Virginia to Los

Angeles. The initial proposal was for this road to stay north while continuing west from Springfield, Missouri, not turning south to California until Utah. But this northern route didn't meet with Avery's approval. He knew this highway would bring business to his home state so he argued, successfully, that the Rockies be avoided and a southern path taken from Springfield through Oklahoma before continuing west through Texas, New Mexico and Arizona.

Giving numbers to the highways came next. Congress wanted all north-south highways to be given odd numbers and if they went east-west, they should have even numbers, a practice followed to this day. There was disagreement over the numbers for several highways, including the one from Chicago to Los Angeles. Avery wanted the number 60 for his Chicago-Los Angeles route but Kentucky, also wanting that number, told Avery to take 62. For whatever reason, Avery disliked 62 but when he found out 66 was available, he accepted it. The rest is history, as they say.

Red's Giant Hamburg, believed to be the first hamburger stand with a drive-up window, opened in Springfield in 1943. "Red," whose full name was Sheldon Cheney, painted the name of his business onto a cross-shaped sign. The word "Giant" was on the horizontal arm and the word "Hamburg" on the vertical. Because Red measured wrong, he didn't have room for the "er" in hamburger. When he retired in the mid-1980s, the sign still had no "er." In 1997 his hamburg stand was torn down and another colorful Route 66 business disappeared into oblivion.

It wasn't long before I came to the five-story Abou Ben Adhem Shrine Mosque. Built twenty years before Red's, it is now on the National Register of Historic Places. The dark red bricks used in its construction didn't distinguish the outside of "The Shrine" as anything out of the ordinary. However, several other architectural features raised it from the mundane, starting with the two terracotta turrets that overlooked the entrance from the front corners of the roof. The area on both sides of the front doors was painted in eye-catching orange, yellow and soft gold. These colors extended upward for four floors and also appeared above and below all the windows on the front. The final distinguishing touch was the thirty-foot white canopy that covered the walkway up the steps from the sidewalk to the front entrance.

Beyond the mosque I rode to the east side of Springfield and checked into a motel. After washing I followed the recommendation of the motel clerk and headed to the nearby Western Sizzlin restaurant. Within a minute my waitress, Cathy, was at my table. While she filled my glass with sweetened iced tea and took my order, a chicken sandwich with a baked potato, her long brown braid swung slowly from side to side. Several minutes later she returned to refill my tea. "I'm really thirsty," I told her. "Could I just have a carafe of iced tea?"

"Of course," she said. By the time I finished eating, I had drunk all the tea in the carafe.

Cathy wanted to talk about Route 66 and I welcomed the conversation. On one of her many trips to my table, she stopped and told me, "I know all about Route 66 in Arizona, New Mexico and California. When I was young my dad would say, 'We're movin to California.' So off we'd go down Highway 66. Twelve months later, he'd say, 'We're movin back to Missouri.' So we'd pack up and come back. We did that several times. Yes, I know about Flagstaff, Kingman, and all those other towns," she said. Even though she spoke fondly of the old highway, I had no doubt she was glad her transient days were over.

Listening to Cathy talk, I paid particular attention to the way she pronounced Missouri. Before I left on my trip, I knew most people pronounced it one of two ways – Mizurah or Mizuree. I had asked Sheila, a woman I knew in Davis who had moved from Missouri thirty years ago, "What's the correct way to pronounce Missouri?"

She smiled, paused a moment and then told me, "People who have lived in Missouri for a long time, as well as most people living in rural areas, usually say Mizurah. The way they pronounce it has been handed down for generations, like a precious tradition. People in urban areas, from out-of-state, or in towns with a university, usually say Mizuree. I've been gone from there so long that I always say Mizuree."

My waitress, maybe because she had once lived in California or because she now lived in the Springfield urban area, pronounced her state, Mizuree.

I strolled back to the motel after dinner and stopped in the office. I wanted something I'd never had – a wake-up call. Asking any motel owner to go to the trouble of waking me in the morning was an imposition I had never wanted to make, until now. Since I was so tired, I was afraid I'd oversleep, even with the curtain partially open. I asked the clerk to wake me at 6:00 a.m. and then watched as he pushed a series of buttons. Curious, I asked, "What's that you're doing?"

"Your call in the morning is a recording that will come automatically. I'm just setting that up for you," he explained.

At that moment my longtime belief that I would be inconveniencing motel staff if I requested a wake-up call any time before sun-up came to a silent and embarrassing end.

Back in my room, I called Donna. As we talked, my eyes teared as I told her, "If everything goes okay, in one more week you'll fly to Illinois and we'll be together again. I can hardly wait."

> *Dug made it to Springfield, Missouri – 99 miles today. Terrain: more rolling hills – maybe pitching hills is a better description.*
>
> *Update on gas prices: The new low was at a Coastal Gas in Springfield. It was $1.819 for a gallon of unleaded regular. Dug wonders why it's called "Coastal" in Missouri. That cheap gas should be in California where the ocean would give real meaning to the word.*
>
> *Here is a summary of how Dug is doing physically:*
>
> *1) The inflamed redness in his left eye only startles people if they get real close.*
>
> *2) His right knee (the one with the two kneecaps) has a distinctive click but only when he's pedaling, something he did for 8 hours and 40 minutes today.*
>
> *3) The pulled muscle in his right calf seems to have eased off for the time being.*
>
> *4) The rawness of his buttocks has turned into two giant calluses, thanks to copious applications of A&D diaper rash ointment from a thirty-year-old tube left over from his children's babyhood.*
>
> *5) The swelling of his lips has gone down and the cracks seem to be healing.*

6) True to the theory of evolution, his legs, because of constant use, have become two tired pistons while his brain, as a result of limited use, seems to have shrunk to virtually nothing.

7) His left wrist is still sprained from yesterday's crash but of more concern the numbness in the base of the palm of his left hand – a pressure point.

Other than these minor maladies, Dug feels great!

He thanks friends Dick and Margie Shunk for the "Route 66, Main Street of America" plaque they sent in recognition of his enthusiasm, endurance and optimism.

The swallow theories refuse to die. From Art Mills: there are no moderate/middle-of-the-road swallows. If they're in the middle of the road, they're dead.

I think it's time to call it a night. Many blessings to you all. Love, Donna.

Before falling asleep, I washed my riding gloves. They were grimy, soaked with sweat and smelled like moldy oranges. I draped them over the heater and turned the fan to low so they would be dry by morning.

Washing clothes was not an everyday part of my routine but calling home, keeping my journal up to date, repacking my panniers, stashing the coins I'd found, lubricating the bike, taking a shower and taking care of my butt were. The friction between my sweaty shorts and my bottom was always at work trying to turn my rear from a rash to an open wound instead of a callous. So every night, just before falling into bed, I would smear A&D ointment on my tush. If it felt sore to the touch, by morning that sensitivity was always gone.

With my evening chores completed, I tried to fall asleep but the noise made by the heater fan kept me restless and I was too lazy to turn it off until I got up at 5:45. Fifteen minutes later, dressed and ready to go, I left the key on the TV and flipped the lights off. As I closed the locked door, headed to the Waffle House for breakfast, I heard the faint ringing of my room phone. I'd have to listen to my first wake-up call at another motel.

29

Frozen Custard Ahead

Leaving Springfield, Route 66 paralleled I-44, taking me into a light breeze blowing head-on out of the northeast. I had hoped to leave the rolling hills behind when I got to Oklahoma but they continued into Missouri. There was, after all, no reason why crossing an arbitrary line should bring about a change in geography, especially if that change was just to make my going easier.

As the morning unfolded, I rode through Strafford, Northview, Marshfield, Niangua Junction, Conway, and Phillipsburg. Their populations varied from 5,800 in Marshfield, to 1900 in Strafford, and 650 or less in the other four. Along the way, men on tractor mowers kept me company, waving as they cut the grass in their expansive yards. Due to abundant precipitation, the grass grew lush making it next to impossible to use a simple walk-behind power mower to keep the grass cut to a manageable length. Their work looked rewarding, evidence of their progress immediately visible behind them. To fit in as one of the guys, if I ever moved to Missouri one of my first purchases would have to be a tractor mower.

If competition for my attention this morning had been limited to men cutting grass, the morning would have passed without drama. What I had been trying to ignore were the abundance of dead turtles cluttering the roadway, having lost their lives under the wheels of passing cars. Their efforts were filled with futility unbeknown to them as they embarked on their slow motion trek from one side of the road to the other. When I came to the next live turtle in the traffic lane, I stopped, determined to improve its odds of reaching its destination.

This turtle was about six inches long and showed no fear when I picked it up. With its head fully extended, it seemed to enjoy the elevated view as we safely crossed the highway. Further on I repeated this routine three more times, telling each turtle to be careful as I nestled it down in the roadside grass. It was the same admonition that many people had given me.

I would have also tried to play hero with the armadillos, called 'dillos' for short, but I had yet to see one alive. Starting in Texas and continuing through Oklahoma, Kansas and now Missouri, nearly 700 miles, Route 66 was littered with their bodies, both long dead and freshly killed. I'd read somewhere that the armadillo population in the United States is estimated to be between 30 and 50 million, a statistic that, for the time being, places them far from extinction-by-car.

The back of an armadillo is covered by a bony shell that makes it look like an over-inflated football. Hitting one with a car must involve a violent thump, much worse than that heard and felt after hitting a rabbit, cat or small dog. Most of the ones I saw had died where they were hit. They must have died a slow, agonizing death that became acceptance when the pain was too overwhelming, a death they didn't deserve.

By lunchtime I arrived in Lebanon, its population nearing 13,000. The sixty miles from Springfield had taken me all morning but I'd made good time. I was hungry, as usual, so I stopped at a diner named Fay's and ordered a roast beef sandwich. While waiting for my lunch I perused the information I had about Wyota, the name of the American Indians who once lived here. At some time in its recent history, the town's leaders deliberately abandoned their historical attachment with the Wyotas and changed the town's name from Wyota to Lebanon, the hometown of a local minister from Tennessee.

While I was tempted to lollygag in Lebanon, I was more interested in following the letter schemes on the road signs. Doing duty as Route 66 since Springfield, the signs had started with 00 which became CC and then W. After lunch in Lebanon I followed the North Outer Road, called a frontage road in California, then F, The South Outer Road, AB and then AA into Waynesville, arriving there in the late afternoon.

Back in 1961, with the Berlin Wall under construction, the cold war warming, my draft date nearing, and my inability to find a teaching job, I had enlisted in the Army. The recruiting sergeant in Santa Fe had all but promised me that Fort Leonard Wood in Waynesville, Missouri was where I would be sent for basic training. My orders were later changed and I ended up in the bitter winter cold of Fort Carson, Colorado where I went from civilian to trained killer in three months.

Now pedaling through Waynesville fifty years later, I was having trouble finding a motel. An Army officer, waiting for a downtown light to change, seemed like he knew his way around so I asked him. He told me I'd find several motels if I continued east to the town of Saint Robert. I walked my bike up a long steep hill and soon thereafter found The Budget Inn. As she handed me my key, the woman at the front desk warned me, "It may get a little noisy tonight with the soldiers." Seeing the quizzical look on my face, she explained, "It's Friday night and many get weekend passes."

"Thanks for the heads up. If it gets too loud, I'll make good use of my ear plugs."

Spaghetti caught my eye on the menu at The Country Kitchen. I'd been riding for three weeks and hadn't once eaten spaghetti. Like last night, I also ordered a carafe of sweetened iced tea. What I didn't request were the smokers. My appreciation for smoke-free California restaurants had grown with every smoky meal I'd eaten in Missouri.

While the smokers made eating difficult inside, it was the storm grates outside that presented another form of danger. In a word, they were built to accommodate vehicles and not bicycles. When the traffic lane was too narrow and I had to move to the right and ride in the gutter, I encountered metal strips that ran parallel with the roadway. These strips were just far enough apart for a bicycle tire to slip through the opening. If that happened to me, I was sure to be abruptly separated from my bike and sent packing seriously injured to the nearest hospital. So every time I neared a storm grate I moved left into the traffic lane where I avoided the grate danger but improved my chances of being hit by a car, both choices demanding my utmost attention.

After dinner I returned to the motel, showered, called Donna, reorganized my panniers, put away the twenty-seven cents I'd found today, and crawled between the covers. As warned, around mid-night the noise woke me. The soldiers were taking full advantage of being out from under curfew and other base restrictions. Yelling, purposeless laughter, and loud car radios were accompanied by car and motel doors being slammed, beer cans being thrown, bottles breaking and car alarms going off. My ear plugs helped…some.

The following morning I was up by 5:30, glad to leave the now quiet but littered motel. A short distance away I found a small restaurant. The eggs, hash browns, toast and a side of ham were filling and cost only $3.99, the best deal yet on my trip.

During breakfast I gave thought to leaving Route 66 and following the shorter and more direct Route 66 freeway alignment, I-44. Two things were holding me back from making this change. The first was the old feeling that I would be cheating if I took the slightly shorter freeway instead of the nearby county road. But my bigger concern was not knowing if bikes were even allowed on the freeway.

Along the way most waitresses had been dependable sources of travel information but when I asked mine this morning she admitted to not knowing the freeway rules for bikes. In an effort to be helpful, she offered to ask several of her customers. Watching from a distance I could see heads shaking and people pointing in my direction. When my waitress-courier returned to my table, she told me nobody knew. I suspected everyone she talked with thought the idea of riding a bicycle on the freeway was insane and none of them wanted to be a party to my death by telling me it was legal, even if it was. Absent an answer to my question, I decided there was only one way to find out.

Beyond Saint Robert, Route 66 was County Road Z. I followed it for two miles and then, for the first time since Texas, pedaled onto the freeway. I decided the absence of a sign prohibiting bicycles meant they were permitted. Nearing the Big Piney River, I plunged into a thick fog bank. The air cooled rapidly and my dark glasses fogged over, making it almost impossible to see. I coasted downhill at 30 mph, trying to steer around debris while at the same time wiping condensation from my glasses. I was fortunate not to take a spill, having let my excitement of being on the freeway cloud my judgment every bit as much as the fog had clouded my glasses.

Being on the freeway gave me a big psychological boost. The draft following the trucks pulled me along and riding on the smoother surface with more gradual ups and downs helped me ride faster. It was a relief not having to share the shoulder but a disadvantage was the ever present hazard of running over wires protruding from pieces of steel-belted semi tires that had blown out. I first experienced this hazard in the Mojave Desert and now nearing Rolla, pronounced "raw-la," a wire stabbed my front tire, the piece of rubber attached to it slapping the concrete every time the wheel revolved. I stopped and, hoping the wire hadn't pierced the front tube, I jerked on it. The sudden hissing signaled my third flat. I unpacked the bike, turned it over, and while patching the tube, realized this probably wouldn't have happened if I had stayed off the freeway.

With my tube patched, I returned to Route 66 and rode on to Rolla. Named after Raleigh, North Carolina, but with a simpler spelling and slightly different pronunciation, Rolla is home to 18,000 people. Pedaling through town I came to the Christ of the Highway statue at St. Patrick's Catholic Church. This peaceful scene of Christ, standing in a marble alcove with his arms upraised, surrounded by plants, some blooming, was yet another reminder to be safe.

Route 66 and I paralleled I-44 east of Rolla. I stopped when I came to Route 66 Motors. While waiting for the owner to open the store, I strolled around admiring the 1950s Fords. When the store opened, I fought the temptation to load up on Route 66 memorabilia, instead limiting my purchase to postcards for family and friends.

In all the time I'd spent studying my two Missouri Route 66 maps in preparation for this trip, until now I'd never noticed the many towns in this area that had the word "saint" in their name. Behind me were Saint Robert and Saint James. Still ahead were Saint Cloud, Saint Clair and then Saint Louis. The town of St. Clair had originally been named Travelers Repose before it was renamed for a railroad engineer. Sandwiched in the middle of these five towns was one named Bourbon, having gotten its name in 1850 as advertising for a retailer who sold whiskey to the railroad crews.

After lunch, a Spartan affair, peanut butter on crackers and trail mix, I decided to return to I-44, regardless of the semi debris littered there. In the vicinity of the town of Sullivan I came to a roadside memorial in the unfenced grassy median shared by both highways. Since starting my trek, I'd seen at least one-hundred of these cross and flower bedecked monuments, some elaborate and others falling apart in the weather. The one this morning was only the second I'd stopped to see. The plastic flowers in the containers were accompanied by a garland of green wrapped around the cross arm. What made this memorial particularly poignant was the picture of the young man who died here. His smile and inquisitive eyes could have been those of my son, Ryan. Around his picture was written, "Our Son Brandon." A mistake had taken his life, snuffing out his potential. A nearby highway sign stated that Brandon's family and friends were, in his memory, keeping this section of road litter-free.

Riding away from this gripping memorial, I thought about what I'd seen and the sadness I felt. Recalling the chorus of an African-American spiritual, I sang the words over and over, welcoming the emotional release they gave to my feelings.

Nobody knows the trouble I've seen
Nobody knows my sorrow
Nobody knows the trouble I've seen
Glory Hallelujah

The freeway and I were getting along just fine. My guilt about not riding on adjacent Route 66 had passed. We were both, after all, going in the same direction to the same destination. My worry about being stopped by the Highway Patrol had also waned, helped by the continuing absence of signs prohibiting bicycles on the freeway. I rode through Stanton, St. Clair and Villa Ridge. At Gray Summit I had planned to exit I-44 and follow Manchester Road, the original path of Route 66 into St. Louis. But when I reached that off-ramp, on the spur of the moment I changed my mind. Instead I followed I-44 to Pacific where I exited onto another Route 66 alignment into St. Louis and stopped at the first motel I came to, a Comfort Inn. The clerk told me he had a room for $98. Since I wasn't interested in buying the motel, just using a room for the night, I moved on.

The road took me through quiet meadows and groves of trees. I came upon a KOA and stopped to see if they had a vacant Kamping Kabin. They didn't but the owners were very helpful, giving me directions to motels and places to eat in Eureka, the next town. They also insisted I take a large AAA street map to guide me through St. Louis. Little did I know how important this gesture would help me tomorrow. A short distance beyond the KOA was the Six Flags Amusement Park, several restaurants, and motels. I checked into a Super 8 – $55.50 with my AARP discount – and then found a restaurant where I joined exuberant families who were sharing the fun they had had at Six Flags.

Back in my motel room after dinner, before zeroing my computer I logged into my journal the numerical results of this, my 25th day:

Maximum speed: 29.5 mph
Time pedaling: 9 hours and 24 minutes – the highest so far
Average speed: 11.1 mph
Total miles: 104.5
Last four days: Averaged 99 miles/day

My long distance phone conversation with Donna was cheerful, loving and relaxed. She mentioned that a friend from Chicago, Tim Townsend, had come by and given her two CDs. On one, ten vocalists each sang their version of *Get Your Kicks on Route 66*. The other was a PBS special called "Across the Tracks," narrated by Martin Milner from the TV show, *Route 66*.

The next morning I awoke to the rumble of thunder. I walked to a nearby Denny's for breakfast, enjoying the cool air and the rain that was turning to mist. After breakfast I resumed my adventure, splashing through puddles that soaked my calves. Pushed by a tailwind, I worked my way back onto I-44. On the freeway the light Sunday traffic sped by, their tires kicking up a fine spray that speckled my glasses and forced me to stop twice to clean them. Shortly before the I-44 interchange with I-270, I exited the freeway. From here I followed Chippewa Street, another alignment into two-hundred and forty-two-year-old St. Louis.

The St. Louis area was chosen as a fur trading post by Pierre Laclede Liguest in 1763. The following year, Auguste Chouteau founded St. Louis and named it after Louis IX of France, the patron saint of Louis XV. It is the largest city on Route 66 between Los Angeles and Chicago, although it is losing population as people move out of the metropolitan area and into the suburbs. In 1950 there were over 850,000 residents and today there are less than 700,000.

The rain clouds had gone and I was being beckoned by the tall buildings in downtown St. Louis, the Gateway Arch, the as yet unseen Mississippi River, and a frozen custard shop named Ted Drewes. I had not a care in the world when my bike started wobbling. I glanced down and saw that the rear tire was almost flat. My three flats up until now had all been on the front, the easier tire to repair. Because this flat was on the rear I would have to unload my two rear panniers, tent and bedroll before I could turn the bike over. Once I accomplished that, I would manipulate the greasy chain before taking the wheel off. I was perturbed about this second flat in two days and its interruption of the beautiful morning.

I pushed the bike onto the tree and grass-covered median of a nearby side street where I removed the tube and pumped it up. I found the hissing hole and patched it. Before replacing the tube, I impatiently ran my hands around the inside of the tire and felt nothing sticking through. A rapid inspection of the tread side of the tire brought the same result. Not being able to find what caused the flat bothered me somewhat but I was anxious to move on. I remounted the wheel, used my drinking water to try and wash my greasy hands, repacked the bike, and rode off. Several minutes later, the erratic wobbling began again. I knew what was happening and didn't need to look at the back tire. I was disgusted. I pushed the bike to a patch of grass in a nearby parking lot and again unloaded the bike before turning it up side down. After removing the tube and inflating it, this time I found two holes. I decided my partnership with the tube was over and it was time to use the new one I'd bought in Albuquerque. This time, after a thorough inside-and-out examination of the tire, I found and removed two small glass shards and several semi-tire wires, one of which stabbed my index finger and led to blood joining the mix of grime and grease on my hands. I could only hope that I'd found and removed everything likely to cause my new tube to go flat. This being Sunday, if I hadn't, I had no idea where I'd find an open bike shop and the help I'd need. While leaving the shopping center, I came upon a Subway Restaurant. The employees were gracious in letting me use their restroom to clean up.

Riding on, my every sense focused on the rear wheel. The hint of a wobble, hiss or exaggerated bump all consumed my attention. When none of the tire-going-flat symptoms materialized after several miles, I regained confidence in my flat changing ability and began to relax. Gradually I forgot about the tire and resumed my anticipation of eating frozen custard, a first time experience.

It Only Hurts When I Sit Down

Frozen custard forever!

In 1929, an enterprising man by the name of Ted Drewes opened a frozen custard stand in Florida. He later built three more, all in St. Louis. For 2,000 miles I had been looking forward to patronizing the one he built here on Route 66 in 1941. It was 10:45 a.m., fifteen minutes before opening, when I cycled up to the building. I felt welcomed by its high-gloss white paint, pitched roof, and the large red wooden letters, Ted Drewes, on the west end. White wooden icicles of various lengths hung from the eaves on the east and west ends, adding to the cheerful décor while increasing my anticipation of the cold confection to come. I parked my bike and walked up to one of the order windows. Several people were already in line, waiting for the staff inside, dressed in their yellow "Ted Drewes, Frozen Custard Since 1929" t-shirts, to open. I took a menu and pushed my bike to a nearby bench. Cars in the parking lot bore license plates from Florida, Michigan and Pennsylvania, my bike license the only one from California.

The menu included the history of this St. Louis destination, and listed thirty-six flavors, including Tedad's (Scotch Oatmeal Cookie) and two I had no idea what they were – Frisco and Abaco Mocha. I contemplated ordering a Concrete, a milkshake named for its thickness. Traditionally it is served upside down with not a drop of custard running out. The All Shook Up Concrete is a Ted Drewes original, inspired by Elvis' favorite snack, peanut butter and bananas. I finally settled on a vanilla sundae called Terramizzou, which was listed as "a combination of Ted's secret blend of chocolate and pistachio nuts." The name is a take off on the Italian dessert Tiramisu, and the University of Missouri nickname, Mizzou, pronounced Mah-zoo.

I returned to the lengthening line, ordered a regular-sized sundae, paid $1.60, and stepped lively to my bench, feeling like a child anxious to open a Christmas present. My salivary glands worked overtime as I swirled the custard, sweeter than ice cream and silky-smooth, around in my mouth. I was tempted to bolt down this delicious treat but knew the faster I ate, the sooner I'd have to leave. So I picked at it, teasing my taste buds with a small amount of custard cradled in each spoonful, wondering all along why I hadn't ordered a jumbo or even a super.

Before I left I wanted a question answered. So I returned to the order window and asked one of the employees, "What's the difference between ice cream and frozen custard." The smile that graced her face must have been provoked by the fact that this question was asked often.

"Well," she said, "Frozen custard is more fattening." And then she laughed. "A richer cream is used in making the custard and there are eggs too. We only run vanilla through our machines and then we add the various flavors to create the Concretes and specialties like the Terramizzou you had." And there it was. I had an answer and I didn't.

A short time after I returned to California I stopped by the University of California-Davis and was given the Food and Drug Administration requirements for ice cream and frozen custard. The primary difference between the two is that frozen custard has more egg yolk solids than ice cream. This information only heightened my yearning for frozen custard as did knowing that the only frozen custard shop in the Sacramento area, Elk Grove, was fifty round-trip miles away. In time I drove those fifty miles, purchased several flavors of custard and shared them all with my fellow writers in the Davis Art Center. The only thing missing? Ted Drewes.

30

Fear and Prejudice

Everything was right with my world as I moved on. Frozen custard had trumped rolling hills, flat tires, and headwinds. Route 66 led me over a long, arching bridge from where I saw Busch Stadium, home of the St. Louis Cardinals. In the distance the Gateway Arch rose 630 feet, carving a graceful stainless steel arc in the clear sky. Completed in 1965, the Arch commemorates the Louisiana Purchase and is the tallest human-made monument in the United States. Somewhere I read it is built to sway one inch in a twenty mph wind and eighteen inches in a 150 mph hurricane. I had no desire to confront my acrophobia by taking the four minute ride to the top, wind or no wind.

Ahead of me north of downtown St. Louis were the Old St. Louis, Hyde Park, Bissell-College Hill and Baden Riverview neighborhoods, and my final destination in Missouri, the Chain of Rocks Bridge over the Mississippi. As I pedaled along I couldn't help but notice the many dilapidated and deteriorating two and three-story brick homes. Some, obviously unoccupied, had their doors and windows boarded. Where houses had once been there were now vacant lots filled with weeds, cluttered with garbage, discarded tires, non-working appliances and abandoned automobiles. I had unknowingly planned a path that was going to take me through some of St. Louis' blight.

As I moved along slowly, I began to feel conspicuous and vulnerable. People had begun to gather, standing around, drinking and gambling. As their heads turned their eyes followed me. I tried to convince myself that on the surface this was nothing more than people being curious, enjoying their friends on a Sunday afternoon. There was no reason for

The world famous Arc.

poverty, loitering, and trash to cause me to feel scared but for the first time on my trip, I did. Without evidence to the contrary I jumped to the conclusion that among the strangers keeping an eye on me there must be some who would find pleasure in running me down and accosting me. The only motivation they needed was to see me on a bicycle, a stranger in the neighborhood who obviously didn't belong here.

Driven by fear and prejudice and my emotions running amuck, welling up from within me, I remembered previous bike trips when people in passing cars had yelled, honked, and thrown things at me. Nearing Shiprock, New Mexico, a car with dark-tinted windows swerved to hit me, missing me by mere inches. Remembering these events only intensified my fear in St. Louis. To keep from having my bike and all my gear stolen, I needed to keep moving, pedaling with purpose while avoiding eye contact, acting as if I knew where I was, which I didn't because I was lost.

Instead of paying attention to the names of streets, I had been worrying about things over which I had no control. The streets I was following seemed to be leading me away from the congestion of stores, traffic, and the Mississippi, somewhere off in the distance to my right. As I blundered along, I remembered the St. Louis AAA map the KOA owners had insisted I take with me yesterday afternoon. If I could find a place to stop where I wouldn't be seen, I could study the map and figure out where I'd gone wrong.

Ahead I saw a church. To one side grew a tree with low hanging branches, a place where I could be somewhat hidden. I stopped, unfolded the large map and slowly picked out the streets I'd missed. I didn't want to retrace my path, passing people who, seeing me again would figure out I was lost, but that was my only option.

Reversing direction, to my surprise nobody showed any interest in my presence as I made the turns I should have made earlier. I rode through an industrial area and then a park along the Mississippi, every imagined personal threat disappearing as gradually as they had begun. What I was still carrying, however, were my unfounded, unreasonable, and unsubstantiated prejudices.

When planning this part of my trip, I wasn't sure how I would get across the Mississippi. The McKinley Bridge was the original Route 66 crossing but in the mid-1930s, Route 66 was moved to the MacArthur Bridge. Later it was rerouted again, this time to the Chain of Rocks Bridge, built in 1929 and closed in 1977. In her recent *Historic Route 66 Booklet,* Teri Parker wrote that the Chain of Rocks Bridge had reopened in 1999 for use by pedestrians and bicyclists only, making it, at 1.1 miles, the longest pedestrian bridge in the world.

The bend in the Chain of Rocks Bridge over the Mississippi.

When I turned off Riverview Drive and rode to the entrance of the cantilever through-truss bridge, I felt relieved. My fear of being belayed disappeared, its place taken by people walking and bicycling on the bridge giving conclusive evidence to its being passable. I stopped and snacked, enjoying the vibrant colors of the blue sky, red bridge framework, and the bright blue, hip-high wire mesh fence that prevented people from accidentally falling into the great river below. Riding a bicycle with training wheels, a little boy wobbled by, giggling and shouting an exuberant "Hi." I returned his greeting and wondered if years later he would remember riding on this historic bridge like I remembered the first time I walked with Donna across the Golden Gate Bridge in northern California. My fear of heights faced a stiff challenge that Sunday decades ago but the view of Alcatraz, San Francisco, the ships and sailboats on the Bay, and the utter enjoyment everyone was having tempered that fear.

I wasn't anxious to hurry across the Chain of Rocks Bridge so I walked my bike to the famous twenty-two degree bend near the halfway point. It was this angle that gave rise to stories of traffic backing up for miles. Semis, having to swing wide into the oncoming lane so as to negotiate the curve, forced vehicles in both directions to stop. I had read two reasons for this structural anomaly. One claimed Missouri had started to build its half of the bridge before Illinois found stable footing for theirs, resulting in the two sides meeting at an abrupt angle rather than straight on. The second reason argued that the bend was intentional, needed for the stability of the foundation while at the same time allowing barges to line up with the current so they wouldn't collide with the support beams.

Beyond the bend I rode to what I guessed was the middle of the river. I looked for the "Welcome to Illinois" sign but there was none. Just like the Missouri border, I would enter Illinois without a signed welcome, stopping only long enough to put the Missouri Route 66 sticker onto my crossbar.

31

TTT

Every time I entered a new state I was filled with unbounded anticipation. Looking down at the Mississippi, these feelings were stronger this time. I was on the home stretch, my goal the eastern end of Route 66 only five days away in Chicago. My enthusiasm came in part from also knowing that by tomorrow evening I'd be in Springfield where my son and daughter-in-law, Ryan and Julie, and their dachshund, Austen were waiting to welcome me.

Unlike at the start of the Chain of Rocks Bridge in Missouri, I was alone at the Illinois end. I left the river and bridge behind and unexpectedly came to a second bridge. This one over the Chain of Rocks Canal was used by barges to bypass rock hazards in the Mississippi. Up the canal I saw a convoy of twelve barges headed my way. Joined together they formed a group three barges wide and four long, all being pushed by a tug. The cargo in each barge was covered by a different colored hatch, creating a Technicolor procession of turquoise, gold, green, white and red that sliced silently through the silver-blue water below me.

A short distance beyond the barge canal, I was lost…again. My map and route cards lacked sufficient detail and as a result, I had wandered away from the Mother Road. The house up ahead looked deserted but I saw feet sticking out from under a car. Someone was either taking a nap or playing mechanic. I shouted, "Hello," and watched a man wiggle into full view. Propped on his left arm, he gestured with his right, giving me directions that turned out to be accurate, something I hadn't always been able to count on.

Ryan and Julie surprise me in Springfield.

Route 66 eventually joined Highway 157 that paralleled I-55, the fifth and final freeway to take the place of Route 66. By dinnertime, I arrived in Edwardsville. The pictures of pizza on the windows of a restaurant were all I needed to lure me to stop there for dinner.

Following the direction on the sign just inside the door, I seated myself. When my waitress arrived she gave me a glass of water and menu, and told me, "I'm Peggy. I'll be your server," to which I replied, "I'm Doug and I'll be your eater." She smiled and walked away, leaving me unsure as to how she'd taken my flippant attempt at being funny.

Peggy gave me plenty of time to memorize the menu before she returned. Whether she had forgotten my first name or just wanted to keep our conversation all business, she asked, "Are you ready to order, sir?"

Breakfast, my sundae at Drewes, and trail mix snacks throughout the day was the only food I'd eaten so whatever I had for dinner needed to be enough to put my ravenous appetite to rest. So I told Peggy, "I'd like an all-you-can-eat salad, spaghetti and sweetened iced tea.

The mound of noodles she set before me a few minutes later was adorned with two huge meatballs the size of large plums, everything buried under a generous ladling of spaghetti sauce that was slowly inching its way to the edge of my plate. Within half-an-hour I had upheld my end of the bargain, both plates empty and my hunger sated.

While paying my tab, I asked Peggy if there were any motels north of Edwardsville. She assured me that Hamel, the next town, despite having a population of less than 600, had one motel. I pedaled leisurely for an hour before arriving at Hamel, called by its residents, "the best little town on Route 66." On the outskirts, a colorful 8x12-foot sign greeted me, making up for the missing welcome sign at the Illinois border. Painted on the sign were blooming tulips, a Corvette, a red-and-white two-door Chevy sedan, a silver water tower with Hamel emblazoned on its side, and a large white license plate that read, *Welcome to Hamel, Illinois.*

Cycling on a beautiful Illinois day.

Black and white banners attached to the top of power poles also welcomed visitors. On each banner were a Route 66 Highway shield, the words, *Get Your Kicks on Route 66*, and the name Hamel. Following Peggy's directions I found The Innkeeper Motel at the I-55 off-ramp into town.

After settling in I used my room phone to call Ryan and Julie, intent on letting them know when I would arrive in Springfield tomorrow. Julie answered and said she was just leaving to pick up Ryan at the St. Louis International Airport. She would be passing Hamel on her way, so I suggested she stop. Her short visit an hour later left me thankful for my family once again.

Dug's in a motel halfway between Edwardsville and Staunton, Illinois tonight. Since crossing the Mississippi he has seen no more road-kill armadillos, turtles or possums. He wonders why, especially the 'dillos. He told me that the Mississippi shouldn't prevent them from crossing from Missouri to Illinois. They swim with a strong dog-paddle and have the ability to gulp air into their intestines making themselves buoyant.

Dug sends this message to his Tuesday night writing class. "Thanks for your good thoughts. I know struggle provokes dimensions of emotion that don't erupt when everything is going one's way. I am trying to keep everything in perspective because I know people don't want to hear about travail all the time. By the way, as I get closer to Chicago, I am asking more people if they've heard of Don Schwartz (the teacher of the writing class), who is from Chicago. So far, nobody has."

I gave Dug a message from his cousin, Dick. His daughter flew over Dug yesterday while going from Philadelphia to San Francisco. When I told this to Dug he said, "If her jet was flying 480 mph, in twelve minutes she would go ninety-six miles, a full eleven hour day of pedaling for me."

Well, it's hard to believe that the end is in sight. Dug and I can't thank you all enough for your interest and support. Until tomorrow night, blessings to you.

Love, Donna

Monday morning. May 23rd. Day 27. I thought I saw the light of morning through the parted motel curtains so I got up. But it was only 4:54 a.m., the light coming from a nearby street lamp. The restaurant didn't open until 6:00 a.m. so I went back to bed for another forty-five minutes.

Keeping me humming at breakfast was music from the 60s, coming through the speakers in the Innkeeper Restaurant. "The beat goes on, la de da de deee, la de da de daaa," was Sonny and Cher's incessant message as I drank my orange juice and spread two packets of grape jam onto my butter-soaked English muffin. I sat alone, the only person in the non-smoking section. The locals, eleven so far, all men, were in the smoking section, enjoying one another's company as they laughed and solved the world's problems. The music continued over the speakers, The Teddy Bears providing the lyrical repetition, "To know, know, know him is to love, love, love him, and I do," while I attacked my bacon strips, hash browns, and eggs. Phil Spector had gotten the idea for this song while visiting his father's grave. When I finished eating, I paid my bill and walked outside into the cool, bright morning, the refrain of "Wooly Bully," offering the musical benediction to my breakfast. This recording by Sam the Sham and the Pharoahs had been selected record of the year in 1965. Domingo Samudio (Sam) had given the song its unusual title. It was the name of his cat.

Since leaving Tulsa five days ago, I had averaged ninety-four miles a day and didn't feel like I was hurrying. The distance to Springfield today would be short, a manageable seventy-nine miles. Pedaling north from Hamel, I didn't feel cocky, just strong. The adrenaline was flowing and I felt pulled by my goal of being with Ryan and Julie by the end of the day.

Before starting this adventure I had joked with family and friends, telling them that when I got to Springfield I might just decide, "I've gone far enough. Forget Chicago. I've had it. Two hundred more miles are not to be." But ending in Springfield short of my goal wasn't even on my mind this morning.

One thing that was on my mind (again) was the futile effort to name my bike. I had named trout I caught (lunkers), my '62 Ford Falcon (the bird), the college I graduated from (a diploma mill), my unicycle (BC), and my occupation in the Army (trained killer). But every time I tried to name my bike, I always came up empty. This morning, after fifteen minutes of considering and rejecting uninspired names, like Blue Bomb, I gave up.

To encourage me when I was battling the hills back in Oklahoma and Missouri, Ryan had told me, "When you get to Illinois Dad, it's flat." The one thing he'd forgotten to mention, however, was that Illinois would make up for any absence of hills with an abundance of wind and nothing to impede it. This morning it had started early, a headwind out of the north.

Several miles beyond Hamel and south of the town of Staunton, I decided to change roads and follow the original 1926-30 alignment of Route 66 which was Highway 4, the first fully paved highway in Illinois. It would veer northwest, away from I-55 and into rural farmland. I anticipated most of the traffic would stay on the freeway, leaving Route 66 as the safer route.

Northwest of Staunton I rode through the villages of Sawyerville and Mount Clare, both with populations under 500. In Mount Clare I saw no mount, four legged or geological. Next was Gillespie, population 3,500. Nearing Carlinville, its population nearly double Gillespie's, I took a short detour, following a section of old Route 66 into a forest where the trees blocked the wind that had increased in intensity. Stopping to rest, I sat on the old highway curb, snacking on trail mix and enjoying the quiet that was intermittently interrupted by the melodies of unfamiliar and unseen birds.

When I got to Carlinville I walked around the storied Macoupin County Courthouse, also called The Million Dollar Courthouse. In 1867 after the Civil War, there was an effort made to make two counties out of Macoupin County. To prevent this, county leaders, with a budget of $250,000, began building a courthouse. By the time it was finished in 1870, the cost had risen to $1,500,000. Its construction had been accompanied by scandal and openly referred to as the "courthouse swindle." It took county residents fifty years to pay it off. When it was finished, there was only one other courthouse in the United States that was bigger and it was in New York City. The beautiful limestone building looked like a state capitol. Its tall silver dome, high pillars and massive stone blocks spoke importance. I climbed the steps to the north entrance and at the top I was surprised to see The Ten Commandments on a plaque.

Leaving Carlinville, I ran into road construction. Somehow I missed a turn, unaware that instead of following Route 66/Highway 4 North, I was now on Highway 108 West. The wind, still howling but no longer blowing head-on as it had been coming into Carlinville, should have been an immediate clue that I had made a directional mistake. I was about five miles beyond Carlinville, pedaling back to Missouri, when I came to a Highway sign with the number 4 on it. Disgusted, I stopped on the side of the road, my chin falling to my chest. I didn't want to retrace my way back to Carlinville. My only way to avoid this would be to find a secondary road that wandered east-north-east through farmland until it intersected with Route 66 north of Carlinville.

Just up the road was a farmhouse. At the end of the long gravel driveway, I leaned my bike where it was conspicuous against a tree in the front yard. After a series of loud raps, an elderly couple opened their front door just a crack and ever so slowly. I introduced myself and through the still closed and presumed locked screen door, I explained my predicament. They argued back and forth in the dark entryway before settling on directions that would get me back to Highway 4/ Route 66 without having to return to Carlinville. I thanked them for their help and as I left, I wondered if they had ever before answered a knock on their door and been greeted by a lost California bicyclist.

I followed their rights and lefts, my confidence in their complicated directions fading. Coming toward me on the dirt road was a pickup. I flagged down the driver and he assured me the directions I'd been given were accurate. Twenty minutes later I had lost an hour but was glad to be back on the right highway.

As the morning continued to unfold, so did the headwind. I had no hills to climb but the wind was more than making up for their absence. My original hope that the heavy traffic would stay on the freeway was proving to be wishful thinking. In addition to the congestion, the absence of a shoulder forced me to compete for riding space in the traffic lane while the wind kept me from moving in anything that resembled a straight line.

While bucking the wind, it was impossible not to notice, mile-after-mile, the seemingly endless acres planted in corn. The stalks were all about one foot tall, flailing in rhythm as the wind tried to wrench them from the soil. Before today, whenever I had thought of corn, it was Nebraska – the University of Nebraska Cornhuskers – that came to mind. To my short list of corn states I would add Illinois.

Riding through Nilwood, population 300, whatever little patience I had left was nearing an end. The roar of the wind whistling through my helmet, the imperative to stay in my lowest two gears, and the sight of the pitiful tenths of-a-mile as they rolled over painfully slow on my handlebar computer all provoked me to scream my frustration. When

I came to Girard, the next town, it was 1:15 p.m., well past time to eat lunch. Hoping that food would tame my anger, I stopped at a fast-food stand. Since there was no indoor seating, I had no hope of getting out of the wind. I ordered a fried fish sandwich, which turned out to be neither palatable nor nutritious.

In an attempt to divert my attention from the disappointment I was stuffing into my mouth, I struck up a conversation with the only other customer, a man sitting at the picnic table downwind from mine. His black jacket and helmet were on the bench next to him. Like me, he was riding a bike but his was a Harley. As the wind whipped dust and trash around us, I introduced myself and asked him, "You wouldn't be interested in trading bikes would you?"

He laughed and said, "This is bad but the wind out on the freeway is really bad." After a short silence, he added, "One thing for sure I won't be doing today is falling asleep on the bike."

I thought about this as he was leaving, wondering how someone riding a motorcycle, especially a Harley with its loud, grumbling exhaust, could possibly fall asleep.

Several wind-blasted miles after Girard came Virden. In 1898, seven miners and five coal company guards were killed here when miners and strike breakers clashed during the Virden Mine battle. This was a landmark event in the history of the labor movement in the United States. Miners Day is celebrated in Girard every October 12th.

Since early this morning I had started looking for the water tower that every town seemed to have. Virden's was silver. Some had the town name on them, like Maryville and Glen Carbon. They served as an attraction, each one pulling me toward it as I pushed against the wind. Hunched over, trying to make myself more aerodynamic, the towers would slowly grow larger, simple and appreciated evidence that I was inching forward.

Remembering back to my last unforgettable experience with headwind two weeks ago between Gallup and Grants in New Mexico, I knew impatience was the root of my frustration with the wind. Growing up in New Mexico I had learned, if something couldn't be done now, there was always tomorrow and the tomorrows after that. New Mexico was The Land of Mañana as much as it was The Land of Enchantment.

But in the intervening fifty years since living in New Mexico, I'd forgotten most of my lessons in patience, nowhere more evident than when I rode my bike up hills or into headwinds. What mattered was the wind and hill that slowed my forward progress. When they were no longer an issue, the time spent on my bicycle was precious, in a word, joyful. The power of self-propulsion engaged my being. Bike riding became a spiritual experience where I felt fully alive, albeit living the life of a fair weather cyclist.

What I needed to do on days like today when biking got hard was to reclaim patience, and in the process feel the same joy I felt when I was on level ground and with a tailwind. But this wouldn't come until I tamed the idea that everything had to be done on my terms.

As thoughts of patience swirled like the wind around me, I remembered something that happened my first day of teaching thirty-five years ago. I had opened the top drawer of my desk and found, in addition to neatly arranged clerical supplies, a 3x5-inch card taped where I couldn't miss it. On the card an unnamed co-worker had written, TTT, followed by the words, *Things Take Time*.

With the wind doing its level best to blow me back to Missouri, I knew the changes in my attitude that I needed to make. Over the years as a teacher I'd taken TTT to heart but never more than now did it seem so important, so relevant. Time was on my side and all I had to do was engage it and be thankful for the privilege of living this amazing experience.

32

Miss Full-of-Life

The towns of Thayer and Auburn, the Redbud City, came next. In Auburn, I'd reached my limit, worn out and frustrated over my pitiful progress. I found a pay phone and called Ryan. When I got close to Springfield our plan had been for Julie to pick him up early from work and bring him to meet me somewhere south of Springfield. From there we would ride together as he led me to their home. I'd been looking forward to doing this the whole trip but now, with the experience nearing, I told him, "I'm exhausted. You'd better just forget coming out to meet me because at the rate I'm going, I probably won't get to Springfield until way after sundown."

Rather than join me in my discouragement, in his calm and positive manner he suggested, "Dad, why don't you just rest a bit? Chatham is only seven more miles. Take your time and when you get there, call me again and we'll decide what to do then."

Later when I thought about what he had said, I realized he was suggesting I stop thinking of the full distance I had to go and instead break it up into manageable segments, starting with the short distance from Auburn to Chatham.

After we hung up, I pushed the bike to a nearby gas station/deli where I could rest. As I walked in, a girl I guessed to be about ten years old, wearing a white blouse, blue shorts, and tennis shoes, skipped over to greet me, said "Hi" and then followed me as I headed to the men's room. It was impossible to ignore her since she was talking non-stop. "Where are you going? Is that your bike? My dad owns this place," and on and on. She seemed intent on following me right into the restroom so after I got inside, I made sure the door was locked.

When I came out the little girl was waiting for me. As I started my search for something to eat, I didn't have the heart to tell her I could manage on my own. She wanted to know what I was looking for and when I told her, she led me directly to the V-8 Juice, sunflower seeds, and ice, all the while suggesting chips, candy bars and other sugar-loaded goodies I was trying to avoid. After paying I went to a booth, my escort tagging right along. Slumped in comfort I sipped my drink and sucked on ice while she kept up a constant chatter, entertaining me with her Kung-fu and Star Wars light saber moves, her ponytail flipping from side-to-side. When she exhausted this part of her repertoire, she moved on to pirouettes and other ballet moves. I suspected cartwheels were coming next as she flitted back and forth behind the booth opposite me. While all this was happening, I began to wonder: What in the grand scheme of things brought this cheerful pixy and her entertainment into my life? All I wanted was to wallow in my self-pity but her unrestrained joy was making it impossible to concentrate on anything but her gaiety. As she continued to entertain me, I felt a thankfulness come over me. Her distraction had enabled me to take my mind off the wind while I reinforced my physical and emotional resources.

When I finished my snack, I walked to the door, my guide right alongside, twirling and still talking incessantly. She wanted to see my bike and then in her next breath told me all about hers, which was at home. Outside, she pointed to a nearby man and, with pride in her voice, told me, "That's my dad." He was brushing red paint onto the steel posts that prevented cars from running into the gas pumps.

I showed his daughter my bike, and when I said goodbye to her, she got the hint and went back inside. I wasn't quite sure how to start my conversation with her dad but I introduced myself and told him, "Your daughter is sure a lively sprite and she's proud of you."

He set down his paint brush, used a rag to wipe paint from his hands, and asked, "Did she bother you?"

"At first, yes. But her cheerfulness changed my attitude about my struggle with this wind," I told him. "I wouldn't call her spontaneity "bothering me" but she does need to be reminded not to follow strange men into the restroom."

As he thanked me for my concern, I detected some resignation in his voice. Maybe others had told him the same thing.

Leaving Auburn I dug down (not intended to be a play on my first name) and reconnected with the motivation that had brought me this far. The rest had given me time to adjust, accept the wind, and all I had going for me.

Chatham, population slightly over 10,000, came into view an hour later. I was now within eleven miles of Springfield. I found a pay phone, called Ryan and made sure he knew I would be on Highway 4/Route 66 until Route 66 went east and then north onto Chatham Road. Since I had no cell phone, the last thing I wanted was for him and Julie to drive all over the countryside south of Springfield looking for me.

I was about seven miles from Springfield, descending an overpass when I saw them heading toward me. The struggle with the wind wasn't quite over but the hugs we exchanged on the side of the road would make the remaining distance manageable.

Ryan unloaded his bike and we decided he would lead. We rode along, his conversation taking my mind off how tired I was. He told me that friends in Springfield wanted to welcome me when I arrived at his home, among them Katie Spindell, head of the Illinois Route 66 Heritage Project. But he knew I would be worn out and not ready to socialize, so he had convinced everyone to wait several days and come to the party he and Julie were planning to celebrate the successful finish of my ride to Chicago. Nonetheless, waiting for us at his home were one of Ryan's running friends who happened to be driving by, two neighbors, one with her little girl, and Julie holding a poster she'd made that read, "Welcome to Springfield Dug." The tears of happiness and relief welled in my eyes. I later described to people how my son, without any visible sign of a rope, had pulled me the last few miles into Springfield.

Unfortunately, there was no time yet to sit and visit. I had noticed a broken spoke on my rear wheel this morning. The chain was starting to slip on the sprockets again as it had 2,000 miles ago in California so it needed some professional attention. I was also traveling with no spare tube since my flat in St. Louis. We put the bike into the trunk and Ryan drove me to a nearby bike shop. He had called ahead and alerted them to my needs. When we arrived the mechanic said, "So you're the guy riding from California to Chicago. We'll get to work on your bike right away and it'll be ready to go before we close tonight." Talk about service.

Back home, Ryan barbequed burgers and Julie made a green salad and a big bowl of macaroni salad, her grandmother's recipe. We sat at a picnic table in the backyard, eating, talking, and being entertained by their dachshund, Austen, as she ran around looking for the squirrel that liked to tease her. My tank was empty and I ate accordingly. From time to time Ryan would disappear into the house to answer the phone, get more iced tea, bread or anything else we needed. During one of his absences, unbeknownst to me, he sneaked out the front door, drove to the bike shop and returned with my overhauled bike. After dinner I gave the bike a little test ride to the end of the block and back. The bike was just like new, ready to go.

Later in the evening I repacked my panniers. I decided to take three days worth of clothes, just enough for my three-day sprint to Chicago. Included in what I would leave behind were my bedroll, rain gear (the forecast for rain wouldn't come till tomorrow evening), and one water bottle. The only weight I added was my new spare tube and Ryan's re-supply of trail mix.

> *Hi Everyone. Dug is in Springfield, Illinois tonight with our son and daughter-in-law. Today he traveled seventy-eight miles. The headwind blew a gale, forcing him off the highway several times.*
>
> *I told Dug that $1,500 has been given to Yolo Habitat so far. A friend of Ryan's who is living in New York has pledged $66 for every state Dug rides through.*
>
> *We talked about how difficult it is for his body to shut down at night. He lies sprawled on the bed, still feeling like he is on his bike, his body tense. He tries to relax but deep inside he feels subtle twitches. It's like his nervous system is still reacting to potholes, trying to keep him balanced in the wind, avoiding a spill and traffic. He has learned to deliberately relax his jaws, cheeks, and lips. He untenses the muscles in his shoulders, unclenches his fists and lets his body gradually droop, seeming*

to melt into the mattress. As he does this, he can feel his nervous system shutting down and sleep following.

Tomorrow he leaves for Chicago and hopes to arrive in three days.

Blessings and peace to you all. I'll check in tomorrow night. Love, Donna.

Ryan, Julie and I talked into the late evening. I knew I could manage the final two-hundred miles in the remaining three days so I set aside my compulsive need to get nine hours of sleep tonight.

I took a shower and in the process found a tick preparing to engorge itself with my blood. This was no time to get Lyme disease and its attendant heart and arthritis problems. Before getting into bed, I figured my average speed for the day: 9.3 mph, the lowest on my trip.

Lying in bed with the window open, I thought about Ryan and Julie's kindness. They had extended themselves to make sure my every need was met and that the last three days of my trip would be successful. I listened for the sound of wind blowing through the trees outside. There was none. The only sound was that of crickets serenading me to sleep around midnight.

Despite my plan to sleep a little later, I awoke as usual shortly before 6:00 a.m. Maybe it was the headache, my first of the trip. Fortunately, after I was up and about, it went away.

Last night Julie had told me that I was going to get an early phone call from Ben Yount, a local radio personality. Julie and Ryan knew Ben from their church. Several days ago while walking Austen she had run into Ben when he was visiting a neighbor. After mentioning my adventure to him, he told her he would like to interview me and use our conversation as a human interest segment on WTAX radio in Springfield.

Ben's call came shortly after his news on the hour. His questions covered the basics, enough to create a brief story, a teaser that he distributed to thirty-nine Illinois Radio Network stations. Several days later after my trip was over, Ben gave me a copy of what he had said that morning:

A California man is pedaling from California to Chicago along Route 66 in celebration of his 66th birthday. Doug Waterman has *been on the bike trip for about a month, having started in Santa Monica, Calif. He hopes to finish the 2,448-mile ride this week. He expects to pass through Lincoln, Bloomington and Pontiac in central Illinois today (Tuesday). Waterman says he started the trip to see his brothers in New Mexico and Oklahoma and his son in Springfield. After seeing eight states from the seat of his bicycle, Waterman plans to take it easy on the return trip. He already has a train ticket that'll get him back to California.*

Following my interview with Ben, I got another phone call, this one from an *Illinois Times* photographer. He wanted a photo so I delayed leaving, giving him time to hurry over and take one.

It was 9:00 a.m. when I hugged Ryan and Julie goodbye and pedaled away. Everything was falling into place for a successful end to my month-long journey. After reaching Chicago I would return to Springfield on the commuter train. Donna was planning to fly from California and the four of us would enjoy a few days together visiting attractions in Springfield. But I had to reach Chicago first, the process of which would hold new challenges to my well-being.

Chicago is nearing.

33

Following Orders

The in-bound commuter traffic had waned by the time I cycled north out of Springfield. The morning was cool, there was a gentle north wind, and I felt comfortable wearing a long-sleeve cotton running shirt with my red long-sleeve fleece pullover. Lost in the euphoria of my adventure and enjoying my smooth running bike with its lighter load, I saw a woman unloading the trunk of her car alongside the road up ahead. As I neared she waved and hollered, "Are you heading to Chicago?"

"Yes," I answered and stopped.

Katie Sheehan introduced herself as a reporter for Springfield TV station WCFN, Channel 49. She explained that WCFN has a news agreement with WTAX radio and that Ben Yount had called her and suggested she track me down and interview me. She had hurried to this spot hoping I hadn't already passed by.

We chatted while she completed the set-up of her video-taping equipment. Once that was accomplished, she began recording my answers to her many questions. I started out somewhat embarrassed by the attention but gradually I relaxed and enjoyed the experience. She focused her video-camera on my crossbar, photographing the Route 66 stickers, one for each of the seven states I'd been through. She followed with shots of my panniers, my rudimentary GPS System – the 4x6-inch handlebar route cards – and my computer. As her interview continued, people in nearby offices came outside, watching and wondering what was going on.

When Katie was finished, we talked as she disassembled and repacked her equipment. It wasn't until we parted that I realized I had forgotten to have her sign my journal. My list of things to do when I returned in several days would include arranging to see her again.

A short distance north of Springfield was Sherman. I stopped there at the U.S. Route 66 Memorial Rest Area to check the directions on my route card. It indicated I would soon transition to I-55 for a short distance. Looking ahead I could see the onramp leading to the Interstate. I shed my fleece and continued on, passing a brown and white, 4x8-foot sign on my right. The directions on it read: Historic Illinois U.S. Route 66 Use Interstate 55 to Exit 109. My first experience on an Illinois freeway was about to begin.

I had been riding for about five minutes on the freeway shoulder when I heard a siren. It sounded for only a second. Over the course of my trip I had had so many dogs bark at me and people yell and honk their horns that I had learned not to be startled by loud and unexpected noises like this. I glanced casually over my left shoulder to see where the sound had come from and saw an Illinois State Trooper in his patrol car less than ten feet directly behind me. I hadn't seen him

Bicycles are entitled.

the last time I looked in my rear-view mirror and wondered how long he'd been there.

I stopped and watched as he opened his door, unfurled his six-foot, four-inch frame, put on his Smokey Bear hat, closed his door, and walked over to where I stood straddling my bike. Immediately I felt diminished. His first words to me were, "So how're ya' doin'?"

"I'm doin' great," I answered, the shock of being stopped starting to ease with his friendly greeting.

"No you're not," he said. And his reprimand began. "You're not supposed to be on this freeway. No freeway in Illinois allows a bicycle on it."

Trying to decide how to explain my situation without appearing confrontational, I pointed back to the way I'd come and explained, "I just got on the freeway at that last on-ramp back there. I'm following Route 66 and the sign said to use I-55 until exit 109. My guess is Exit 109 is the next one," and I pointed ahead about one-half mile.

"There was another sign you missed that said 'no bikes'. You aren't allowed on the freeway, period." He pointed to the fence on the opposite west bound side of the freeway, and said, "You should be on that frontage road over there."

"I can assure you I have no desire to be on the freeway when I don't have to be. I was just following the direction on the sign back at the on-ramp."

Ignoring my explanation he said, "I need your ID," his tone an impatient command.

I gave him my California driver's license and he got back into his patrol car. I presumed he was running a check to see if I had any outstanding warrants. While he did his work I took advantage of this break and wondered how much the ticket was going to cost me.

Before I had left Davis to begin this leap into the unknown, I had requested from Stu Bresnick, the Yolo County Director of Habitat for Humanity, that he write a letter of introduction for me on Habitat stationery. I figured his letter would explain and legitimize my fund raising for Habitat if I happened to get into any difficulty. Here on the shoulder of I-55, I considered showing this letter to the State Trooper but decided it wouldn't help.

When he reemerged from his patrol car he returned my license and explained he was giving me a written warning, an 11-711, for disobeying a controlled access highway restriction. He gave me the yellow copy and told me, "If you're caught riding again on any Illinois freeway, you'll get a ticket. You're in our computer now."

I took the warning and as I was putting it into my handlebar bag, he lowered his final boom. "What I want you to do now is cross these three east-bound freeway lanes, go through the median ditch, cross the three west-bound lanes, climb that low bank and lift your bike over the fence onto the frontage road."

"Couldn't I just ride to the off-ramp up ahead and exit the freeway there?" I asked.

"No. I want you off the freeway right here."

I had no doubt about his insistence. But before acting on it, I had one more request. "This is a little unusual I know, but, since starting my Route 66 bike ride in Santa Monica, people along the way have been signing my journal. Would you be willing to sign it too?"

My request must have seemed like I was asking him to sign my High School Yearbook but he said nothing as he took the book. He wrote down only the basics. No good wishes or inspiring comments. Just his illegible name, his badge number and the words, "Il State Police." Then he returned to his patrol car and watched.

I was well aware that following his directions could cost me my life. While I waited on the shoulder for a chance to cross, I was surprised how fast cars and semis going sixty-five mph, or faster, filled the staggered occupancy of the three lanes making it nearly impossible to judge when to start my dart across. When what I hoped was a safe time to cross finally came, I pushed my bike quickly across the first three lanes, suppressing thoughts of what would happen if I stumbled and fell in any lane. I then went down and up in the ditch separating the two directions, thankful it wasn't filled with water. The west-bound traffic was more congested, forcing me to wait on the shoulder several minutes before I began my dash across those three lanes. I saw the Trooper drive off as I struggled to push my bike to the top of the bank. When I got there I was confronted with a fence that had two strands of barbed wire on top, the top strand chest high. I tried twice to lift the loaded bike but was unable to get the tires high enough to clear the fence. After the second attempt I dropped the bike in frustration, unaware that the Trooper had doubled back and was alongside the freeway below me. "Can you do it?" I heard him holler through the lowered passenger window and over the traffic noise.

"No, I can't. The fence is too high, my bike is too heavy, and these barbed wire strands on the top are stabbing me," I hollered back while trying to restrain my frustration.

I fully expected him to tell me to unload my bike and try again but instead he said, "Okay, here's what I'll let you do. Stay on this side of the freeway and go back the direction you came from." He pointed west and said, "Do you see that truck weighing station?"

Looking ahead I could see the buildings about one-half mile away so I told him, "Yes."

"It's closed today. When you get there you'll see an open gate in the fence. Go through that gate and you'll be on the frontage road."

I thanked him and watched as he sped away. Several minutes later I found the gate. Moving northeast again, now on the frontage road, my thoughts were consumed by the experience I'd just had. I didn't disagree with being stopped and given a warning. If the officer had ignored me on my bike and I had been hit, seriously injured or killed on his patrol, it might have cost him his job. But my chances of getting hit and killed while following his directions to cross six lanes of a busy freeway were much greater than if he had just taken a few minutes and escorted me, with his lights flashing, down the shoulder to exit 109 which we both knew was no more than half-a-mile away. That distance, in fact, was the same distance he allowed me, unescorted, to use the freeway shoulder until I got to the gate in the fence.

34

Kindness at Funks Grove

The frontage road paralleled I-55 through the village of Williamsville, population around 1,500. Six miles later came Elkhart, about one third Williamsville's size. Alleviating my hunger had become my top priority so I stopped for lunch at a small café in Elkhart.

I walked in, sat down at the only empty table, and watched as the overworked waitress hurried around trying to meet the needs of the customers at the fourteen occupied tables. The scowl on her face exuded unhappiness and was accompanied by a snappy, bitter, impatience in her voice. Further complicating her frustration as she scurried from table to table were the strands of errant brown hair that refused to stay behind her ears where she repeatedly tried to contain them. On one of her forays into my vicinity she silently flung a menu onto my table. I looked it over and decided a cold turkey sandwich with the soup of the day sounded good. I waited patiently for her to return and when she did I asked, "What's your soup of the day?"

She didn't even look up from her order pad as she barked, "We don't serve soup in the summer!"

I had lost track of the date several times on my trip but I knew summer was still weeks away, today being the 24th of May. Regardless, my waitress was in no mood to debate the season. Suspecting she would punish me with a boycott if I tried, I decided to just be done with it. With my allotted five seconds to order now over and with it the time to re-examine the menu, I ordered a glass of iced tea, fries and a cheeseburger with no onions. As she walked away, I wondered if there were others in Elkhart who thought it was already summer.

My lunch passed without additional drama, giving me time to consider the ritual of tipping. Not wanting to contribute to further strife and frustration, I left a tip larger than the normal twenty percent, an amount I hoped would tell her I cared.

Five miles beyond Elkhart I came to Broadwell, a village of just under 200 people. In 1937, Ernest (Ernie) Edwards and his wife, Frances, opened the Harbor Inn here on Route 66.

Eventually they changed the name. The accepted folklore as to why they did this centers on an unnamed customer who came in one day and wanted a sandwich. When asked what kind, he said, "Just give me one off that pig's hip." From that time on, Ernie's ham sandwiches, served with his secret sauce and a bowl of Jell-O, attracted locals and travelers and led Ernie to change the name of their business to The Pig-Hip Restaurant. According to Teri Parker in her *Route 66 Booklet*, Ernie, while discussing the ham he used in his sandwiches, explained, "When a pig has an itch, it tends to scratch with its right leg, thus resulting with that side producing tougher meat. So I only use meat from a pig's left side." If nothing else, it was a colorful myth.

In 1992, Ernie and Frances closed the restaurant. With help from a National Park Service grant, the Route 66 Association of Illinois helped restore their establishment and it reopened in April, 2003, this time as the Pig-Hip Restaurant Museum. Ernie, in his eighties and known affectionately as "the old coot on 66," daily engages visitors to the Museum. Since my day had been filled with many interruptions and I wanted to get some miles behind me, I missed meeting Ernie, stopping at the Pig-Hip only long enough to take a picture. Two years later, on March 5, 2007, the Pig-Hip burned down. A stone marker now identifies the site. As a finale to his story, in 2012, Ernie passed on. While he isn't with us anymore, we can still relish his contributions to the lore of Route 66.

Eight miles further on, I came to the city of Lincoln. It is the only town in the United States named after Abraham Lincoln and this was done before he became President. Abraham (he disliked being called Abe) practiced law here from 1847-1859.

Many times on this adventure, people had pulled up alongside, most to talk and a couple to harass. Here in Lincoln, a driver shouted at me, "Where ya' goin'?"

"Chicago."

"And where'd ya' start?"

"Santa Monica. I've got about 2200 miles behind me now."

After hearing my up-to-date progress report, he thrust his right thumb into the air and before speeding off, hollered, "Praise God." Encouragement came in many forms and usually when I least expected it.

The afternoon wore on with small towns continuing to pop up every few miles. Atlanta was next and five miles later, McLean, the location of the Dixie Truckers Home. It opened in 1928 and is the oldest truck stop in Illinois. A piece of pecan pie would have been a treat but since the day was rapidly slipping by, I had to make a choice: drop by Funks Grove, which was just four miles ahead, or the Truck Stop. My unanimous vote went to Funks Grove.

It was just before five o'clock when I arrived at the gravel driveway. I read the Route 66 Roadside Attraction sign and learned how, in 1824, Isaac Funk and his sons began making pure maple sirup from the sugar and black maple trees found here. Now 181 years later, the seventh generation of Funks annually makes 1,800 gallons of sirup at this historic place.

I rode the short distance through the beckoning trees to the store and leaned my bike against the front wall. I tried to turn the door knob but it was locked. The business hours posted on the door showed it closed at 5 p.m. Discouraged, I turned to leave and saw an elderly woman heading in my direction. She must have seen me from inside the house across from the store and decided if I had enough energy to pedal to the store she could in kind return and open the store for me. Without a doubt I was touched by her absence of selfishness.

As she approached I introduced myself and she did likewise, the smile on her face helping to breach her anonymity as she told me her name was Glaida Funk. To ward off the cool air under the trees, she wore an unbuttoned sweater over her blouse. She unlocked the door and while I browsed inside we carried on our conversation. "I'm from Oklahoma and I don't know if they consider me a Funk since I'm a Funk by marriage," she said.

I enjoyed talking with her but felt like I was imposing. After her long day in the store, I presumed she wanted nothing more than to just sit and relax at home. So I hurried, finally settling on the purchase of a small bottle of sirup, a gift for Ryan and Julie after my trip was over. My transaction complete, I asked Glaida if she would sign my journal. She readily agreed, and along with her name, she wrote, "Funks Grove Pure Maple Sirip; Keep Pedaling!"

Before I left I had to ask her the question she must have been asked hundreds of times. "Why is sirup spelled with the letter 'i' replacing the 'y'?"

"Pure maple sirup is spelled 'sirup,'" she explained. When sirup has sugar or other sweeteners added to it, the spelling changes to 'syrup'. As a footnote, Webster in his dictionary preferred the spelling currently used today.

It was so simple. I thanked Glaida for her kindness in opening the store for me. Having read how they sometimes run out of sirup, I was glad she still had some to sell me.

The fifteen miles from Funks Grove to Bloomington took me nearly two hours. I wasn't having any luck in finding a motel so I stopped a pedestrian and asked if he knew of any nearby. He thought a moment before telling me, "If you continue following Route 66 to Normal, you'll find some near I-55." So I pedaled on for several more miles, finally coming to a Motel 6 just after 7:00 p.m. I checked in, arranged for my first wake-up call…again, and washed up. Before walking across the street to a Pizza Hut, I unclipped my computer from the handle bar and saw that it had taken me ten hours to go a very eventful sixty-eight miles today. At the restaurant, unlike at lunch, a staff of six was there to serve a family of four and me.

> Hi everyone. I just got an email from old friends, the Masons, who now live in Urbana, Illinois. They failed to find Dug on Route 66 today, however, they did see him on the evening news tonight and said, "He looked good."
>
> Dug's day included interactions with, among many, a TV reporter, an Illinois State Trooper, and a raccoon scampering toward him in the grass alongside the road. When he saw Dug he took off in the opposite direction.
>
> Tomorrow Dug has some serious cycling to do. Hopefully the storm headed his way from Colorado won't interfere.
>
> Peace and blessings until tomorrow night. Love, Donna.

The following morning the phone rang, waking me out of a deep sleep at 5:45 a.m. Momentarily confused as to where I was and who would be calling me, I picked up the receiver and heard the pre-recorded wake-up message: "This is Tom Bodett calling to tell you, you've just won ten million dollars. Just kidding. Actually, it's time to get up." I hung up the phone, rubbed my eyes, smiled and did as I was told.

My two-eggs-over-hard breakfast in a nearby Denny's was uneventful and fast. I was headed northeast out of Normal by 6:30, a light breeze already blowing head-on. I hoped this wasn't the start of the storm Donna had warned was headed my direction. Without complications, if I pedaled at least one-hundred miles today, I would be close enough to reach the end of Route 66 at the shore of Lake Michigan by noon tomorrow, and then find the train station where I'd catch the last commuter train of the day back to Springfield. I resolved to be joyful, patient, and strong in my last full day of riding.

Leaving Normal my mind was cluttered with names and numbers. As a mental exercise, I tried to remember the names of the ten towns I'd ridden through over the distance of sixty-eight miles yesterday. I couldn't, my mind a blank. I thought back three weeks to the five days it had taken me to cross Arizona. Over those 375 miles, Route 66 had gone through only ten towns and I remembered the names of all of them. I was earning a "C" in this geography lesson.

Like most of yesterday, I-55 continued nearby, this time on my left. Six miles from Normal was Towanda. It was here I noticed an old abandoned but passable section of Route 66 sandwiched between Route 66 and I-55. I moved over onto it and wondered how much longer it would be before the grass growing up through the cracks would completely fracture and cover it.

Enjoying having this stretch of road all to myself, I came upon two groups of signs on opposite sides of the road. The eight on my left were roughly 4x8 feet in size. Each one represented one of the eight states that Route 66 went through. I stopped at the Texas sign and read the words, "Howdy from Texas US 66." Within the outline of Texas were drawn The Alamo, a Brahma bull, Prickly Pear cactus, Stetson, lariat and rattlesnake. Route 66 was represented by a line across the upper panhandle.

The six red signs on my right were smaller. On each was a line from a Burma Shave rhyme. West-bound motorists could read:

*A beard
That's rough
And overgrown
Is better than
A chaperone.
Burma Shave.*

On the reverse side of each sign, travelers heading east saw:

*The wolf
Is shaved
So neat and trim
Red Riding Hood
Is chasing him.
Burma Shave.*

Burma Shave signs like these were once all along Route 66, entertaining travelers with clever advertising for shaving cream. The only other ones I'd seen on my trip were in the yard behind the store/visitor's center in Truxton, Arizona.

Seven miles after the visual entertainment in Towanda, I came to Lexington, a town of 2,000 named after Lexington, Massachusetts where the first battle in the American Revolution had been fought. For 2.2 miles I rode on the Ollie and Dorothy Myers Walkway, a thin, smooth layer of asphalt that had been paved over the west-bound lane of abandoned Route 66. Little did I know that this short stretch would be the most enjoyable and safest the whole day.

As I pedaled along, I thought back to my phone conversation with Donna last night. She had asked, "Are you sad to see your trip nearing the end?" I couldn't remember my answer but I had probably said something like, "I haven't thought much about it." And that was true. I had consciously avoided thinking about the end, but now, over the two hours from Lexington to Pontiac, her question wouldn't go away.

I thought about the times when the going had been hard – the hills, wind, rain, flat tires, the lightning storm I had been caught in, my fall, the fear I felt in St. Louis, and when the trooper ordered me to cross I-55. Grouping these experiences together made it easy to feel only gladness about them being over. But that was too simple. I knew that when dealing with these adversities I was very much alive, my emotional, physical, and intellectual resources working at their very peak to help me. The times of struggle gave me a more complete and realistic perspective and I knew that without them, my experience would have been incredibly boring, a stifling sameness.

Continuing to think about Donna's question, I knew after my adventure was over it would take time to back away and see what came to the surface. As for the end being sad or happy, the surprises still ahead would weigh heavily in determining that answer.

35

Here and There

The gentle waves of air blew all morning, gradually changing from north to northeast as the hours wore on. The Colorado storm Donna had warned me about was a no-show, so far anyway. If the weather stayed as it was and the traffic didn't get too rambunctious, my hundred-mile day would be a joy.

I breezed through Pontiac and its 12,000 residents. In 1837, it had been named after Chief Obwandiyag, an American Indian whose name in the Ottawa language was pronounced Bwon-diac. I laughed at the thought of General Motors mass producing Obwandiyag Bonnevilles.

By noon I pedaled into Odell, having already ridden forty-five miles. I sidled into an empty booth in the nearly full Wishing Well Café, aware of the stares and diminished conversations that greeted my arrival. Occupying the booth between me and the front window was an elderly ruffled, unkempt woman. Judging from the overflowing ashtray in front of her, she must have spent most of the morning chain smoking here. Two teenagers followed me inside and sat in a nearby booth with a thud and a sigh. The entire time I was there, they never ordered any food, content to sprawl in their booth, taking up space while talking loudly. From time to time they leaned their heads backward, a position that permitted them to more easily admire the smoke rings they were releasing into the increasingly foul air.

For several days I had wanted soup for lunch and this craving had again built to an obsession. I decided there was no way I could be rebuffed like yesterday. So I tried again, this time ordering chicken dumpling soup with a roast beef sandwich and iced tea. The soup brought back the memory of one of my first dates with Donna when we were courting forty years ago. In a restaurant in Scottsdale, Arizona, I had ordered chicken and dumplings. We still laugh when we remember that nearly every bite contained a chicken bone. When I finished eating, the bones formed a sizeable pile on my plate. Today, thankfully, my soup was boneless.

Before leaving Odell and its 1,000 residents, I stopped at the Standard Oil gas station. The small white brick building trimmed in blue had one red gravity-fed gas pump in front. The building had stood vacant and crumbling for many years before being placed on the National Register of Historic Places and restored to serve as a Route 66 Visitor's Center. I went inside and looked at the pictures taken during its hey-day, then decay and now its restoration. Seeing this structure added yet another small piece to the enjoyment of my trip.

Route 66 continued as it had since Normal, running parallel to I-55 from a few hundred feet to a mile away. I was surprised at the number of cars and semis that had joined me on the frontage road instead of using the freeway. Their presence was keeping me on both the edge of the road and my emotions. Eight miles from Odell was Dwight. Founded in 1854, its motto is "Not Just a Bump in the Road." Just over 4,300 people call Dwight home. Somehow I missed the First National Bank of Dwight, built in 1905 and one of three banks designed by Frank Lloyd Wright.

The miles rolled by and I entered the village of Gardner, the discovery of coal the reason for its founding. Route 66 became Highway 53 leading me through three other old towns where coal had once been mined – Braceville, Godley, and Braidwood. In Braidwood coal had been discovered by accident when a water-well was being dug. Today, the 5,000 people who live there share their town with a nuclear power plant.

Wilmington, situated on the banks of the Kankakee River, came next. Families here could proudly point to a time in their history when they opened their homes as refuge to those escaping slavery through the Underground Railroad.

Seven miles from Wilmington was Elwood and then in another seven miles, Preston Heights, both towns with under 3,000 residents. Four miles later I entered Joliet, "the fastest growing city in the

Midwest." The eighteen miles from Elwood to Joliet turned out to be the worst of my trip. The two-lane highway was narrow, there was no shoulder, the speed limit 55 mph, and the traffic crowded in both directions. The edge of much of this highway, including the white line, had broken up into large three-inch thick chunks of asphalt that extended as much as fifteen inches into the traffic lane. Riding on this fractured surface was like trying to cycle over miles of children's blocks. Fearing I would be hit or fall, I rode in the dirt on the sloping shoulder, or walked the bike while keeping an eye on my side view mirror.

I had learned, when leaving Victorville, California, that two-lane roads without shoulders were the most dangerous whether they were between towns or in them. In 2003, 622 bicyclists in the United States had died in accidents involving motor vehicles. I wondered how many of them had been killed on a road like this one from Elwood to Joliet.

In Joliet I crossed I-80, the freeway that bisects my home town, Davis, California. I started looking for a motel but block after block there were none. The facetious rumor that pronouncing Joliet, "Jolly-ette" would result in a $5.00 ticket was on my mind as I approached a police officer and asked for directions. He told me, "Unless you go back the way you've come, the nearest motel is between ten and twelve miles up ahead. I'd suggest you continue to follow Highway 53/Route 66 to Romeoville."

I knew until I ate first I didn't have another hour of energy left so I changed my request, asking him to recommend a place to eat. He suggested a nearby fried chicken fast-food restaurant where I made short work of mashed potatoes, a biscuit, soda and three pieces of chicken.

It was 7:30 when I found a Super 8 motel in Romeoville. I paid the highest price of any evening on my trip, $58.92. After thirteen hours and 105 miles, I didn't care. I was glad to be in a place where I could get a good nights rest. Today would be my last night in a motel. Chicago was only thirty-five miles away and by the end of the day tomorrow, I hoped to fall asleep in the comfortable sofa-bed at Ryan and Julie's home back in Springfield.

Hello everyone. I just heard from Dug's friend, Art Mills, and Dug's brother, Kim, that Dug made the national news on TV tonight – at least in Albuquerque and Sacramento.

Tim Townsend, a Davis friend, sent an email. He asked, "Do you suppose it is merely coincidence that to cover the exactly 200 Rand McNally miles from Springfield to Chicago in three days, Mr. 66 will have to pedal 66 miles/day on Rt. 66? To be more precise, I suppose it's 66 and 66/100ths of a mile per day."

After a lot of thought Dug has figured out why he should have taken a cell phone:

1. He could have called a local therapist for psychological counseling.

2. He needed the extra weight.

3. If he had been hit by a semi he could have called an ambulance from the ditch.

4. He could have called ahead for a pizza to be delivered and waiting for him at his motel every night.

Well, tomorrow will be my last email update. Blessings and many thanks to all of you for your support.

Love, Donna.

Before falling asleep, I called Cynthia Day, a friend of Julie. Ryan had asked her to take my picture when I got to the end tomorrow so she and I arranged to meet in Grant Park. The excitement was building, so much so that I didn't fall asleep until nearly 10:30.

36

A Surprise Awaits

Day 30. May 26, 2005. Like every other day, I awoke before 6:00 a.m., again without the need for a wake-up call. This was it, the last day, arrival day, I-made-it day. Could I hope? My giddiness refused to be restrained.

Nearly every morning on my trip I had been anxious to eat and get going. But today I awoke determined to take my own sweet time. That is until while walking to the motel office for a cup of coffee I saw the overcast sky. If this was the storm Donna had warned me about two days ago, I knew I shouldn't lollygag over breakfast. So I skipped a second cup of coffee, hurriedly packed my panniers, left the motel and headed north on Route 66/Highway 53, a glut of commuters keeping me company. When I got to I-55 I knew that bicycles were forbidden on this Route 66 alignment so I continued north on Highway 53 for several miles before turning right onto Highway 34, named Ogden Avenue.

Vehicles on this Route 66 alignment had two lanes for each direction and the gutter for me. The traffic from behind came in bumper-to-bumper waves, forced into this pattern by having to stop and gather at stop lights at major intersections. I welcomed each lull when it came and used those brief one-to-two minute interludes to sprint as fast as I could in the right-hand lane until the next onslaught of impatient drivers caught me, forcing me back into the gutter. Last night on the phone, I had mentioned to Donna my anticipation of this traffic. She had suggested I wait for it to thin if it was too dangerous. Now caught in the midst of this headlong rush, I thought about taking her advice.

But with the threat of rain continuing to literally hang over me, I decided to keep going, stopping only when I saw semis approaching in my rearview mirror. Because of their width and the narrowness of the right-hand lane, their right-side dualies took up part of the gutter. If I didn't stop and push my bike beyond the gutter, I risked being hit as they brushed by just inches away. They had no intention of slowing and, without space to do so, didn't move to the left before passing me.

How tragic it would be to come this far and be hit and injured, or killed, mere miles short of my destination. The driver of any vehicle could hit me if they misjudged the width of the right-hand lane or turned their steering wheel even slightly to the right while reaching for their coffee, cell phone or anything that was starting to fall onto the floor mat. The slightest distraction on their part could mean disaster for me because, in reality, there were no inches for error.

My erratic forward progress continued for over an hour as I rode through Downers, Clarendon Hills, Hinsdale, Western Springs and La Grange. These towns reminded me of the Los Angeles area – miles of businesses with no indication where one town ended and the next began. Along the way I welcomed the parting clouds. I picked up a slight tailwind, the sun came out, and the traffic gradually thinned. I stopped at a gas station to check directions and top off my water bottle. Passing a Mexican Restaurant I saw a pay phone and on the spur of the moment decided to call Ryan at work, just to tell him how I was doing. No answer. So I dialed Julie, in the process finding a dime on the floor of the phone booth. I added it to the collection of coins, nearing $5.00, that I had picked up for Habitat since Santa Monica. Julie told me Ryan was working away from his office this morning but she would tell him "hi" for me when he called around noon.

Continuing on Highway 34/Ogden Avenue, I came to the intersection where it crossed Highway 43. I cycled through Berwyn and headed to Cicero made famous by Al Capone when he moved his base of organized crime here from Chicago. Up ahead I saw a highway overpass.

When I reached it, I parked my bike and climbed the stairs used by pedestrians to get to the roadway above. At the top I took pictures of downtown Chicago, its skyscrapers visible in the distant haze.

The first afternoon of my adventure I'd ridden through Los Angeles, the second largest city in the United States. Now just ahead was the third largest, Chicago, its population nearing ten million. Commonly referred to by its nickname, "the windy city," the origin of this phrase is still bantered about. The explanation I like traces the label to the debate between New York and Chicago over who would host the 1813 World's Fair. New York newspapers had used the term derogatorily, referring to the Fair supporters in Chicago as "long-winded."

Ogden Avenue was still multiple lanes heading to downtown Chicago. As I entered a busy intersection, a van going my direction passed me on my left. The high profile of the van prevented the driver of an on-coming car from seeing me as he waited for the van to pass before he turned left. When the van was out of his way, the car driver headed directly at me. I slowed, waved for him to pass and he crossed in front of me.

The driver of a second car following the first one, was also turning left, playing follow-the-leader. He had assumed that the way was clear for him to turn and he headed straight toward me. At the last second

Downtown Chicago.

he swerved right, passing behind me. Then came the semi, turning left like the two cars before him. The center of his massive chrome bumper and the grill over the radiator were aimed right at me. I remember seeing the green light that gave me the right-of-way and thinking I could never survive being hit broadside by this truck. Everything happened so fast that I have no recollection of how he missed me. Maybe I closed my eyes. I heard no brakes squealing. When I reached the traffic island, I stopped to gather my wits. Looking back I saw that the semi-tractor had no trailer which must have given the driver enough mobility to swerve behind me. Maybe he had stopped until I cleared the intersection. Whatever, I was thankful to be alive.

One block later I found the excuse I needed for a break – a Dunkin Donuts. I settled into a booth with a maple-cake and a cup of caffeinated coffee. Gradually my heart stopped racing and my body relaxed. I thought about taking out my journal and writing about the experience I'd just had but it wasn't until three days later that I could bring myself to do that.

Ignoring the din of customers coming and going, I thought about the numerous stops I had made since the clouds had begun to part: taking a picture of downtown Chicago, calling Ryan and then Julie, filling my water bottle that was far from empty, asking for directions when I wasn't really lost, and now eating a donut, all excuses. I knew I had been procrastinating, avoiding the end, having decided that I didn't want to confront my sadness of finishing. It was as if, with my goal just ahead, I didn't want to reach it, even with a photographer waiting to document the moment.

Continuing on Ogden Avenue I came to Douglas Park where I made another unplanned stop. I leaned my bike against a fence and walked into the park, stopping occasionally to watch two teams of older men play soccer.

When I resumed pedaling, I rode by a street sign that buoyed my feeling of entitlement. It read, "*Shared Lane, Yield to Bikes.*" I sure could have used this sign when I was struggling to stay alive in the abundance of dangerous situations.

When Ogden and one-way Jackson Street met, Route 66 and I continued east on Jackson, the buildings towering above me. I was so fascinated in looking up, not paying attention to where I was going, that several times I came close to running into stopped vehicles. I rode by Union Station where I would board a train headed back to Springfield later this afternoon. Beyond the South Branch of the Chicago River I passed the 110-story, 1450-foot tall Sears Tower, the tallest building in the United States. It was joined by the Aon Center, the John Hancock Center, and the AT&T Center, all stretching upward over 1,000 feet. I later read that two other skyscrapers were over 900 feet, four over 800 feet and twenty-four more between 600 and 800 feet tall.

The traffic crawled and the noise intensified, obliterating any remnant of quiet. I passed cars, delivery vans, taxis, and cable cars filled with tourists. We were like mobile families, gathering at the end of every block to exchange nods and smiles while waiting for another traffic light to change.

My final destination was where Jackson Street, after going through Grant Park, would meet Lake Shore Drive. Before meeting Cynthia and her young son there, I wanted to do two things, the first to find a sign. The street on the west side of Grant Park is Michigan. Where Jackson met Michigan, I pushed my bike onto the sidewalk, stopped a man moving with the throng in the opposite direction and asked, "Can you tell me where the sign is that marks the Chicago end of Route 66?"

He pondered a moment before telling me, "I have no idea what you're talking about," before he walked away. Undaunted, I picked a second person, selecting her for no other reason than she was walking with intent, as if she knew where she was going, definitely a native, erect and smiling. As she approached I said, "Excuse me, do you know Chicago well?"

She stopped and said, "I've lived here for over twenty years so I guess I can say I do."

"Maybe you can help me then. I'm looking for the sign that marks the Chicago end of Route 66. I couldn't find it on east-bound Jackson Street."

"That's because the sign you're looking for is one block north on west-bound Adams Street. I'm going that direction. If you'd like, I'll show you where it is."

As we walked north on the jammed sidewalk, people coming toward us parted with precision, as if making way for someone pushing a loaded bicycle was something they did all the time. At the next corner, we crossed Adams and turned west. We walked another twenty feet and she stopped, pointed to a light pole just ahead and with a cheerful feeling of accomplishment in her voice, said, "There's your sign."

Sure enough, about twenty feet above the sidewalk was the brown and white sign I had been looking for. It read, "*Begin, Historic Illinois U.S. 66 Route.*"

While we talked, it dawned on me that we hadn't introduced ourselves. I told her my name, and as we shook hands she told me hers was Sydnie. I wondered out loud how many people in Chicago knew about this sign. "My husband and I hope to drive Route 66 someday so we've been reading about it. That's how I knew. I'm glad I was able to help you."

I asked Sydnie to sign my journal and she wrote, "Congratulations! I'm writing this at the corner of Adams and Michigan Avenue. Sydnie Kampschroeder. Chicago, Il."

After she left I took a picture of the sign, went back to Jackson Street, crossed Michigan, and continued east on Jackson through Grant Park to my destination, now only three blocks away. It seemed strange to be pushing my bike the short remaining distance after riding it for 2300 miles but I was still delaying.

Celebrating my finish. Photo by Cynthia Day.

I glanced at my watch and saw that I had less than thirty minutes, plenty of time to do the second thing I wanted to do – make phone calls to my family before meeting Cynthia at noon. My search for a pay phone was coming up empty until one block out of my way I saw a park maintenance crew eating lunch on the grass. I interrupted them and asked if they knew where I could find a pay phone. After a spirited discussion among themselves, they decided there was only one pay phone in the park and it just happened to be back on Jackson, one block from my destination.

I found the phone and made my first call, to Donna at work. I tried to control my emotions but I choked up. Half whispering, I told her, "I made it." Those three words had never meant so much. I followed that call with one to my parents, and then my brother Chris. I left messages for my sister, Lynn, my daughter, Darlene and her husband, Dean, and my brother, Kim.

With my family in the loop, it was time to end my adventure. I pushed my bike the last block on Jackson through the park toward Lake Michigan. While waiting for the light to change at Lake Shore Drive, I looked across the multi-lane street and saw a woman I assumed was Cynthia, standing next to a stroller. The man talking with her had his back to me. When he turned and looked my direction, I couldn't believe who I saw. It was…..Ryan!

I recalled my earlier phone conversation with Julie when she had told me, "Ryan's out of his office." Never had I suspected he was here in Chicago, 200 miles from his work. He would later explain that his boss had asked him yesterday if he was going to Chicago to meet me. He had told her, "I don't have any vacation left," to which she emphatically responded, "Don't come in tomorrow! Go meet your dad." So he had caught the 6:00 a.m. train from Springfield, arriving with just enough time to tape to the fence his green and orange colored posters that welcomed me to Chicago.

My sprint across Lake Shore Drive ended in an elongated hug with Ryan. I had contemplated many times on my trip what this moment would be like when I got to Lake Michigan. With no family or close friends to meet me, I resigned myself to standing alone on a busy Chicago street corner, loneliness surrounding me as I vented my emotions in tears that only I would understand. But now, in an embrace with my son, everything had changed. Instead of spontaneous tears of sadness for my trip being over, I felt joy, surprise and overwhelming gratitude for him caring enough to want to share the final revolutions of my wheels with me.

Lake Michigan joins Ryan, Cynthia, and Isaac.

37

The End of a Wonderful Day

People enjoying their lunch break strolled by our joyous scene. They smiled, nodded, said, "Hello," and stopped to read Ryan's posters welcoming me. It was a Chamber of Commerce day – no clouds or wind and the temperature in the 70s. Only the absence of palm trees gave away the fact that I wasn't in Santa Monica where the weather had been just like this when I started out thirty days ago.

After Ryan introduced me to Cynthia and her two-year-old son, Isaac, she started taking pictures. For some I held a Route 66 highway shield, a gift to me from Steve, one of Ryan's co-workers. Other shots included Ryan, my bike, Grant Park, Lake Michigan, and sailboats berthed in the yacht harbor behind us.

When she finished, Ryan and I took turns keeping an eye on Isaac as he toddled around and his mom wrote in my journal: "Your journey is an inspiration. Congratulations on completing a dream. All the best. Cynthia and Isaac, Chicago, Illinois." When she packed to leave, I whispered to Ryan, "I don't have anything to give her in thanks." I needn't have worried. He went to his backpack and pulled out a bouquet of flowers, a gift to her from both of us.

After Cynthia and Isaac left, Ryan and I took down his posters and ambled over to 319-acre Grant Park. I tried to imagine the thousands of people gathered here to protest the Vietnam War during the 1968 Democratic National Convention. In 1979, 350,000 people joined Pope John Paul II as he celebrated Mass here.

Ryan and I bought ice cream cones at a refreshment stand and sat down at the Buckingham Fountain, one of the world's largest. Was I really here? For that matter, was Ryan really here? As we talked, every minute 14,000 gallons of water shot into the air from the fountain's 133 jets. What Ryan hadn't told me was the nearing variation in this routine. It was on the hour that the center jet shot a plume of water 150 feet into the air. We watched as children laughed, splashing in the spray being pushed by a gentle breeze.

We had time to eat before catching the train so Ryan suggested we have lunch at Bennigans on Michigan Avenue, a downtown eatery popular with Chicagoans. As we ate and talked, I began my second long journey – coming to grips with my trip being over. The more we talked the more I knew how very lucky I was to have a son who wanted to be a part of my adventure.

When leaving my motel room this morning, I'd worried I wouldn't have enough time to find Union Station, purchase my ticket and keep track of my bike before loading it onto the last train of the day to Springfield. But now that Ryan was with me I relaxed, knowing he would help me through a routine he knew well.

After twelve years of construction interrupted by World War I, Union Station was completed in 1925. The fact that it takes up 9 ½ blocks is deceptive since most of it is underground. Ten northbound and ten southbound tracks allow the Station to handle up to 700 trains a day. Ryan and I would be two of approximately 126,000 passengers passing through its doors today.

Ryan intentionally took me into Union Station through the Clinton Street entrance. We walked down a long ramp through a drab and dimly lighted hallway, turned right and entered The Great Hall. I stood in awe. Rising at least 100 feet above us was a vaulted skylight that covered the entire roof. The station floor was made of pink Tennessee marble and the walls were fronted by large Corinthian columns. Enormous wooden benches gave travelers ample room to stretch out while waiting for their train. In 2002 Union Station was declared a Chicago Historic Landmark, an honor that many felt was long overdue.

The routine at the station went smoothly until time to board. While hefting my loaded bike up the steep steps into the train and then working my way around a narrow corner into the car, I got the panniers wedged. The conductor stood nearby, watching my predicament.

As the line of passengers waiting to board grew longer, he made no attempt to help. Ryan was several passengers behind me and when he saw my predicament he came to my rescue.

On the way back to Springfield I was like a volcano, spewing stories and stream-of-consciousness thoughts without interruption. Ryan listened but he had had a long day. In the middle of one of my stories, he got very quiet. When I glanced at him I saw he had fallen asleep, giving me the opportunity to figure out how many times my feet had revolved over my 2,333 miles. I started with the guesstimate of eighty revolutions per minute which I multiplied times the fifty-three minutes I pedaled each hour (I was overly optimistic that I had coasted seven non-revolution minutes every hour), a total of 4240 revolutions per hour. I pedaled an average of ten hours per day, totaling 42,400 revolutions per day. This amount times twenty-seven full days of cycling (I had two full days and 2 half days of rest) gave me a rough estimate of around 1,144,800 revolutions from Santa Monica to Chicago. If nothing else, this number would qualify me for having a high tolerance for repetitive movement.

Ryan woke in time for us to meet Julie at the Springfield station and before long we were eating dinner. I gorged on two helpings of spaghetti, a large bowl of salad, and brownies I snitched from the pan every time I went through the kitchen. My voracious hunger had taken hold and wouldn't abate for another week.

Before I fell asleep, Donna and I talked on the phone for the second time today. A sense of relief and being safe led our conversation to being more lighthearted than it had been in awhile. Our joy also came from knowing that tomorrow she would fly to St. Louis and we would soon be together.

> *Well folks, he made it! He called me at work to let me know and sounded great. "I can see Lake Michigan," he said. As he neared the end, he looked across the street and saw our son, Ryan. What a surprise! Julie's friend, Cynthia, snapped pictures of his arrival. It was fitting that a family member, especially Ryan, be there to welcome Dug.*

> *Our friend, Tom Lauderbach, emailed me. "Over NPR yesterday I heard the announcer mention this 66-year-old guy pedaling Route 66."*

Dug sends this message to all of you: From the bottom of my heart I thank you for your support during the difficult times, and there were lots of them. I understand the importance of community and relationships and how good it feels to hear folks say, 'How are you?' and 'You be careful.' I also thank you all for your donations to Habitat."

Many blessings and best wishes to all of you and much thanks for your gracious interest in following Dug's progress through my updates. You were a wonderful support to me in that way.

Love, Donna

38

Loose Ends and Celebration

The next morning I awoke just before daybreak. Standing in the semi-darkness I began my pre-riding routine, deciding first whether to wear padded or unpadded riding shorts and a long or short-sleeve shirt. As I looked around the bedroom for my bike and panniers it dawned on me that my ride was over. I didn't need to wear riding clothes, look outside to see if the wind was blowing and from which direction, tuck my shoelaces into my shoes so they wouldn't get tangled in the chain, or zero my computer functions.

As the birds filled the air with their melodies, their songs coming through the open bedroom window, I laid back down and listened, reveling in my accomplishment. I was on top of a mountain and would come down eventually, but for now, all I wanted to do was enjoy the view.

While my adventure was over, my trip wasn't. The plan for today was for Julie's parents, the Rollers, who lived across the Mississippi from St. Louis in Godfrey, to pick Donna up at the airport. Meanwhile, Ryan, Julie and I would drive the eighty miles from Springfield. But I had lied to Donna, telling her we wouldn't be coming until tomorrow, setting up our arrival one day early at the Rollers as a big surprise.

Ryan came home from work early and before we headed to Godfrey he gave me two Illinois State Trooper shoulder patches and a CD of train songs, gifts from two security guards in the Federal Courthouse where he worked as a law clerk. Ryan had told both guards about my experience of being stopped by a State Trooper on I-55 and they intended their gifts to take the edge off that life threatening experience, a gesture I would soon thank them for in person.

The drive to Godfrey wasn't fast enough. On the way I taped a cotton patch over my right eye, put my left arm in a makeshift sling and wrapped an ace bandage around my right knee. When we got to Julie's parents' home, I got out of the back seat, leaned on Ryan's shoulder, and with an exaggerated limp, hobbled to the front door where Donna greeted us with an exuberant laugh. She knew I had finished my ride intact and my act didn't fool her. After one month apart, it was great to be together again. We fell into each others arms and hugged in a long embrace before looking at each other intently, trying to see what, if anything had changed. Right away she saw the thinness in my jowls. Later she would comment on my ribs showing. Before dinner we took a long walk through the neighborhood, ambling along hand-in-hand, our conversation non-stop as we began our catch-up.

Falling asleep that evening, we listened to the storm that had settled over southern Illinois, thrashing the house with wind and rain. I was thankful my ride was over and I wouldn't have to confront the windy deluge the next morning, bent over soaking wet on my bicycle seat.

The following morning we returned to Springfield and I started making plans to meet with several people. The first person I wanted to see was Bob Cavanagh, a freelance reporter for the *Illinois Times*.

One morning several weeks before my trip began, the phone rang. Bob introduced himself and explained he was calling from Springfield, Illinois. He told me he had met Ryan on a city bus one morning as they headed to work in downtown Springfield. Ryan had told him about my upcoming Route 66 bike trip and Bob had said he'd like to talk to me and write an article about my trip for the *Illinois Times*.

Our phone conversation had been punctuated with both laughter and serious reflection. I felt comfortable answering this stranger's questions as he crafted his piece. It was his question, "Have you considered you might not succeed in your trip?" that gave me pause.

In fact, I hadn't and I told him so. Intentionally probing beneath the surface, Bob had delivered a reality nudge to what I was about to undertake – a solo 2300-mile bike ride that would test anyone let alone someone my age. We ended our phone conversation with the promise to get together when I got to Springfield. Using the information from his phone interview, Bob wrote his introductory, pre-ride column in the *Times* (See Appendix A). As my trip unfolded, he used Ryan and Donna's e-mails to write four weekly updates as I inched my way to Chicago.

Bob arrived at Ryan and Julie's home promptly at 9:00 a.m. on Sunday, the day before Memorial Day. As we walked to his van he told me he wanted to show me something before we went for coffee. We drove a short distance north of Springfield before parking in a small nondescript gravel parking lot. I had no idea where we were as we walked in the early morning stillness down a lane overgrown with trees, bushes and knee-high grass, vegetation that was slowly cracking and covering the remnants of a concrete road. After approximately 200 feet, our walk ended abruptly at the abutments that once supported a bridge. "I thought you'd like to see this," he said. "We've been walking on old Route 66 and this is where it once crossed the Sangamon River." My thoughts scrolled back to the morning in Santa Rosa, New Mexico when Rudy Sandoval had driven me to the eastern edge of town. Like today, I had no idea where he was taking me until he stopped, pointed to an opening that went over a low rise between the forest of piñons and junipers, and said, "That's where Route 66 went." In both situations, a local resident had taken the time to show me history that I would have otherwise missed.

Bob and I got our coffee and settled into chairs at a sidewalk table in downtown Springfield. The normally busy streets were nearly deserted. In response to my asking, Bob told me about his job in the Interlibrary Loan section of the Lincoln Library, about his wife, and their four children, three of whom were triplets. But he didn't want to talk about himself. He deftly turned the conversation to my trip, saying, "When I read in one of Donna's early e-mails that you were having trouble with your right knee, I knew you were toast, that you'd never make it."

"You know Bob, here's the rest of that story. I was having trouble with my knee **before** I started my trip. I kept it to myself, never told anybody about it, even Donna, until I was well along. I don't know why but my knee stopped hurting after the first couple of weeks."

I thanked Bob for taking a chance writing about me. "After all," I explained, "You had never met me and I could have come up with any number of poor excuses to give up and nobody would have known the difference… but me." I should have asked Bob how he would have handled that with his readers, explaining to them why he was writing about a quitter, but I didn't.

An hour later, our conversation and coffee drawing to a close, I asked Bob to sign my journal. He wrote, "Doug (or Dug?!), I'm sure glad to meet you. I'm a history lover with a great nostalgic streak so I am somewhat envious because I can't just pick up and leave. So thanks for letting me experience your sense of freedom vicariously. Best. Bob Cavanagh."

Memorial Day began with Ryan's special Chilaquile breakfast: fried bite-sized pieces of corn tortilla, scrambled eggs, peppercorn cheese, sautéed onions, and hot salsa. We followed his hearty offering with another drive to Godfrey. Friends of the Rollers took us on a boat ride up the Mississippi, the day cloudy but pleasant. At dinner that evening with Julie's parents, relatives, and friends, we toasted the successful completion of my trip. I enjoyed answering questions and telling stories, no longer surprised over how interested people were in my adventure.

The following day we headed back to Springfield. The fun of tying up more loose ends would start today at the Cozy Dog Drive-in. When riding through Springfield on my way to Chicago, I hadn't the time to stop and eat at this Route 66 landmark. The Cozy Dog story began in the 1940s when Ed Waldmire was stationed with the Army Air Corps in Texas. He had been experimenting with a way to coat hot dogs with a batter while deep-frying them. He finally perfected his hot-dog-on-a-stick, calling it "The Crusty Cur."

Ed returned to Springfield after World War II and decided to debut his gastronomical delight at the 1946 Illinois State Fair. But before doing so, his wife convinced him to change the name of his creation to "The Cozy Dog." His success at the Fair led to Ed opening The Cozy Dog House in Springfield. After his death in 1993, The Cozy Dog continued as a family business.

Donna, Julie, Ryan and I arrived there just before noon the day after Memorial Day. The short line moved quickly and after placing our order at the counter I asked, "Is the owner here?"

"She's busy right now but I'll tell her you want to see her."

We were finishing our Cozy Dogs and fries when a woman walked up to our table. She was wearing blue jeans and a light gray pullover

With the Cozy Dog owner, Sue Waldmire.

with the words Cozy Dog Drive-in on the front. "Hi. I'm Sue Waldmire. You wanted to see me?"

I introduced us, briefly explained why we were there, and told her about my bike trip. Our conversation was relaxed, like that between old friends who hadn't seen each other in a long time. She explained that as a result of her divorce from Ed's son, she was now the owner of The Cozy Dog. I asked Sue to sign my journal and she wrote, "Thanks so much for stopping by The Cozy Dog for lunch today. I really enjoyed meeting your family. Happy Trails, Sue Waldmire." She rubber stamped my journal with the Cozy Dog logo – two smiling hot dogs, arm-in-arm, the same logo that was on her shirt – and then said she wanted me to do some signing. The first was a copy of the *Illinois Times* that had one of Bob Cavanaugh's weekly updates about my trip. Following that she led us to a large, Plexiglas covered round table on the other side of the restaurant. Nobody was sitting at the table so she slid the glass to one side, partially exposing the surface. Using her pen I signed my name in this special location where it joined the names of many others, who, like me, had stopped to eat here while following Route 66.

Following lunch at the Cozy Dog, Donna and I visited the recently opened Lincoln Museum. The displays and action dioramas brought Lincoln to life. In so many ways his was a tragic life – losing jobs, elections and children. Had I visited this museum before my adventure, the inspiration I would have derived from Lincoln's life would certainly have buoyed me during the difficult times.

After leaving the Museum, we swung by the Amtrak station to purchase a bike box to use in shipping my bike back to Davis. At the station the ticket agent told me, "You're lucky. I have one box left."

"What's the penalty?" I asked.

"Five bucks. When you're ready to head home to California, just bring your boxed bike and for another five dollars, we'll ship it for you."

What a deal.

Two days after Memorial Day I met with two media people who had used TV and Radio to bring my trip to the attention of the public. First was Ben Yount of WTAX radio in Springfield. It was Julie who had arranged for Ben to interview me over the phone the morning I left Springfield headed to Chicago and I wanted to meet him in person. Ryan and I arrived in time to watch him wrap up his 8:00 a.m. News on-the-Hour. We talked for a short while before he gave us a tour of the station. As our visit ended, I thanked Ben for his interest in my ride. His immediate response was, "I want to thank **you** for letting us tell

Cozy dogs for Donna, Julie and Ryan.

your story; it's a fantastic story."

The second media person I wanted to see was Catie Sheehan from TV station WCFN/WCIA. It was Catie who one week ago had followed up on a tip from Ben and intercepted me as I was biking out of Springfield. Her video-taped interview of me had been released by her station to The Associated Press and it had been broadcast on the evening news in cities across the U.S., including the San Francisco Bay area and Albuquerque. Sitting outside with Catie, I thanked her for her interest in my trip and since I had forgotten the first time we met, I asked her to sign my journal. Later I read, "What an exciting adventure – biking across America – alone and to raise money for Habitat for Humanity. Someday I'd like to run a marathon. You've inspired me to #1: do it and, #2: do it for the good of a charity."

Another person I wanted to see today was Heather Pounds, an employee of the Central Illinois Tourism Development Office. When planning my trip, I had both corresponded and spoken with her on the phone. She had given me lots of information, including seven maps of Illinois that had a bicycle safety rating for every highway in the state. When I walked into her office the first thing I noticed was her desk, piled with work. But she ignored it, welcoming my unannounced visit and the opportunity to talk with me.

Ryan's boss, Federal District Court Judge Jeanne Scott had invited Donna, Julie, Ryan and me to have lunch with her. It was fun to sit and listen to Judge Scott talk about Lincoln, the history of Springfield and her praise of Ryan. After lunch we walked over to the courthouse for a tour. Just inside the front doors I innocently breezed through the metal detector and triggered a loud buzzer. Two security guards rushed over to me immediately and before I knew what was happening, one of them grabbed my wrists and handcuffed me. With his hand firmly grasping my upper arm, he led me into a small holding cell several feet away and clanked the door shut. The resulting echo reverberated, competing with everyone's laughter, including those of Donna and Ryan. The guards had told Ryan ahead of time that they intended to do this as a follow-up to my having been pulled over by a State Trooper when leaving Springfield. Most of the courthouse guards were ex-state troopers and while they said nothing about what had happened to me on I-55, I interpreted their laughter and playful handcuffing as sympathy for how I'd been treated.

My bike ride had been over for several days now. Conversations were gradually moving away from being about my ride, a fact I welcomed. But that was about to change at the reception that Ryan and Julie were having in my honor this evening. They were excited about welcoming their friends, co-workers, and neighbors to meet me and to share in the success of my trip. I in return was finding it hard to receive this gift from them. I urged them to cancel the event or at least invite fewer people but my efforts were futile. Ryan had enlarged and copied Donna's daily e-mails and tacked all thirty of them in chronological order on their back yard fence. They had bought refreshments and ordered a large cake with white frosting on which was the outline of a cyclist, the Route 66 shield, and the words "66 on 66." Their only request of me, other than to enjoy myself, was to repack my bike so people could see it and if they wanted, to try and lift it.

End of trip party cake.

Despite my initial misgivings about being on stage, the party was a blast. The first surprise was when I turned around and saw old Davis friends I hadn't seen in twenty-five years, Don and Donna Mason. They lived nearby in Urbana and had driven a section of Illinois Route 66 one afternoon a week ago, unsuccessful in their search to find me. Don handed me a post card as we hugged. I laughed as I read what was written on the front:

> *You can't make footprints in the sands of time if you're sitting on your butt. And who wants to make butt prints in the sands of time?*
> *By Bob Moawad*

Julie's parents drove up from Godfrey. Bob Cavanagh and his family came as did Ben Yount and Judge Scott. Among the many people I got to meet were Ryan's running friends, his three Little Brothers (from the Big Brothers/Big Sisters organization), members of the youth soccer team he coached and their parents.

Near the end of the evening, Katie Spindell, head of the Illinois Route 66 Heritage Project, got everyone's attention and asked me to join her. She presented me with pins, key chains, a pen, Christmas tree ornament, t-shirt, shopping bag, everything with "Route 66" on it. She also gave me a baseball hat that had the path of Route 66 on one side along with its mileage in each of the eight states.

Dan Frachey, the Director of Habitat for Humanity in Springfield (Sangamon County), followed Katie and gave me a certificate honoring my efforts in support of Habitat.

When it was my turn to talk I tried to thank everyone for their support and Katie and Dan for their recognition but the emotion of the moment made it difficult.

Before he left, Ben Yount interviewed Katie and me for his WTAX news broadcast the following morning. After everyone left, Ryan, Julie, Donna and I sat outside in the balmy evening, listening to the crickets and talking until late as we basked in the enjoyment of an event that had been so much fun.

The following day was our last in Springfield. Ryan made waffles and we covered them with the Sirip I had bought at Funk's Grove on my way to Chicago. I was sorry I hadn't purchased another bottle to take back to California.

After lunch I got a phone call from David Singer, the manager of radio station KNX in Los Angeles. He wanted to know if they could interview me. I agreed and several minutes later news anchors Jim Thornton and Vickie Cox called. They had learned about my ride from the Associated Press. It was a fun interview that gave me another chance to plug Habitat and relive parts of my adventure.

Donna and I were up by 5:00 a.m. the next morning. The commuter train to Chicago was due in Springfield in an hour. I watched the sky brighten while listening to the ever-present birds welcome the day. As I sat listening, I wondered where the week with Ryan and Julie had gone. It had been a wonderful time. I had grown closer to them both and felt blessed. Our parting at the train station was a study in mixed emotions. I took comfort in knowing that in another year Ryan and

Welcome home greeters, Davis, CA, Amtrak station. From left, Susie O'Bryant, Gail Nishimoto, Mark Nishimoto, Marcus Clark (chair, Yolo County Habitat for Humanity Board), Doug, Donna, and Tim Townsend.

Julie would be moving back to California and we would get to see them more often.

When we got to Chicago, Donna and I had several hours to wander before our train left for California. We followed the path I took down Jackson Street to Grant Park, our destination the pay phone from where I had called her. When we got to it, it was gone. All that was left was the iron stand that had held the phone. The only pay phone in Grant Park had been taken away in the last week, decommissioned just like Route 66 had been.

At Lake Michigan we sat on the steps overlooking the yacht harbor. The high fog obscured the skyscrapers but not the boats and the lake. We strolled around Buckingham Fountain and after lunch, I showed Donna the "Route 66 Begins Here" sign as we walked west on Adams to Union Station. Amtrak #5, the California Zephyr, left on time and we were headed home to Davis.

Davis neighbors, Miguel and Diego Sedillo, welcome Doug home.

Epilogue

In 2007 I began writing my story about biking the length of America's most famous highway, Route 66. My writing companions during this time were a clipboard filled with unlined paper, a black-ink pen for first drafts, and a red one for rewrites, my journal, and occasionally my portable Smith-Corona typewriter, "Old Manual." I usually wrote at home in the morning, but sometimes in the quiet of the Beulah Hughes Room in our Davis Library. My words flowed from pens at our family summer cabin at Bucks Lake in the Sierra, at Gualala on the California coast north of San Francisco, and while visiting my parents in Santa Fe. More than once I fell under the inspiration, the glazed-raised kind, as I savored a donut from Fluffy Donuts just off the UC-Davis campus. As my stories slid into place, I committed them to the sometimes confusing inner dance of the computer Donna and I shared. Writing gave me the opportunity to look back and remember my Route 66 experiences. I welcomed the hours of reliving my ups and downs, fears and joys, confidence and apprehension, and the overwhelming high when I got to Chicago. And while I expected my feelings to fade by now, they just haven't. I'm still on my mountain, stopping daily to enjoy the view, in large part because people won't let me come down.

Even now I'm asked, "Do you have another trip planned?" (I did begin another trip, which I called "Around the State at Sixty-eight," but I got sick 1,000 miles into it and had to abort) or, "How much do you ride every day?" (Staying in shape by running eight to eleven miles every week cuts into time I would otherwise be riding). I'm amazed at how often people start a conversation, telling me, for example, "My wife and I just came back from the Grand Canyon and we can't believe you rode on I-40 with all the speeding cars and semis roaring past you at 75 mph or more." They ask if I ate where they ate, or saw the statue, building, tower, motel, sign, or the shoes hanging from a tree they had seen on Route 66.

Before I left on this adventure, little did I realize how my solo, 2330-mile trip on a fully loaded mountain bike on a highway whose number matched my age, would draw me close to strangers and closer to family and friends. Some hung road maps in their offices or at home, following my daily progress where every one-hundred miles I pedaled equaled one inch on their maps. Their e-mails to Donna were funny, encouraging and supportive of us both. Some got so involved in my trip that as I neared the end they wondered how they'd make it through the days ahead when there would be no daily e-mail update from Donna waiting for them on their computer every morning.

My sister, Lynn, had a friend, Damini, in India to whom she had been forwarding Donnas' e-mails. One e-mail Lynn received from her friend touched us all, especially knowing how hungry I was most of the time.

> "Oh i wish i cud help him in some way, like giving him a nice packed Indian meal for his journey. Anyway wish him all the luck from Katju family!!!! All the best. Damini.

When my ride was over, I was overwhelmed knowing that people interested in my ride had donated over $6,000 to Yolo County Habitat for Humanity. The Director, Stu Bresnick, told me that this money (and the $5 worth of change I'd picked up) would pay for a roof on one of the three homes being built.

Putting my experience on paper helped me to more fully realize how privileged I was to live it. A whim, an itch, a momentary flash of an idea that could have vanished into the void, had stuck around. I was given a wonderful gift and thirty days to unwrap it. Since then, more than once I've told people, "We've only one life and if yours is anything like mine, it's going way too fast. So when we have the opportunity to pursue a dream, we should go for it." The reminder on the back of the postcard that my friends, the Masons, gave to me makes the point this way:

> *The journey has always been about laughing together, loving each other, seeking adventure, believing in our dreams and making a difference…but sometimes we forget.*

I know had I not pursued my dream of riding the length of America's Main Street, that I would have, at the point of dying, deeply regretted not having done so. It takes a lifetime of experiences to make a life but it may take only one unrealized, set aside adventure to make a life feel unfulfilled.

As my writing progressed, I noticed how my memory tried to diminish the reality of my struggles by leveling the steep hills, calming the gales, warming the early morning cold and cooling the midday heat and humidity. When writing about those times I came close to serious injury and death, I've had to be particularly aware of being true to each one.

With the first pedal strokes in Santa Monica, I knew that my daily pre-ride life was too ordered, too comfortable, and too predictable. While I had no hard-and-fast goals, I did want to use this opportunity to sort out what the last third of my life, my legacy might look like. I wanted to find goodness along the way and use every example as a way of being less selfish and more caring. And it was Ryan, knowing my way of rushing through things, who reminded me, "This is probably the only time you'll make this trip so take your time."

From the luxury of hindsight, I look back and see how my trek began with a heavy emphasis on me. I was afraid of being hurt either accidentally or intentionally, by a vehicle or someone afoot who had no desire to share their space with me. But it didn't take long for this fear to be overwhelmed by kindness that came in the form of unsolicited gifts: a pen, directions, a reduction in the cost of a purchase, semi drivers changing lanes to give me room, Habitat donations, and the love of my family along the way. Strangers cared, acting on a multitude of opportunities to help me along. It was as if by ensuring my safety and success they were doing the same for themselves.

Throughout my life I've found it easier to give then receive. My difficulty in accepting things was bound up in my belief that I didn't deserve gifts, congratulations, advice or even praise. As my trip went along, this attitude changed. I welcomed help, all of it given without expecting anything in return. It was Donna who reminded me that by being more open I would build community as people went out of their way to help me.

One wonderful example of giving/receiving occurred at the party in Ryan and Julie's back yard. As the evening was ending, two young boys, Travis and Tyler Vogel, accompanied by their dad, walked up to me. We shook hands and then they handed me $66, telling me it was for Habitat. Their father explained they had raised some of the money on their own and the rest they had taken out of their piggy banks. I will never forget the look of pride on their faces at that moment of their joyful giving.

When my trip was over, I felt that I'd come up short in my goal of ambling along. One place I'd hurried through was Seligman, Arizona, the home town of Angel Delgadillo. I hadn't taken the time to meet Angel, the driving force in convincing the Arizona legislature years ago to designate Route 66 as an historic highway from Seligman to Oatman. It was to him I felt I owed a big thank you.

This mistake of not seeing Angel sat heavy on my mind over the years since ending my bicycle trek so on our way to visit family in New Mexico a year ago, I made the specific point of stopping with Donna to see Angel in Seligman. In his barbershop filled with Route 66 memorabilia, I asked the lady stocking t-shirts if Angel was around. She told me she was his daughter, that Angel was retired now and taking a nap, but if I could wait a minute, she'd call him at home and maybe he'd be able to come and talk with me.

Angel, with his infectious smile, showed up a few minutes later. Seldom have I felt such an immediate liking of a person. We laughed and joked, our conversation turning momentarily serious when I asked him about his efforts to bring Route 66 back to life. "When the freeway opened and we were bypassed, they didn't even give Seligman a sign on the freeway. So I decided I couldn't wait for others to do something about this," he said.

For ten minutes Donna and I had this remarkable man to ourselves, until his curio shop began filling with people who had gotten off the tour bus parked out front. I knew they'd want to meet Mr. Route 66 so we took pictures of Angel laughing, his arms around us. Before he moved on to greet the people streaming in, he signed a postcard that had a picture of him and his deceased brother, Juan, both of them laughing while sitting on lawn chairs in the middle of The Mother Road. We shook hands and then he joined his new visitors. As we left we saw Angel sharpening his razor in preparation for shaving the beard off one of his visitors.

How many experiences like this I had hurried past, I can only guess. I do know that every adventure Donna and I have had has always ended with one of us saying, "Next time we'll have to see or do this or that," regardless of the amount of time we've taken to see everything.

So I can't be too hard on myself for missing some things. I'll just have to be sure and come back again.

Two people I'm glad I took the time to see along the way the first time were Harley and Annabelle, the Mediocre Music Makers in Erick, Oklahoma. They had sung a song to me that had made a lasting impression but I couldn't remember the lyrics, just the melody which I hummed for days after I left them. Several weeks after I returned to Davis, I called them. They remembered me and with both of them on the line, I asked, "I'd like to know the name of the song you sung while I was there." I repeated the first line and Harley immediately said, "We really like that one. It's called *'For the Good Times'* and was written by Ray Price thirty-five years ago."

Harley was kind enough not to point out that I had the words a bit mixed up. He and Annabelle corrected them, as they sang:

> *"Lay your head*
> *Upon my pillow*
> *Hold your warm and tender body*
> *Close to mine*
> *Hear the whisper of the raindrops*
> *Blowing soft against the window*
> *And make believe you love me*
> *One more time*
> *For the good times."*

Before we hung up, I was curious about something. One of the newspaper articles they'd given me had an article about the Pixar production crew having come to Erick to film them both singing *Get Your Kicks on Route 66*. Harley told me, "They've been here twice now. We're being included in the animated movie *Cars*. It'll be in theaters by June, 2006, the 80th anniversary of Route 66." With that timely information, I thanked them and said goodbye, again.

Since my phone call, life has changed for them. I've come to learn that Annabelle lost her fight with cancer. Unlike my first time through Seligman, I'm glad I took the time to stop and see Annabelle and Harley and listen to them sing "The Good Times."

Route 66 has undergone many changes since its birth in 1926, and will continue to change as the years go by. I have my own special thirty-day snapshot, a treasured experience I've shared with you in the preceding pages.

So where do you and I go from here? What are we to do with our opportunities to interact with the world around us? I like the answers Seymour Krim gives in his essay, *For My Brothers and Sisters in the Failure Business*:

> "Our secret is that we still have an epic longing to be more than what we are, to…above all, keep experimenting with our lives all the way to Forest Lawn, to see how much we can make real out of that prolific American dream machine within."

Appendix A

April 28, 2005
Illinois Times
Road Trip
By Bob Cavanagh

Doug Waterman, a retired teacher from Davis, Calif., plans to visit his son Ryan and daughter-in-law Julie here in Springfield next month. There's nothing remarkable about that, except that Waterman's choice of transportation has raised some eyebrows, even among his family.

Starting today, April 28, Waterman plans to cycle the length of old U.S. Route 66 from Santa Monica to Chicago. Waterman, who turned 66 this week, is calling the trip, "66 on 66."

You can almost hear the faint strains of Bobby Troup's classic song as Waterman details one of the most difficult parts of the journey: getting out of the Los Angeles area. "I'll go from Santa Monica to Pasadena to San Bernardino, over the hills, and into the desert," he says. "I'll climb out of the LA Basin over the Cajon Pass at about 4,200 feet."

Waterman is making the trip for myriad reasons, but suffice it to say that it's a personal goal that he's duty-bound to fulfill.

"In 1896, a woman named Margaret Valentine LeLong bicycled across the country. Can you imagine what that journey must've been like? He asks. I figure if she could do it, then I can do it."

"I'm also a member of a writing group at the local arts center, and we write and submit short papers about our experiences. I kept a journal on my New Mexico trip"– seven years ago, Waterman cycled to New Mexico over the Carson Pass at about 8,200 feet – "and turned it into a short booklet. The interaction I had with people on that trip really meant a lot to me. We live in a strange world, and sometimes it's hard to be charitable to our fellow human beings. But I found a heck of a lot of good in people. I want to continue to stay in touch with the goodness of people, and I'm optimistic that I'll find that."

To that end, Waterman is giving a higher purpose to his journey by soliciting cash donations for Habitat for Humanity of Yolo County, Calif. He says that the group's small staff is entirely volunteer, save for one employee whose small salary is paid by AmeriCorps, "so every penny raised will go for wood, nails, Sheetrock, and concrete." Contributors may pledge a dollar amount per mile or per day – Waterman optimistically thinks he'll spend 28 days en route – but he would like people to know that Habitat for Humanity-Sangamon County would undoubtedly appreciate any contribution, of any size, to its worthy cause as well. For information about Habitat's local efforts, call 523-2710.

Waterman's son Ryan is completing a two-year clerkship in Springfield for U.S. District Judge Jeanne Scott. He and his wife have lived on the west side of town since 2003 but are making plans to relocate to California in September, where Ryan Waterman will enter the private practice of law. He says that he wasn't surprised when his father announced plans for his two-wheeled peregrination because he has long spoken of just such a trip.

"I wasn't surprised," says the younger Waterman, "but I am excited and somewhat nervous. You don't have great adventure without risk. I understand that, and so does my mom. She's been married to him for 38 years, and she knows that when he is determined to do something, his mind is made up. The question of him *not* doing this is gone now, so we are behind him."

The knowledge that so many people are supporting him in his endeavor – Yolo County Habitat for Humanity received more than $600 in donations before he had even begun his journey – is keen motivation for Waterman to persevere to the end. He hopes to dip his bike into the chilly waters of Lake Michigan sometime before June 1. By combing books and maps, he has compiled about 75 index cards bearing directions to help him scrupulously adhere to the original Route 66 wherever possible.

"I don't want to die in 15 years wondering 'What if?'" says Waterman. "We are given each day as a gift, and it is up to us to make the most of our gift."

Acknowledgements

My bike trip from Santa Monica to Chicago was a success thanks to my family and friends, but especially because of my wife, Donna. Her love was always there, steady through all the many challenges of planning and pedaling. I will ever cherish your gift, Donna.

In the early stages of planning I knew if my ride was to be a success as a fund raiser for Habitat, my charity of choice, I needed the support of Stu Bresnick, the Executive Director. When we got together and he said, "Yes," I had the go-ahead I needed from a fellow cyclist and friend.

I have struggled with how to acknowledge the many people who helped me negotiate this Route called "66'. They were my village, scattered over 2300 miles, urging me along, helping me craft my narrative. Thank you Julia, author, editor and daughter-in-law. You got me started by editing my first fifty pages and here I am, almost finished.

So many fell in line to support me and it is with gratitude I recognize them. My sister Lynn, daughter Darlene and her husband, Dean, my cheerleaders from a distance: I thank you from the depth of my heart. The neighbors and friends who welcomed us at the Davis Amtrak station: next-door neighbors Gail, Jerry and, Mark and Kate with her two young sons and their "welcome home" home-made posters. How thankful I am for Susie O'Bryant and the United Methodist Church of Davis for providing space and the opportunity to show my slides.

Others whose names appear throughout my book and deserve my thanks are my brother Kim and his wife Sheila; my other brother Chris, and my cousin Dick. My thanks go to Tom Lauderbach, Donna and Don Mason, Ben Yount, Tim Townsend, Katie Sheehan, Margie and Dick, Glaida, Marie Reil, Neil and Marilyn Roller, Judge Jeanne Scott, Bob Cavanaugh, Sue Waldmire, Katie Spindel, Dan Frachey, Angel Delgadillo, Kim Alderwick, Shane and Rise Miller, Kyle and Suzi Miller and everyone who got behind me in ways known and unknown.

I would be remiss if I didn't thank Don Schwartz, the creative writing teacher at the Davis Arts Center for many years. He has taken many budding writers, myself included, and with patience molded us week by week into what could be called writers. To all my friends under

Don's tutelage, I thank you for helping unlock the world of words.

To my son Ryan, I thank you infinity: for all the many things pre and post-ride that you did to ensure that my adventure would be a success, not the least of which was coming to Chicago to welcome me, along with Cynthia Day, her camera and young son.

In conclusion I thank Marti Childs and Jeff March, owners of EditPros LLC. With guidance they helped me work my way through the world of self-publishing.

If only Mom and Dad were here to read my finished product.

About the Author

Doug Waterman taught Special Education/Work Experience high school students in the Sacramento City School District for 35 years. Retirement gave him the opportunity to prepare in earnest for yet another bicycling adventure – 2300 miles on historic Route 66, Santa Monica to Chicago. He lives in Davis, California, with his wife of 49 years. They have a son and daughter, and three grandchildren.

Doug Waterman in Chicago. Photo by Cynthia Day.

www.ingramcontent.com/pod-product-compliance
Lightning Source LLC
Chambersburg PA
CBHW062056290426
44110CB00022B/2614